THE SILENT TAKEOVER

Noreena Hertz is the Associate Director of the Centre of International Business and Management at the Judge Institute of the University of Cambridge, where she obtained her PhD. She is the author of *Russian Business Relationships in the Wake of Reform*.

THE SILENT TAKEOVER

Global Capitalism and the Death of Democracy

NOREENA HERTZ

WILLIAM HEINEMANN : LONDON

First published in the United Kingdom in 2001 by William Heinemann

3 5 7 9 10 8 6 4 2

Copyright © Noreena Hertz 2001

Noreena Hertz has asserted her right under the Copyright, Designs and Patents Act, 1988
to be identified as the author of this work

William Heinemann
The Random House Group Limited
20 Vauxhall Bridge Road, London SW1V 2SA

Random House Australia (Pty) Limited
20 Alfred Street, Milsons Point, Sydney,
New South Wales 2061, Australia

Random House New Zealand Limited
18 Poland Road, Glenfield,
Auckland 10, New Zealand

Random House (Pty) Limited
Endulini, 5a Jubilee Road,
Parktown 2193, South Africa

The Random House Group Limited Reg. No. 954009

www.randomhouse.co.uk

A CIP catalogue record for this book is available from the British Library

Papers used by Random House are natural, recyclable products made from
wood grown in sustainable forests. The manufacturing processes conform to
the environmental regulations of the country of origin

ISBN 0 434 00933 4

Typeset by SX Composing DTP, Rayleigh, Essex
Printed and bound in Great Britain by
Mackays of Chatham plc, Chatham, Kent.

For my late mother – Leah, my father – Jonathan and sister – Arabel.
With deepest love and gratitude.

ACKNOWLEDGEMENTS

I would like to thank Professor Robin Matthews and Professor Debora Spar for their insightful comments on earlier drafts and unstinting support for the project and also Charles Hampden Turner, Professor Peter Nolan, Professor John Child, Professor Sandra Dawson, Christos Pitelis, Jamie Mitchell, Richard Symons, Tanya Schwarz, and Jamie Miller for their intellectual input.

Catherine Needham and Beth Ahlering for their excellent research assistance and enthusiasm for the project and also Angela Spatharou, Chryssa Kanellakis-Reimer, Christopher Garner, Robert Sabbarton, Nadia Kokourina, Becky Morris, Tom Gross, Raj Lalsare, Virginia Graham, Paul Davies, and Rob Koepp for their help on various chapters.

Gillon Aitken, David Lloyd and Samir Shah, for believing in me and the project in its most early days and Clare Alexander for providing me with support and care all the way through.

All those at Random House especially my editor Ravi Mirchandani for helping turn my initial idea into a reality.

Julia Hobsbawm, Sir Martin Sorrell and John Lloyd for their encouragement. Len Blavatnik and Henry Porter for their overwhelming generosity and support.

Pat Lilley for keeping me organised, Andrew Flower for keeping me well, and Ralph Hancock for his eagle eyes.

My friends – who put up with the fact that they did not see me for months on end and not only rarely complained, but continued to phone. Especially Orson for making the writing period a magical time; Alexis for continuing to be an incredibly important part of my life and always being there when I need him; James for those special treats that did make the bad bits better; and Juliet for her kindness.

THE REVOLUTION
WILL NOT BE TELEVISED

Dancing with the Pink Fairies

S-26. For those in the know the acronym is easily decipherable: September 26, 2000, the call for action transmitted to hundreds of thousands at the click of a mouse. S-26 – Prague.

I learnt about the Prague protests through the Net, as did most of those who gathered there. A chain letter sent to thousands and forwarded to thousands more eventually reached me. Cyberwar with a clear message: be there, if you think that globalisation is failing. Be there if you want to protest against global capitalism. If you think multinational corporations are too powerful. If you no longer believe your elected representatives will listen. Be there if you want to be heard.

On 26 September Prague was host city to the IMF and World Bank's annual conference, and the place to be for the veterans of Seattle, Melbourne and London's City and Parliament Square riots. They flocked there in droves, pink fairies in drag, red devils handing out Boycott

Bacardi leaflets, Italian anarchists in *It's a Knockout* padded body armour, environmentalists with mobile phones, suburbanites with cameras snapping as if they were on a day trip to Blackpool – a babel of different languages and different objectives gathered under the one 'anti' banner.

I was prepared for the tear gas: I had read the Ruckus Society handbook, required reading for protesters, and had brought the requisite lemon and vinegar and a handkerchief to wrap around my face. I was prepared for the police standoffs: I had studied the tactics of civil disobedience and direct action at the non-violence workshop I had attended earlier that week in a hangar-like meeting place on the north-west outskirts of the city. My crash course in 'The Movement' had been provided by 24-year old Chelsea Mozen, a white-bread former Washington city government employee, who looked as if she had just come off the set of *The Waltons*.

What I was not prepared for was the sense of community amongst the divergent and often conflicting interests, the sense of camaraderie and unity around a shared opposition to the status quo. Neither was I prepared for the sheer rage, inflamed by the insistent drumming and by the mournful wailing of the rainbow-stringed whistles sold at a dollar a piece. Least of all, perhaps, was I prepared for the extent to which those I spoke with were utterly disillusioned with politics and politicians, corporations and businesspeople alike, and the lengths to which they were prepared to go to break what they saw as a conspiracy of silence.

Ten years after the tanks last drove on to Red Square, twelve years after the Berlin Wall came down, after the longest period of economic boom in modern times, dissent is nevertheless growing at a remarkable rate, voiced not only by those who gathered in Prague, not only by the rainbow warriors, but by disparate and often surprising parties – ordinary people with ordinary lives. All over the world, concerns are being raised about governments' loyalties and corporations' objectives. Concerns that the pendulum of capitalism may have swung just a bit too far; that our love affair with the free market may have obscured harsh truths; that too many people are losing out. That the state cannot be trusted to look after our interests; and that we are paying too high a price for our increased economic growth. They are worried that the sound of business is drowning out the voices of other interest groups.

The fairy tale ending of the story that began in Westminster on 3 May 1979, the day Margaret Thatcher came into power, and was later reproduced in the United States, Latin America, East Asia, India, most of Africa and the rest of Europe – the story of the streets being paved with gold, and the realisation of the American dream – is no longer taken for granted. Myths that were perpetuated during the Cold War era, out of fear of weakening 'our' position, are beginning to be debunked. Wealth doesn't always trickle down. There are limits to growth. The state will not protect us. A society guided only by the invisible hand of the market is not only imperfect, but also unjust.[1]

The world that is emerging from the Cold War is the antithesis of the shrink-wrapped One World of the hyperglobalists. It is in fact confused, contradictory and mercurial. It is a world in which a litany of doubts is starting to be recited, not at the ballot box, but in cathedrals, shopping malls and on the streets. A world in which loyalties can no longer be determined, and allegiances seem to have switched. While BP was running a programme for its top two hundred executives on the future of capitalism in which the merits and demerits of globalisation were debated, a British Labour government was fighting to privatise air traffic control.

The *Space Odyssey* world of 2001 is getting dangerously close to the apocalyptic visions of *Rollerball, Network* and *Soylent Green*. It is a world in which, as we will see, corporations are taking over from the state, the businessman becoming more powerful than the politician, and commercial interests are paramount. As I will show, protest by the consumer public is fast becoming the only way of effecting policy and controlling the excesses of corporate activity.

The Benetton bubble

We can date the beginning of this world, this world of the Silent Takeover, from Margaret

Thatcher's ascendency. The hairspray-helmeted Iron Lady proselytised a particular brand of capitalism with her *compadre* Ronald Reagan that put inordinate power into the hands of corporations, and gained market share at the expense not only of politics but also of democracy. And it has been a durable product. Apart from a few discreet tweaks theirs remains the dominant ideology across much of the world. Politics in the post-Cold War age has become increasingly homogenised, standardised, a commodity.

Benetton provides an apt metaphor for politics today. Over the last eighteen years this Italian fashion company has run the most provocative advertising campaigns ever seen. Twenty foot billboards with the picture of a starving black baby; the AIDS victim at his moment of death; the blooded uniform of a dead Bosnian soldier; the 'United Killers of Benetton' campaign, a ninety-six page magazine insert with photograph after photograph of condemned prisoners languishing on America's Death Rows. Benetton shocked us to attention, but shock is all it provided. It didn't rally us into action. Nor did it try and address these issues itself. Their advertising provided no exploration of the morality of war, there was no attempt to relieve poverty or cure AIDS. The only goal was to increase sales, not to start a discussion of the issues behind capital punishment. And if it profited from others' misery, so what?[2]

We are living in a Benetton bubble. We are presented with shocking images by politicians who try to win our favour by demonising their opponents and highlighting the dangers of other parties – remember the Conservatives' highly controversial 'demon eyes' campaign prior to the 1997 election which put a photograph of Tony Blair with red satanic eyes, above the slogan, 'New Labour, New Danger'. They speak of making a difference and changing our lives. Different parties offer us supposedly different solutions and choices: conservatism, republican values, and now the Third Way, all in an attempt to secure our votes.

But the rhetoric is not matched by reality. The solutions our politicians offer are as bogus as those of Benetton: a Chinese girl standing next to an American boy, a black woman holding hands with a white woman. Models with unusual faces, strong faces, sometimes beautiful, sometimes not. Multicoloured people in multicoloured clothes.

Political answers have become as illusory as the rows and rows of homogenised clothes, standard T-shirts and cardigans, folded in your local Benetton store. High-street conservatism and conformity *par excellence*. The Third Way? The Third Coming is more likely. Politicians continue to offer only one solution: a system based on laissez-faire economics, the culture of consumerism, the power of finance and free trade. They try and sell it in varying shades of blue, red or yellow, but it is still a system in which the corporation is king, the state its subject, its citizens consumers. A not com solution for a dot com world.

But, I will argue, the system is undeniably failing. Behind the ideological consensus and supposed triumph of capitalism, cracks are appearing. If everything is so wonderful, why, as we will see, are people ignoring the ballot box and taking to the streets and shopping malls instead? How meaningful is democracy if only half the people turn out to vote, as in the Bush-Gore American elections, even though everyone knew it was going to be a close race? What is the worth of representation if, as I will show, our politicians now jump to the commands of corporations rather than of their own citizens?

Capitalism on tap

It took time for people to rise up in protest, to see that the weightless state was unlikely to deliver the clean safe world that they wanted their children to grow up in. For a long time people didn't question the one-ideology, homogeneous world. Why should they? For many, life was good and getting better. For most of the past twenty years the stock market has risen and interest rates fallen. More people than ever before own their own homes. Two thirds of us, in the developed world, have television sets of our own.[3] Most of us, in the West that is, have cars. Our children wear Nike and Baby Gap. The middle class has grown and grown.

We are drip-fed images that reinforce this capitalist dream. Studios and networks beatify the very essence of capitalism. Prevailing norms and mainstream thoughts are recorded, replayed and reinforced in Technicolor, while any criticism of the orthodoxy is consciously quashed. The peaceful element in the protests of Seattle and Prague hardly made it to our screens. Procter & Gamble explicitly prohibits programming around its commercials 'which could in any way further the concept of business as cold or ruthless'.[4] Programmes are sought that reinforce the advertisers' message. 'Each time a television set is turned on, the political, economic, and moral basis for a profit-driven social order is implicitly legitimised.'[5]

In 1997 Adbusters,[6] a Canadian 'culture jamming' organisation, tried to air a counter-consumerism ad in which an animated pig superimposed on a map of North America smacked its lips while saying, 'The average North American consumes five times more than a Mexican, 10 times more than a Chinese person, and 30 times more than a person from India . . . Give it a rest. November 28 is Buy Nothing Day.' But US stations such as NBC, CBS and ABC flatly refused to run it, even though the funding for it was there. 'We don't want to take any advertising that's inimical to our legitimate business interests,' said Richard Gitter, vice-president of advertising standards at the General Electric Company's NBC network.

Westinghouse Electric Corp's CBS went even further in a letter rejecting the commercial, justifying its decision on the grounds that Buy Nothing Day was 'in opposition to the current economic policy in the United States'.[7]

Corporate behemoths

Such is our legacy. A world in which consumerism is equated with economic policy, where corporate interests reign, where corporations spew their jargon on to the airwaves and stifle nations with their imperial rule. Corporations have become behemoths, huge global giants that wield immense political power.

Propelled by government policies of privatisation, deregulation and trade liberalisation, and the advances in communication technologies of the past twenty years, a power shift has taken place. The hundred largest multinational corporations now control about 20 per cent of global foreign assets; fifty-one of the hundred biggest economies in the world are now corporations, only forty-nine are nation states.[8] The sales of General Motors and Ford are greater than the GDP of the whole of sub-Saharan Africa; the assets of IBM, BP and General Electric outstrip the economic capabilities of most small nations; and Wal-Mart, the US supermarket retailer, has higher revenues than most Central and Eastern European states including Poland, the Czech Republic, Ukraine, Hungary, Romania and Slovakia.[9] The size of corporations is increasing. In the first year of the new millennium communications giant Vodafone merged with Mannesmann, pharmaceutical conglomerate Smith Kline Beecham with Glaxo Wellcome and internet service provider AOL with media corporation Time Warner. These mega-mergers dwarfed the M&A activity of the 1980s. Each merger seems bigger than the one before, and governments rarely stand in the way. Each new merger gives corporations even more power. All the goods we buy or use – our petrol, the drugs our GPs prescribe, essentials like water, transport, health and education, even the new school computers and the crops growing in the fields around our communities – are increasingly controlled by corporations which may at their whim choose to nurture, support or strangle us.

This is the world of the Silent Takeover, the world at the dawn of the new millennium. Governments' hands are tied and we are increasingly dependent on corporations. Business is in the driving seat, corporations determine the rules of the game, and governments have become referees, enforcing rules laid down by others. Portable corporations are now movable feasts and governments go to great lengths to attract or retain them on their shores. Blind eyes are turned to tax loopholes. Business moguls use sophisticated tax dodges to keep their bounty offshore. Rupert Murdoch's News Corporation pays only 6 per cent tax worldwide; and in the UK, up to the end of 1998, it paid no net British corporation tax at all, despite having made £1.4 billion profit there since June 1987.[10] This is a world in which, although we already see the signs of the eroding tax base in our crumbling public services and infrastructure, our elected representatives kowtow to business, afraid not to dance to the piper's tune.

Governments once battled for physical territory; today they fight for market share. They see their primary job as that of ensuring an environment in which business can prosper, and which is attractive to business. The role of nation states has become to a large extent simply that of providing the public goods and infrastructure that business needs at the lowest costs and protecting the world free trade system.

Divided we fall

In the process, justice, equity, rights, the environment and even issues of national security fall by the wayside. Social justice has come to mean access to markets. Social safety nets have been weakened. Union power has been smashed.

Never before in modern times has the gap between the haves and the have-nots been so wide, never have so many been excluded or so championless. Forty-five million Americans have no health insurance. In London, car windscreen washers armed with squeegees and pails of dirty water ambush drivers at traffic lights, while in Manhattan people fish empty drink cans from bins, to claim their five cents redemption value. Americans spend $8 billion a year on cosmetics while the world cannot find the $9 billion the UN reckons is needed to give all people access to clean drinking water and sanitation. The British Labour party has gone on record as saying that wealth creation is now more important than wealth redistribution.[11]

In America during the ten years from 1988, income for the poorest families rose less than 1 per cent, while it jumped 15 per cent for the richest fifth. In New York the poorest 20 per cent earn an annual average of $10,700, while the wealthiest 20 per cent earn $152,350.[12] Wages for those at the bottom are so low that, despite the country's low unemployment figures, millions of employed Americans are living in poverty.

Capitalism has triumphed, but its spoils are not shared by all. Its failings are ignored by governments which, thanks to the very policy measures they introduced, are increasingly unable to deal with the consequences of their system.

And that system is rotten. Political scandals are unveiled all too frequently: Kohl, Schmidt and Mitterrand are among those we already know or suspect. Even those politicians not on the take are increasingly indebted to or enmeshed with business, and nowhere was this more apparent than in the 2000 American presidential elections, whose candidates' very ability to run depended upon their securing of corporate funding. George W. Bush's campaign war chest was $191 million.[13]

No wonder the politicians' star is fading. People sense the growing impotence of traditional politics and the unwillingness of politicians to champion them, and are beginning to abandon politics *en masse*. The British Women's Institute – the very symbol of comfortable Middle England – battled the Sainsbury supermarket chain over GM foods, but also slow-handclapped Blair. Whereas the 1980s saw democracy emerging over the world as the dominant mode of government, imbued with a unique legitimacy and commanding mass support, by the 1990s voter turnout almost everywhere was falling, party membership declining and politicians were rated below parking wardens as worthy of respect.[14] All over the world, from the old democracies of the United States and Western Europe to the young nations of Latin America and the Far East, people have less confidence in the institutions of government today than they had a decade ago. Only 44 per cent of British voters aged 18 to 24 voted in the 1997 general election. The product sold by politicians is seen as broken, no longer deemed worth buying.

Breaking the silence

This is the world of the Silent Takeover I will explore in this book. My aim is to make sense of this world and understand where it is likely to take us: a world in which corporate resources dwarf those of nations, and businessmen outrank politicians; in which three quarters of Americans now think that business has gained too much power over many aspects of their lives;[15] and in which, despite the ever harder sell of party politics, fewer and fewer trouble to vote. Economics is now accorded greater respect than politics, the citizen has been abandoned and the consumer is all that matters. 'Participation in the market has [been] substituted for participation in politics.'[16]

My argument is not intended to be anti-capitalist. Capitalism is clearly the best system for generating wealth, and free trade and open capital markets have brought unprecedented economic growth to most if not all of the world. Nor is the book intended to be anti-business. Corporations are not amoral but, I will argue, they are morally ambivalent. In fact, under certain market conditions, business is more able and willing than government to take on many of the world's problems. 'Social responsibility', 'sustainable development', 'environmental impact' are terms more likely to be heard today from CEOs than from government ministers.

Neither do I intend to glorify government. Although, as I will argue, the state has a clear role to play in society, I remain highly sceptical of government's ability to play this role, especially now that the boundaries between business and government have blurred so much and there is such a lack of true political leadership or will.

What my book *is* intended to be, however, is unashamedly pro-people, pro-democracy, and pro-justice. I mean to question the moral justification for a brand of capitalism that encourages governments to sell their citizens for a song; to challenge the legitimacy of a world in which many lose and few win; and to reveal how the takeover endangers democracy, and to argue that there is a fundamental paradox at the heart of laissez-faire capitalism, that by reducing the state to its bare minimum and putting corporations at centre stage the state risks jeopardising its own legitimacy. I will explore the implications of a world in which we cannot trust governments to look after our interests and in which unelected powers – big corporations – are taking over governments' roles, and examine the consequences of a political mindset which values the pursuit of market share above all else. I will chart the unfettered pursuit of profit, and confront those who justify pork-barrel politics as an expression of free speech, and those who justify non-intervention in other countries' affairs for reasons of their own trade interests.

Over the last two decades the balance of power between politics and commerce has shifted radically, leaving politicians increasingly subordinate to the colossal economic power of big business. Unleashed by the Thatcher–Reagan axis, and accelerated by the end of the Cold War, this process has grown Hydra-like over the last two decades and now manifests itself in what are diverse positive and negative forms. Whichever way we look at it, corporations are taking on the responsibilities of government.

And as business has extended its role, it has, as we shall see, actually come to define the public realm. The political state has become the corporate state. Governments, by not even acknowledging the takeover, risk shattering the implicit contract between state and citizen that lies at the heart of a democratic society, making the rejection of the ballot box and the embracing of non-traditional forms of political expression increasingly attractive alternatives. Exploring these developments and their consequences will make up the body of this book.

My decision to write *The Silent Takeover* was not a disinterested one. I needed to make sense of my own growing discontent, my own feelings that things were going awry. How could it be that life had in many ways never been better, yet I and so many around me seemed so troubled? How was it that I, the daughter of a woman who devoted much of her life to putting women into politics, now saw politics as a co-opted, increasingly meaningless arena – a sideshow whose best act was the farce of the last US presidential elections? How could it be that ten years after landing in Leningrad to set up Russia's first stock exchange – a travelling saleswoman with capitalism in my briefcase – I now felt a burning need to question its very tenets? Why was it that at Cambridge University's business school, where I teach, when I made it clear that I was willing to supervise on the issues that this book examines, I was deluged with so many requests from students that I couldn't possibly satisfy them all?

We stand today at a critical juncture. If we do nothing, if we do not challenge the Silent Takeover, do not question our belief system, do not admit our own culpability in the creation of this 'new world order', all is lost. As we shall see inequality of income is bad not only for the poor, but for the rich too.[17] The steady erosion of government and politics is dangerous for all, regardless of political persuasion. A world in which Rupert Murdoch has more power than Tony Blair, and corporations set the political agenda, is frightening and undemocratic. The idea of corporations taking over the roles of government might in some ways seem appealing, but risks leaving us increasingly without recourse.

The story will be told through a cast of characters that we shall meet on the way. Granny D, the 91-year-old grandmother who walked across America to champion campaign finance reform; Sister Patricia Marshall, the shareholder activist nun who persuaded PepsiCo to sell off its Burmese bottling plant; Oskar Lafontaine, the former German Finance Minister whose parting comment on his resignation was, 'The heart is not traded on the stock market yet'. These are but a few of the voices we will hear.

But this book is not just the sum of their disparate stories, it is the sum of all our stories. We are all in the midst of a corporate takeover, and no gated communities or six-figure salaries will protect us from its impact.

My subject is how the Silent Takeover crept upon us, why it matters, and what we can do about it.

LIVING IN A MATERIAL WORLD

Boogie Woogie in Bhutan

The kingdom of Bhutan, mythical Land of the Thunder Dragon, last of the independent Himalayan principalities, lies between Tibet and India. Wilfully isolationist, it has managed for centuries to follow its own path. Its population of around 600,000 is among the poorest in the world in terms of GNP per capita – average annual income is $550 – but this is a misleading picture, as it disregards the fact that more than 85 per cent of the population is involved in subsistence farming, and barter transactions are the norm. People in Bhutan are well fed and clothed, and homelessness is virtually non-existent.

'Success' here is determined on the basis of ecological, ethical and spiritual development; morality and enlightenment are valued above material wealth. Buddhist values are upheld and traditions maintained: the country's 2,000 monasteries are active, and Driglam Namsha, the ancient code of conduct, remains part of the school curriculum. According to Bhutan's King, Jigme Singye Wangchuk, 'Gross National Happiness is more important than Gross National Product.'

The path of development has been carefully managed so as to remain consistent with the country's integral belief system. Unlike its neighbour Nepal, which admitted 500,000 tourists in 1998, Bhutan took in only 6,000 that year; and each of them was provided with a strict code of conduct that included the prohibition of tipping and distributing sweets or pens to local children, to discourage begging.

Another significant generator of foreign revenue, commercial logging, has also been shunned because of the damage it would do to the environment – Bhutanese Buddhism lays great importance on ecology. As C. Dorji, the Minster of Planning, puts it, 'We will not be rushed into an uncritical adoption of all things that are modern; we will draw on the experience of those who have trod the path of development before us, and undertake modernisation with caution at a pace consistent with our capacity and needs. We therefore seek to preserve our culture, traditions, value systems and institutions.'

But the tentacles of global capitalism are far reaching, and they reach even Bhutan which cannot escape the one-kilowatt broadcast signals that now bounce between the thousands of satellite dishes that have over the past few years been appearing between the prayer flags and prayer wheels that dot the landscape.

Already the impact of the West is apparent. Basketball has replaced archery as the national sport, thanks to the videotapes of NBA games that the king has shipped to him from New York. *Boogie Woogie,* a game show sponsored by Colgate, now rivals the panoramic Himalayan vista for viewers' attention. *Friends, Teletubbies,* BBC and CNN entertain, inform and brief. Nightclubs intercut N'Sync and Britney Spears with 1980s Wham and Culture Club. A modern telecommunication systems has been put in place and e-mail is replacing letter-writing, despite the ten days of free mail service that Queen Tashi Dorji Wangmo Wangchuk, the eldest of the king's four wives, offered the Bhutanese to combat this very development. Children now make pilgrimages to monasteries offering prayers and lighting butter lamps while clad in Spice Girls T-shirts. Farmers sell apples, oranges, potatoes and cardamom to their

Indian and Bangladeshi neighbours for foreign currency; and there are twenty-five privately owned video stores in the capital city, Thimphu.

So even Bhutan, the last Shangri-La, is being infiltrated. Unable to resist the spoils of the West, unable to continue its isolationist policies, it admits Western influences. The situation raises many questions. How soon before the forces of globalisation and free market capitalism are irreversibly entrenched? How blindly will the population follow their leader once their eyes are opened to the multichannel, multiparty universe? Will Bhutan really be able to travel 'The Middle Path', a way forward that claims to be able to embrace modernity without compromising traditional ideology, or will the worship of Mammon and MTV culture fast replace the homage paid to the Buddha? Are the days of enlightenment and disregard of material success numbered, now that the Bhutanese will be able to see just how little they can afford relative to others? For how much longer will the king and his queens be able to continue to direct the economy and take responsibility for the welfare of their citizens' lives?

If events elsewhere are anything to go by, probably not for very long.

The state in control

But for now at least, the Bhutanese state remains the principal economic force (most of industry is state-owned) and also the main carer for the people's welfare needs – roles the state played in Europe and America too for much of the past century, before the fundamental mindset shift of the 1970s and 1980s when the extreme version of laissez-faire capitalism epitomised by the American model became so dominant, before government fell in love with the free market.

By the end of the nineteenth century, governments in Europe and the United States had begun to accept that they had responsibilities beyond those of internal order and external security. There was a growing realisation that capitalism was responsible for great cruelties, and a sense that the state should play a role in alleviating the harshest elements of the system through some sort of social intervention. And this nascent feeling gained pace over the first half of the twentieth century, through the Wall Street crash and the Great Depression, then World War II, events which brought first mass unemployment, and then even wider human suffering.

In an attempt to address the needs of the poor, and at the same time stave off the threat of Communism[1] – the Soviet Union was by now offering its citizens the most generous of welfare packages – by the middle of the last century most developed states had begun to establish systems of social security and welfare themselves. The components of the package differed between countries, varying from generous schemes for the redistribution of wealth to minimum provision against destitution. But most Western states offered subsidised access to education, health, housing and personal care services, alongside some form of income maintenance. The dominant mindset was that no citizen was to be allowed to fall below a minimum standard of overall well-being. In the UK, for example, between 1945 and the mid-1970s, the proportion of GDP spent on the main welfare services rose from just 5 per cent to around 20 per cent. Expenditure on the National Health Service rose from about £500 million in 1951 to £5,596 million by 1975.[2] In the United States the expansion of social spending came later. It was not until the Kennedy and Johnson administrations (1961–68) that the state appeared truly willing to substantially enlarge its welfare provision. And only in 1964, in the midst of considerable prosperity and sustained economic growth, did President Johnson declare a 'national war on poverty'.[3]

Not only did the state become the main provider of welfare during the post-war period, it also became the key economic actor. In Europe, even before World War II, countries had begun to nationalise industry, and this process accelerated after 1945. The electorate were now open to the thought of government controlling the 'commanding heights', for they had seen the effectiveness of state control of the wartime economy.

But owning industry was not enough. Post-war governments also felt it legitimate to play an active role in controlling the macro-economy and the market. The Bretton Woods agreement, signed by the leading industrialised nations in 1944, brought heavy regulation of financial markets. And neo-classical liberalism – a system that had largely left the market alone to regulate economic life – was displaced, in the West at least, by Keynesian economics.

John Maynard Keynes believed that governments could and should intervene in the economy, and evolved a wholly new model that approached the economy from the direction of money and finance. He argued that the economy has no natural tendency to create full employment, so if self-regulation cannot deliver jobs, governments must intervene to provide them. Since depressions result not from spending too much but from spending too little, government spending must be key. His doctrines, conceived in the aftermath of the Wall Street crash and the Great Depression, called for governments to sustain aggregate economic demand and full employment, within the context of a mixed economy and a welfare state. They fitted the moment. The potential for big government to be a force for good had been demonstrated during the war. The social cohesion implied by full employment and an extensive welfare system matched the prevailing mood for stability and security in the hard-won peace.

By the end of the 1940s the British Labour government had fully embraced Keynesian economics. In the United States, the 1946 Employment Act committed government to the goal of full employment, although it was not until the 1960s that Kennedy and Johnson moved to an explicitly Keynesian programme. Other Western countries, rebuilding their economies after the war, and heavily dependent on American aid, soon adopted a similar model: a large welfare state, state ownership of major industries, and interventionist government. Much of the developing world also embraced state-dominated development strategies.

Rethinking the state

Things began to change at the end of 1973 when the world's major Arab oil-producing states formed a cartel, OPEC, and sent oil prices skyrocketing. With surging oil prices came an upward spiral of prices and wages, triggering economic recession, unemployment and price inflation of over 20 per cent in several countries, and the widespread inability of Third World countries to service their debt.

The prevailing doctrine of Keynesianism, which had been so successful in the preceding thirty years, proved unable to cope in these times of trouble. Not only could it not offer any remedy, many believed that it had caused the crisis in the first place. In any case, events made nonsense of one of Keynesianism's most basic tenets: that inflation could not rise at the same time as unemployment. So a new solution was called for as governments came to believe that 'the problem lay not in the inefficient management of the prevailing consensus, but in the consensus itself.'[4]

The new economic conditions triggered by the oil crisis demanded a new style of management of the economy: fiscal restraint and control of the money supply. Overnight, almost all Western countries' finance ministers could be heard talking about the need to fight inflation and to rein back the public sector. The providers of loans to countries in crisis made the embracing of this new ethos a condition of providing funds. In Britain, when the Labour Chancellor Denis Healey was forced to turn to the International Monetary Fund for a loan in 1976, the reduction of public spending and tight control over inflation were conditions of the IMF's aid.

From that moment Keynesianism, and with it big government, were dying if not already dead. The Prime Minister, James Callaghan, delivered its epitaph in a speech at the Labour Party conference later that same year: 'We used to think you could spend your way out of recession and increase employment by . . . boosting government spending. I tell you in all candour that that option no longer exists.'[5] In the United States, President Carter was reaching the same conclusion, cutting public spending in an attempt to stimulate the economy.

So by the late 1970s Keynes, a man whose teachings had been adopted wholesale by the West in an attempt to rebuild a world shattered by war and establish a secure capitalist bloc as a bulwark against Communism, was relegated to a footnote in history. Yet despite the abandonment of Keynesianism, it took a few more years for a new form of capitalism with a distinct ideology to triumph. During the Callaghan and Carter administrations, the idea still prevailed that the state existed to resolve contradictions within the market, and was a force for good in the economy.

The rise of the New Right

The watershed came in 1979 and 1980 with the election first of Margaret Thatcher and then of Ronald Reagan – politicians from the New Right, who enthusiastically advocated the free market and were determinedly hostile to the concept of an interventionist state. Rejecting Keynesianism, the grocer's daughter and the Hollywood actor embraced the views of economists such as Milton Friedman and Friedrich Hayek. These economists didn't dispute that markets could and did fail; but they believed that the free market was capable of allocating goods and services more effectively than the state could, and that government attempts to combat market failures did more harm than good. They harked back to the ideas that had shaped economic policy from the Victorian era through to the Wall Street crash, that 'The role of the state was to enforce contracts, to supply sound money . . . to ensure that market forces were not distorted'[6,7] and, essentially, to provide the best environment for business to flourish, evoking memories of the 1920s US President Calvin Coolidge's dictum, 'The business of America is business.'

The extent to which this new religion embodied a coherent ideology, a creed of Reaganism or Thatcherism which could be adopted by other states remains a matter of dispute. The two leaders' goals and priorities were often different. Thatcher adopted monetarism – emphasising tight control of the money supply – whereas the Reagan administration was dominated by supply-side economists, who advocated tax cuts to give the greatest incentive to production. But there were themes running through the policies of Reagan and Thatcher that gave a discernible character to their politics, and made it possible to identify their followers in other countries. Their views are easiest to define in the negative: as a rejection of all the pillars of the post-war Keynesian consensus. In place of the goals of full employment and a generous welfare state, the New Right favoured the reduction of inflation and cuts in public spending[8] (which they regarded as a major cause of the current economic malaise); rather than a mixed economy, they wanted the state cut back to its core, with many of its functions privatised or contracted out.

The New Right felt that too much had been expected from government in the post-war period. Its view was that the role of government should be to alleviate the worst evils of the human lot and provide a framework within which people and communities could pursue their various goals – not, as in previous decades, to positively guarantee general welfare.[9] John Moore, Thatcher's Social Services Secretary, explained in 1987: 'For more than a quarter of a century after the last war public opinion in Britain, encouraged by politicians, travelled down the aberrant path towards even more dependence on an even more powerful state. Under the guise of compassion people were encouraged to see themselves as "victims of circumstance".'[10] According to the New Right, the welfare mentality had bred indolence and dependency.

Under these new leaders there was a clear shift of priorities. Interdependence was replaced by independence and egalitarianism was rejected on ideological grounds: the state was no longer to have a role to play in redistributing wealth.[11] Relative standards of poverty were deemed irrelevant; poverty was to be defined by absolute standards of need. As Thatcher argued in 1985, 'You are not doing anything against the poor by seeing that the top people are paid well.'[12] And the state no longer accepted responsibility to provide unquestioning support for those who for whatever reason were denied an ability to be productive. In 1981, in the aftermath of the Brixton riots, Norman Tebbit, the then Secretary of State for Employment, made the infamous assertion that 'My father didn't riot but got on his bike to look for work.'[13] 'Get on your bike' became the moral imperative of Thatcherism.[14]

And greed was declared good. Oliver Stone's *Wall Street,* Tom Wolfe's *The Bonfire of the Vanities,* Martin Amis's *Money* and Michael Lewis's *Liar's Poker* faithfully chronicled the times. Power dressing and padded shoulders clad those aspiring to partake in the capitalist dream. Economists of the Chicago school wrote of man as a selfish utility maximiser and, almost in a self-fulfilling prophecy, *Homo economicus,* or economic man, was born.

The new Conservative government of Margaret Thatcher abandoned the ambitions of both the Labour and Conservative governments of the 1950s and 60s, jettisoned the government's commitment to sustain full employment, celebrated the virtues of private rather than public provision, and set itself to reduce the burden of social expenditure which, it argued, had seriously eroded those economic incentives which alone made sustained economic growth possible.[15,16] The private sector was to be set free, and the state was to be rolled back.

In the UK the 'family silver'[17] was sold off as Thatcher came to see privatisation as the main cure for the ills of the British economy as well as a convenient way of balancing the budget. A massive sale of assets from the public to the private sector was conducted during the eighties and nineties with the Conservative government raising £67 billion[18] between 1979 and 1997.[19] While 'in 1979 government institutions owned much or all of coal, steel, gas, electricity, water, railways, airlines, telecommunications, nuclear power and shipbuilding, and had a significant stake in oil, banking, shipping and road haulage. By 1997, nearly all of this was in private hands.'[20] Nigel Lawson, the then Secretary of State for Energy, summed up the party position, with his argument in 1982 that 'no industry should remain under state ownership unless there is a positive and overwhelming case for it so doing.'[21]

Steps were taken to create an economic culture that rewarded enterprise and innovation. Rates of corporate and individual taxation were reduced; price, dividend and foreign exchange controls were removed with no thought for the vulnerable state in which this would leave the nation. At the Bank of England thousands of people lost their jobs. Restrictions on bank lending and hire purchase were abolished. Controls over broadcasting, telecommunications, transport and advertising were withdrawn. Right-to-buy schemes for council houses were set up, and shares, not least in the formerly publicly-owned utilities, became available much more widely than before. In 1979, there were four times as many trade unionists as share holders. Within a decade the latter exceeded the former.[22] Capitalism was made 'popular' – everyone was to share Thatcher's economic success.[23] Anything or anyone that potentially stood in the way of this success came under attack. Regulation was dismantled, for it was seen as a stranglehold on corporations. The unions were attacked with ferocity, and held largely to blame for the poor economic performance of British industry. The denunciation of trade unionism became an article of faith on the New Right.

In the United States, the long period of increased involvement of the national government in domestic affairs that began with Roosevelt's New Deal was now over, succeeded by the 'New Federalism'.[24] Reaganomics (and Thatcherism too) rested on a firm belief in the 'trickle-down' theory, which claims that if the rich are provided with incentives such as lower taxation, they will in turn have more incentive to act as entrepreneurs and so will boost growth and create jobs. Or that if public service industries are turned over to the private sector, they will be run more efficiently and provide more jobs for people who will then start disappearing off the welfare rolls.[25] Providing incentives for the poor to work, such as making welfare less attractive, was also believed to boost economic growth. Eligibility requirements for benefits were tightened, and rights to food stamps and funds from AFDC (Aid to Families with Dependent Children) were withdrawn from some recipients.[26] Unlike in Europe, public ownership had never taken off in the USA, so Reagan's main tool of liberalisation was deregulation of the economy, a process kicked off by Jimmy Carter in the 1970s.[27] The Reagan administration cancelled oil price controls, loosened restrictions over railroad transportation, broadcasting, and the oil and natural gas industries and was reluctant to enforce anti-trust legislation.[28] Despite the fact that US trade union leaders had never wielded much political clout, Reagan echoed Thatcher in a strong commitment to curbing union power. Shortly after assuming office, he was confronted with a strike by the nation's air traffic controllers. He promptly sacked them all, substituting military controllers and newly trained workers in their place.[29]

As well as making life considerably easier for the private sector, Reagan promised to 'get government off the backs of the people'.[30] Through tax cuts, he aimed to recreate the structure of incentives and rewards that had been frozen by the high-tax policies of his predecessors. The top marginal rate of income tax in the United States fell from 70 per cent to 28 per cent.[31]

By the early 1980s the role of government in England and America had fundamentally and irreversibly changed. Free enterprise was seen as the key to economic success, and the task of government was now 'to create a framework in which individuals and groups can successfully pursue their respective ends'.[32] David Stockman, Reagan's Budget Director, said that 'The . . . vision of a good society rested on the strength and productive potential of free men in free markets.'[33] Successful and unfettered corporations would, it was believed, build the road to Nirvana.

Exporting capitalism

This creed of free market capitalism, Anglo-American style, was soon disseminated across the world. Aided by developments in communications and the media which ensured that ideas spread quickly, and by the single-mindedness of the neo-liberal international lending institutions, the IMF and the World Bank, who were promoting the so-called 'Washington

Consensus', capitalism's foot soldiers marched from Latin America to East Asia, India and most of Africa, from old and declining capitalist nations such as the UK to vigorous capitalist economies with strong traditions of regulation, such as Germany; and eventually even to the former command economies of the Communist world.[34] 'The market' became the catchphrase of the 1980s and 1990s as liberalised states bore witness to the benefits of the capitalist system.

The first countries to embrace Anglo-American free-market capitalism were Britain's former dominions. Sliding economic performance in Australia in the 1980s led Treasury Minister (and later Prime Minister) Paul Keating to warn that the country risked becoming a 'banana republic' if it did not reform. His methods – deregulation, fiscal rectitude and privatisation – were highly reminiscent of Thatcher's. In Canada during the same period, Brian Mulroney liberalised the laws restricting foreign investment in the country, opening up the Canadian market for free trade. In New Zealand, 'One of the world's most comprehensive social democracies became a neo-liberal state . . . Uncompromising neo-liberal ideology animated a programme of radical reform in which no major social institution was left unreconstructed.'[35]

In Latin America, the military dictators who dominated politics in the 1980s also showed themselves to be keen disciples of the New Right. In Chile, under General Pinochet, the lack of democratic constraints facilitated the imposition of painful monetarist economic policies carried out under the guidance of a team of economists from the University of Chicago. And by the early 1990s, all major Latin American leaders, 'President Carlos Salinas de Gortari in Mexico, President Carlos Menem in Argentina and President Fernando Collor de Mello in Brazil [sought] to implement far-reaching programs of economic liberalization accepting the need for market competition and openness to the world economy,'[36] believing that their underdevelopment was due to the 'insufficient degree of capitalism that had been practised in their countries in the past,' and recognising that their only chance of securing IMF loans was by implementing reform packages along the 'Washington Consensus' lines.[37]

Across Europe high levels of inflation and public indebtedness forced governments to question the basis of their economic policies.[38] Helmut Kohl in Germany and Jacques Chirac in France were not New Right zealots like Thatcher and Reagan, yet they appreciated the financial benefits of privatisation; and both showed an understanding of the realities of the new global environment in which they too would have to display willingness to bring down business taxes and deregulate the labour market, or else lose out on inward investment. So under Kohl, 'social benefits and health provisions were restricted, companies privatised, strike laws changed in bosses' favour, business taxes trimmed.'[39] In Italy and France, companies worth roughly $50 billion in all were privatised in the ten years to 1995,[40] resulting in a massive increase in privately held big business.

The end of the Cold War

In the meantime communism, the only other major ideological contender, was dying an ignoble death. In the autumn of 1988 Mikhail Gorbachev travelled to New York to deliver a historic address to the UN General Assembly. The Cold War was over, he proclaimed. Communism had failed in its seventy-year battle against the global capitalist system. A year later the Berlin Wall came crashing down. Three years after that, the Soviet Union collapsed.

But while William the Conqueror took Britain with the Sword, the Soviet bloc was vanquished by the Coca-Cola bottle. Free market capitalism demolished communism by transmitting Rupert Murdoch and Ted Turner's *Weltanschaung,* making it impossible for communist governments to continue to shield their populations from awareness of the prosperity of Western states. McDonalds, Levis, BMWs and rock music had become symbols of the Western way of life as important to the East Europeans as multi-party democracy or freedom of speech and travel. And the Soviet government could no longer resist an international capitalist system that had grown more and more wealthy over the preceding two decades. Huge expenditure on the military had taken its toll. Matching Reagan's proposed Star Wars programme was a financial impossibility. The Soviet Union's need to be ready to fight the rest of the world had become increasingly untenable.

The collapse of Soviet-style communism in turn affected those states outside Europe that had looked to the Russian model in structuring their economies. In India, for example, which traded extensively with communist countries, the revolutions in Eastern Europe spurred the liberalisation of its own economy.[41] It is now moving ahead with privatisation and easing the process of foreign direct investment. In Africa after 1989, Zambia and Tanzania were among several countries that began to convert to more market-minded philosophies.[42] Communism's terminal crisis began in China when the leadership recognised that the country was being left behind by the rest of capitalist Asia and began to feel that it was socialist central planning that had condemned it to backwardness and poverty.[43]

Trade not aid

Even in those parts of the developing world where foreign direct investment had been viewed with suspicion as exploitative and against a host nation's best interests[44] there was a growing acknowledgement of the benefits that the free market and the opening up of the economy could bring. Frustrated with the poor yields of closed economic policy and import substitution, and having witnessed the success of the Asian 'tiger economies' – Singapore, Hong Kong, Taiwan and South Korea – many other developing countries increasingly declared a willingness to open up their markets and welcome the doctrines of free market capitalism. They had seen how these countries had entered into licensing agreements and joint ventures and utilised the capital or the technology of foreign corporations and investors with notable success. Furthermore, with the collapse of the Communist trading bloc and the implementation of international trade treaties such as the GATT Uruguay Round, which promoted liberalisation and deregulation of global markets, developing countries had few options. By the middle of the 1990s there was only one game in town. Governments that were once wary of foreign capital became caught up in the worldwide race for export-oriented growth.

In the meantime, aid, the traditional tool for development, was being steadily withdrawn by First World nations. In 1992 foreign direct investment (FDI) overtook aid for the first time, and the gap has continued to widen. In 1997 FDI in the developing world exceeded $160 billion, while official development flows (that is, aid) in that year reached a mere $40 billion; by contrast, in 1990 aid totalled almost $60 billion and FDI just over $20 billion. Rich countries, now mindful of their public expenditure, were cutting back on expenditure outside their immediate sphere and understandably preferred to cut back on aid rather than on services at home, which were more likely to bring in votes. In any case, the political motive for aid no longer existed. During the Cold War era many developing countries were of strategic importance, and aid had become a currency used by many developed countries to buy allegiance and compliance. Once the Communist threat was gone, aid to 'friendly' countries fell sharply.

Handing over money to other states was hardly in keeping with the new pro-business approach of Western nations. The state was, after all, now seen as a conduit for private sector growth rather than an engine of growth of itself. Better to put money into the private sector in these countries wherever possible. Aid projects often became tied to private sector development.

Ideological consensus

By the early 1990s, the laissez-faire neo-liberal capitalism of Thatcher and Reagan had unquestionably become the dominant world ideology. Even the traditional left now embraces many of its key tenets.

We see this most clearly in the UK and USA, where much of the legacy of the Thatcher – Reagan era is now ineradicable. In Britain, for example, the shareholding class created in the Thatcher revolution has made a policy of renationalisation unfeasible for any party seeking election. Clause Four of the Labour Party's constitution, with its commitment to public ownership of the means of production, has been dropped. Industry will now be in private hands for keeps.

In 1994 the Labour Party, recovering from its fourth successive election defeat, made a decisive break with the past, abandoning its traditional tax-and-spend policies (which were widely seen as the primary reason for its defeat) and embracing neo-liberal free-market economics. The new leader of the Labour opposition, Tony Blair, actually endorsed the framework created by Conservative Chancellor Nigel Lawson in the 1980s, saying that a Labour government would balance the budget and have an explicit target for low and stable inflation. Employment would be managed by supply-side policy.[45]

This ideological realignment was paralleled by developments on the other side of the Atlantic. In the United States the Democratic Leadership Council – an influential group of modernisers within the Democratic Party – pushed the party away from Michael Dukakis' leftish position towards the centre, reinventing it as the 'New Democrats'. In place of the former concern for social justice, the New Democrats, exemplified by Bill Clinton, emphasised business, investment, competitiveness and free trade.

In both New Zealand and Australia in the 1980s, it was 'Labor' administrations, not conservative ones, that presided over the dismantling of the social democratic order and were the first architects of neo-liberal restructuring.

In a world governed by free market capitalism – for no other system has proven as effective in generating wealth – the traditional political spectrum defined decades ago by pro- and anti-capitalists is no longer fitting. The new parties of the centre left no longer place themselves anywhere along a left-right axis. Blair has frequently spoken of the need to 'move the political debate beyond the old boundaries between left and right altogether'.[46] Clinton in his 1992 manifesto denounced 'the brain-dead old parties of left and right'.[47] Today Republicans and Democrats alike are free traders who back the North American Free Trade Agreement (NAFTA) and the role of the World Trade Organisation (WTO). Neither party would want to raise taxes or public expenditure, or change current monetary policies. Neither would be prepared to starve the burgeoning private sector.

In newly emerging markets such as Eastern Europe and South Africa, thanks to the Washington consensus and the influence of private corporations on policy creation, the Anglo-American system has also gained primacy. In Eastern Europe, where explicitly left-wing parties are tarnished by the legacy of Communism, there is no space for a constructive left-of-centre opposition to economic liberalisation. Outside the extremist parties, politics in these countries is premised on the assumption that free-market capitalism is essential to prosperity. In South Africa the Marxist rhetoric of the ANC in the 1990s, which espoused redistribution, social and public spending, and welfare, had by the end of the millennium adopted the now standard Anglo-American line of fiscal and monetary conservatism, trade liberalisation and privatisation.

Only Asia and Continental Europe have seemed reluctant to fully embrace the new consensus. Asian governments continued to intervene in the economy throughout the nineties. To their cost – as the free marketeers later claimed, blaming the Asian financial crisis and subsequent downturn on excessive government intervention, crony capitalism and market inefficiencies. Subsequently, aid has been provided only in exchange for market reforms of the American ilk, and little attention has been paid to the fact that these countries are not at all like America, with significantly different cultures, levels of development and institutions and very different needs.[48]

The ruthlessness of the Anglo-American model never sat well with most Continental European politicians, who still value the underlying principles of the social model – solidarity, achieved through comprehensive welfare systems and economic co-operation, and a belief that the economy should be regulated for the sake of society – and instinctively feel laissez-faire capitalism, with its emphasis on deregulation and privatisation, to be excessive. They see the UK as a Trojan horse, infiltrating Europe with American pro-business ideology. However, concerns about increasingly ageing populations, unemployment pressures, and moves towards monetary union in Europe have meant that even traditional European socialists are having to accept the predominant *Zeitgeist* to a certain degree at least, and are adopting policies that not long ago would have been seen as frankly heretical.

The official age of retirement for public sector workers has been raised in Germany, Greece, Italy and Finland, while the levels of pensions have been reduced.[49] In France, Lionel Jospin's government, facing unemployment levels of 10.6 per cent, has begun to re-evaluate the disincentives for employers imposed by a relatively high minimum wage and extensive social security charges.[50] For the first time, Jospin's advisers talk about the problem of 'poverty traps', whereby generous welfare cheques discourage the unemployed from looking for a job. His economic team is working on tax and benefit changes, along [British Chancellor Gordon] Brown's lines, to steer the jobless into work.'[51] Jospin has also promised tax cuts for the middle classes.[52] Many other countries have introduced unemployment reforms to force recipients to accept work at market driven rates.[53]

Fiscal disciplines imposed on the dozen or so countries striving to join a single currency by the Maastricht Treaty have made centre-left governments as fiscally rigorous as right-wing ones.[54] And in order to meet the convergence criteria, European Union member states have had to adopt conservative macro-economic policies and ensure that fluctuating levels of national debt, government spending or interest rates are not creating major fluctuations in the value of the currency in one state, which the other member states would then have to bail out.

Most of Europe now acknowledges that the social model must be reformed in the interests of economic competitiveness. Increased competition from other countries for inward investment has forced all social market economies to buy in to the free market doctrine to some degree, and deregulate, lower taxes and shrink their welfare states in order to remain a contender in the eyes of increasingly portable global corporations.[55]

Even traditional left-of-centre parties in the 1990s began advocating slimmer government, lower taxes and privatisation, measures to which they were once bitterly opposed.[56] By the end of the millennium Greece's Socialists were slashing state spending to try to squeeze the drachma into the euro. And France's Socialists had privatised more companies than their immediate right-wing predecessors had.[57]

In Berlin, Social Democrat Chancellor Gerhard Schröder has seemed the most willing of the Continental European left to emulate Blair and Clinton by moving towards the right. While still arguing for the importance of social justice, the Blair – Schröder joint manifesto on the Third Way enthused about deregulated markets, entrepreneurship, cuts in taxes and public spending, and a minimalist state.[58] Since being elected in 1998, Schröder has proposed cuts in taxes on both corporations and personal incomes.[59] He has also tried to shrink the national debt, reduce public spending, and lower state pensions and other welfare benefits.[60]

Yet despite the fact that the European social model is clearly being forced to adapt, talk of its *death* is perhaps premature. Jospin believes that he is saying 'yes to a market economy, no to a market society', continues to intervene in the employment market, and has kept taxes at high levels; and Schröder still talks of 'common good' and has now eased back from the Blairist talk of a *Neue Mitte* ('New Middle Way') in favour of 'our German model'. However, all European states have adopted some of the liberalising policies characteristic of the new Anglo-Saxon model, and across Europe there have been moves towards capital deregulation, welfare reform and privatisation. At the beginning of the millennium it seems that, while not renouncing consensus politics and welfare spending as thoroughly as in Britain, Continental Europeans are accepting more readily than before a reduction of the role of the state in guiding national economies, and increasingly believe that corporations and entrepreneurs can generate wealth more effectively than governments.[61]

We are witnessing the emergence of a new consensus, different in content, but similar in tone to that which prevailed prior to the 1970s. In a speech in 1968, Margaret Thatcher said: 'There are dangers in consensus: it could be an attempt to satisfy people holding no particular views about anything. No great party can survive except on the basis of firm beliefs about what it wants to do.'[62] The irony is that the firm beliefs of Thatcher and her contemporaries across the world may have robbed their successors of plausible alternatives. In the triumph of free market capitalism we are left with a single world ideology.

One world

While ideas have been converging, the world has been shrinking. The State has been stepping back, and the market has been taking over. The liberalisation of international finance started in 1960 with the development of offshore lending, continued with the collapse of the Bretton Woods agreement in 1971 and the floating of major currencies, and was completed with the deregulation of the financial sector in the 1970s and early 1980s and the subsequent invention of new financial products: derivatives and options with ever more enticing names – butterflies, straddles and the like.

Access to these new financial products has resulted in an explosion in capital flows, greatly helped by the recent revolutions in communications.[63] The cost of a three-minute telephone call between New York and London has fallen from $300 (in 1996 dollars) in 1930 to less than 45 cents today; the cost of computer processing power has been falling by an average of 30 per cent a year in real terms over the past couple of decades.[64] Billions of dollars are being transferred all over the globe in real time every hour of the day by institutional investors and mutual and pension funds, more willing and able than ever before to diversify risk by putting their money abroad or moving it from one place to another.

Not since the end of the nineteenth century have we seen such an outflow of overseas investment[65] with governments once again increasingly powerless to control or contain these cross-border movements, as clearly shown by the Long Term Capital Management fiasco in which the American Federal Reserve ended up having to bail out a group of American banks, only one among many severe financial crises in the late 1990s.[66]

But it is not just portfolio investment that has been on the rise. Since the early 1980s, corporations, in their quest to secure more cost-effective manufacturing bases and reach new markets in an ever more competitive business environment, have been not only exporting more and more – world exports more than doubled from 1980 to 1997 – but have also been investing in overseas operations and setting up subsidiaries at an unprecedented rate, aided by the increased mobility of international capital which allows them to raise money in offshore locations and move it across exchanges; by the communications revolution, which means that the head office can now easily communicate with its subsidiaries anywhere in the world; by the cost of transportation, which has plummeted especially relative to the value of traded goods; and by the increasing openness of markets that hitherto were closed.[67] Rich countries' industrial tariffs average now only about 4 per cent.

Corporations think nothing nowadays of breaking up their chains of production and locating the links all over the world wherever seems most advantageous. Designing their products in one place, entering into production alliances in another, outsourcing components and service activities somewhere else, sourcing their inputs, capital, raw materials and even labour from wherever costs of production are lower, tax benefits more favourable and access to raw materials or skills cheaper, and marketing in yet another place. Even firms previously comfortably situated within their home territories and relatively domestically oriented have recently disembedded their production and main operations from the parent state, seeking to lower production costs and expand in developing markets.

Multinational corporations, fed to bursting by global laissez-faire capitalism, are now as big as many nation states. Three hundred multinational corporations now account for 25 per cent of the world's assets. The annual values of sales of each of the six largest transnational corporations, varying between $111 and $126 billion, are now exceeded by the GDPs of only twenty-one nation states.

Corporate sales account for two thirds of world trade and a third of world output (Coca-Cola, Toyota and Ford derive nearly half of their revenues outside their base in the USA), while as much as 40 per cent of world trade now occurs within multinational corporations. And these corporations are not only selling globally, they are investing all over the globe. Foreign direct investment has exploded, increasing from around $60 billion in 1980[68] to $394 billion in 1997,[69] with its impact most noticeable in the developing world. While developing countries received an average of $2.35 billion in the early 1970s, this had increased to $80 billion in the period of 1991–96.

Identical products are now manufactured for distribution all over the world. Brands have become universally recognisable, their attributes signalled in the international language of advertisements on far flung satellite television screens. Coca-Cola has been imbued with so much value that it has become the traditional drink at Indian weddings; the blue, red and white of a Pepsi can is now more identifiable than the Union Jack; the swoosh insignia on a pair of Nikes, as familiar in Milan and London as in Saigon, has spawned an entire new global industry of pirated swooshes.

I want to be a millionaire

Globalisation has created a plethora of choice, but a convergence of aspirations and values, which now centre around man's desire to own, acquire and – as Adam Smith put it – 'truck and barter'. From London to Moscow, from Bhutan to Borneo, we all increasingly covet the same products, the same brands. The success of the game show *Who Wants to Be a Millionaire?* which is now shown in fifty-one countries, garnering regular audiences of up to 20 million, shows how much we all want to share the capitalist dream. No longer content with just watching the rich get richer – *Dallas* and *Dynasty* lost their appeal by the 1990s – today we like to believe that wealth is within reach of all of us.

And is it? What is the net result of global capitalism, of a world in which people's economic well-being and physical safety are determined primarily by the strategies and actions of international financial investors and multinational corporations? A world in which the primary service that national governments appear able to offer their citizens is to provide an attractive environment for corporations or international financial investors?

There has been an unprecedented rate of growth of material prosperity not only in industrially developed nations but in countries that, at the close of World War II, were part of the impoverished Third World.[70]

In Britain the proportion of the population who owned their homes rose from just over a half in 1980 to two thirds by the end of the Thatcher period.[71] For many, standards of living increased and sales of TVs, compact discs, freezers and cars all went up.[72] Four in five households in the UK now have a video recorder and 34 per cent of UK households a home computer, this latter figure having almost doubled in the past two years. Sixty per cent of the population now call themselves middle-class, and that includes half of those in skilled manual occupations. Unemployment is at the lowest levels since 1980. Inflation persists, but at a tiny fraction of the levels of the 1970s. More of us have more money to spend than ever before, and more places to spend it. Europe's largest multiplex cinema has just been built in Birmingham, and the British public now spend more on leisure activities than on either food, housing or clothing. Overseas holidays are commonplace: 56 million holidays of four nights or more were taken by British residents in 1998, up a third since 1971.[73]

In New Zealand growth since 1992 has averaged 4 per cent a year, and unemployment has almost halved, to 6 per cent.[74] Australia is enjoying one of the highest growth rates in the developed world. Chile experienced a decade of annual average growth at 7 per cent from

1988 to 1998.[75] In the United States the new century began during the longest period of economic growth in its entire history, with the lowest unemployment rates in thirty years, and the first back-to-back budget surpluses in forty-two years.[76] American corporations have been experiencing remarkable growth rates, and individual CEOs have been amply rewarded for shepherding the boom. Mel Karmazin, the head of CBS, received $200 million in salary for 1998. Michael Eisner, head of Disney, earned $576 million, or roughly the GDP of the Seychelles.[77] America has become a nation of day traders, with more and more US householders gambling their surplus money as if there were no tomorrow, saving virtually nothing and relying on a seemingly ever rising stock market.

The Third World is experiencing a boom too. Net private capital flows to developing countries are six times greater than in 1990, and foreign direct investment has greatly raised the absolute economic welfare of most host countries through tax revenues to government. Royal Dutch Shell, for example, active in over seventy-five developing countries, in 1998 generated tax revenue globally of more than US$46 billion.

Several countries that have opened their arms to free market principles have seen this strategy pay off. Singapore, albeit with an authoritarian regime, has very low unemployment, high single-digit growth rates in GDP and GNP, a highly skilled workforce, a 91 per cent literacy rate, and a per capita income that is the second highest in the region after Japan. Thailand has tripled its GDP per capita since 1975 when only one in six people in rural areas had access to safe drinking water; today it is four out of five.[78] In India, which in recent years has relaxed its hostility to foreign investment and liberalisation, the economy is booming; car sales in cities jumped by 57 per cent during the first nine months of 2000, and Indian software developers are making a global impact with software sales grossing approximately $4 billion in 2000. Along the northern border of Mexico, where the Maquilla export zone has been set up following the establishment of NAFTA in 1994, multinational production created over half a million new jobs where virtually none existed before, often providing better benefits and paying high wages than local companies.

Even in China, where free market reforms have taken place within a nominally communist state, 'liberalising reforms led to a doubling of grain production in five years and provided a new demonstration of the power of market principles',[79] and foreign investment has provided training opportunities, upgraded local facilities and created countless new jobs wherever it has been applied. Companies do not tend to lower their standards in their foreign operations, at least not consistently as one might have thought. Often they improve local operating standards by exporting their own rather than conforming to local norms. When the Polaroid Corporation opened its plant in Shanghai in 1990 it brought engineers from its Scottish facilities to reconstruct the same basic plant design and working conditions as in Scotland. 'The only notable differences were the installation of a high-end stereo system in the plant's main assembly room and an in-house clinic (customary in China, but not in Scotland).'[80] Standardisation is more important to many firms than scrambling to wring cost advantage from local loopholes or regulatory gaps.

Laissez-faire capitalism appears to have triumphed. Handing over the economy to the market seems to have been the right choice. It all looks great. At first glance, that is. But as they say, there is no such thing as a free lunch. So what is the price we will have to pay?

LET THEM EAT CAKE

The Prince and the Pauper

On 4 December 1998 Prince Charles paid a visit to the London offices of the *Big Issue* – a magazine sold by those who have fallen on hard times and who benefit financially from their sales – where he came face to face with homeless Clive Harold, one of the magazine's street sellers. He astonished both the prince and the press by greeting Charles warmly with the words, 'Remember me?'

Harold, dressed in a Father Christmas hat and burly, shabby overcoat, reminded the Prince that both had been in Form Five of Hill House School in Chelsea, London in 1957 when they were nine years old. Their paths had diverged dramatically since then.

The son of a wealthy London financier, Harold had gone from a childhood living in a five-storey house in exclusive Launceston Place, Kensington, to sleeping rough on the Strand. Now he was living on benefit in a £12-a-night bed and breakfast hostel, trying to get his life back on track by selling the *Big Issue* outside Holborn Underground station.

He and Charles had parted ways at the end of the 1956–7 academic year. Charles went to Cheam and then Gordonstoun public school, Harold to Millfield, the most expensive public school in the UK.

By the Seventies Harold had become a successful journalist. He had been a reporter for the *Sun* and in 1980 published a book on UFOs which rose to number eight on the bestseller list. He had been twice married, with three children, by his two wives and a live-in lover. A long-term heavy drinker, Harold's problems stemmed from 1987, when both his father and stepmother died in the same week. He descended into alcoholism, blew the £30,000 inheritance which he received in 1991, and lost his house. 'One day I woke up in a doorway in the Strand,' said Harold. 'I thought to myself, "What the hell have you done?".' He had been sleeping in the Strand until three months before the meeting with Prince Charles – this after a successful, even glamorous life with frequent business trips to Los Angeles and New York, good hotels, all the trimmings.

But the late eighties and the nineties had not been kind to him. Frequent attempts to kick alcohol and revitalise his career had not been successful. After the meeting with the Prince he said: 'Now I'm getting my confidence back. With the help of the *Big Issue*, I'm on benefit and living at a bed and breakfast place. I've joined a writing class and teach others to do what I should be doing.'

The Prince commented to the press: 'Even with a supportive home background young people today can find it hard to maintain their self-confidence against the enormous pressures of modern life. My meeting with Clive Harold was a vivid reminder that homelessness can happen to almost anyone. We live in an increasingly materialist and secular world in which people's identity is determined so often only by the job they do and the money they earn, rather than by what they contribute to society as a whole.'

John Bird, founder of the *Big Issue*, said: 'We've had millionaires' sons, Old Etonians and Army officers in here. Anyone can find themselves on the streets, no matter what start they had in life.' At the time of their meeting, Harold was making £150 a week selling the *Big Issue*. Charles, by contrast, was valued at £100 million.

Harold sold his story to the *Sun* for an undisclosed sum. His former wife Eva and 10-year-old daughter then gave their side of the story to the tabloids, detailing Harold's neglect of his family and the two-week stretch he had done in Pentonville for failing to pay maintenance. For more than a week, he was headline news. A year later, he was still selling the *Big Issue*. The magazine's head office say that he was so traumatised by the press attention that he has asked the company to preserve his whereabouts and anonymity at all costs.

Things do go wrong. Not everyone benefits from the capitalist dream.

The twenty-year neo-liberal experiment that began in Westminster and Washington has not delivered for all of us. Traditional measures of economic growth, such as GDP per capita or GDP growth rate, obscure the truth. Not only has Clive Howard been excluded from the growth process, countless others are being excluded too.

East–west, north–south

The global policy shift towards neo-liberalism that took place during the 1980s and 1990s was supposed, according to its proponents, to bring a convergence of living standards of richer and poorer nations. This never actually happened. For the majority of developing and transitional economies the East–West and North–South income gaps are greater today than before.

The medicines doled out by the World Bank and IMF – 'shock therapy', 'stabilisation', 'structural adjustment', 'trade and financial liberalisation', 'deregulation' – eroded labour institutions and diluted union bargaining power, led to rushed-through mass privatisation programmes that only benefited a minority, and prohibited countries from increasing public expenditure to meet their welfare needs. Not only was the pill bitter, it was often force-fed. The IMF and World Bank can dictate terms to the developing countries that depend upon loans from the international community, by making their loans conditional on the acceptance of their economic views by these nations. Through financial dependence or the threat of sanctions, these organisations coerce errant states into compliance.

Often the patient is made worse. Inequality declined *within* many countries between 1945 and the 1970s, but since the tenets of the 'Washington consensus' became mainstream there has been a reversal of this trend all over the world.[1] In the whole of the former Soviet bloc, most of Latin America, and much of South, South-East and East Asia, inequality has risen significantly over the past two decades. And 'with the notable exception of East Asia, the number of people living in extreme poverty – considered here as living on less than a dollar a day – has increased over this period in every developing country' in the world.[2]

Even countries that assiduously followed Washington's dictates are not benefiting. Since 1994 South Africa has pursued a policy of seeking close integration into the global economy. Trade liberalisation in some sectors has proceeded even faster than GATT/WTO requirements. Effective state support for industries such as clothing and textiles, which are major employers of labour, has been rendered impossible. Exchange controls have been steadily abolished, restrictions and regulations in respect of foreign direct investment have been removed. Yet the rewards have been limited, and economic performance poor and patchy. Post-apartheid South Africa has suffered from slow growth, rising unemployment and an alarmingly poor rate of delivery of social and physical infrastructure.[3] The top ten per cent of households account for almost 50 per cent of total consumer spending while the bottom 10 per cent account for just over 1 per cent.[4] It seems likely that the nation's strictly market-driven industrial policy will undermine rather than promote social reconstruction.

This is a lesson China would do well to heed, now that it has decided to join the WTO. On the terms finally agreed with the US and the EU, not only must China quickly liberalise its trade policy, it must also completely dismantle the apparatus of industrial policy that provided support to its state-owned enterprises. Given that most of these firms are not viable in an unprotected, unsubsidised environment, if China does honour the terms of the agreement the implications are likely to be great. The jobs of 90 million people are potentially at risk, and there is no social safety net to cope with such losses.[5]

Even in those Third World countries that have been experiencing higher levels of aggregate growth through the embracing of neo-liberal economics, for example Chile, the money that is being made is not being distributed among the population. Only a minority benefit from the gains.[6]

Multinational companies that are now able to operate in developing countries as a result of liberalisation policies are among the increasingly few that do benefit. Attempts by Third World governments to attract foreign investment, direct or portfolio – ever more urgent because of the dramatic cutback in aid flows over the past few years – often precipitate what has been called a 'race to the bottom': they limit or dismantle regulation, lower wages, slash welfare requirements, and tacitly allow corporations to create huge social upheavals. Pension contributions have been scrapped, and health care provision paid for by employers reduced. Potentially disruptive groups such as organised labour, which may jeopardise the quest to attract and use foreign investment and expertise, have been silenced[7] – in China hundreds of trade unionists are in prison or labour camps simply for having tried to form unions in special economic zones for foreigners. Short-termism is the norm: 'pollution havens' are created as environmentally unfriendly policies are allowed far below socially desirable levels,[8] human rights abused, a blind eye turned to illegal acts, all in an attempt to attract foreign investment and all in the name of free market capitalism.[9]

But it is not only multinational corporations that benefit from 'open door' policies. Other beneficiaries of such policies are, typically, the host government, corrupt officials, and those fortunate enough to gain employment with foreign firms – they tend to pay better and their standards are often higher than those of local firms. In most of the Third World those outside the ruling elite, or outside the factory gates, are excluded from any gains.

China is the country that has benefited most from the greatest amount of FDI over the past few years, and has had astounding year-on-year economic growth for the past twenty-odd years, yet over a fifth of the population lives on less than $1 a day. India is the Third-World software success story of the decade, yet around half of the population lives at the equivalent of $1.50 a day. And while 80 per cent of revenues generated by oil companies operating in Nigeria remained in the country, they benefited a tiny ruling class.

Rather than the rising tide of the market lifting all boats, structural adjustment and liberalisation policies with no concomitant obligations on redistribution appear to have sunk some social groups, especially the vulnerable and the poor.

A senior oil executive operating in Colombia, said of his company's various activities there:

These projects are good for the government and good for us as a company . . . it's good for whoever can exploit the situation . . . but the majority don't benefit . . . it's only good for the few who can impose themselves.

In some places those who oppose the inflow of investment, fearing that too high a price will have to be paid, fall victim to state officials' greed. There are several reported incidents of Nigerian security forces beating, detaining, or killing people who protested against oil company activities. In November 1995 Ken Saro-Wiwa, the Nigerian political activist, poet and playwright who had led a five-year battle for the secession of Ogoniland and for compensation from Royal Dutch Shell for the environmental damage it had wrought there, was one of nine Ogoni activists executed after a trial that clearly violated international fair trial standards.

In India in May 1997 police beat 180 protesters demonstrating peacefully outside the gate of Enron Power Corporation against an electricity-generating project which locals feared would divert scarce water and kill fish.[10] Enron may not have controlled the chain of command, but the police clearly knew whose interests they were expected to protect. In the pursuit of foreign capital – often used to line their own pockets – some Third World governments have shown themselves willing to literally sacrifice their citizens.

The injustice still seen today in the Third World remains shocking, for all its familiarity. Conventional wisdom explains it as a product of the combination of economic underdevelopment and weak or absent democratic institutions. The conventional analysis is that in the long run, opening up a country's economy and encouraging inward investment will help to improve the people's lot, because it fosters education and training and so produces a better informed workforce and a reflective middle class – both of which, history suggests, are forces that work towards improved democratic participation and concern for rights and equality.

What the conventional analysis ignores, however, is that both the pursuit and the subsequent results of these free-market policies can polarise the population to an increasingly unacceptable extent, so that, as the Nobel prize winning economist Amartya Sen has said, 'famines can happen even when the granaries are full.'[11] This divisive trend can offset the more comfortable conventional prediction of what trade and investment will bring.

Outside your front door

This growing polarisation is not just a Third World phenomenon; we do not see it only in underdeveloped countries with weak democracies. It is also happening here in the West. Clive Harold is just one of many who have gained nothing from the recent boom years even from an initial position of considerable advantage. And the winner of the first million on the UK's version of *Who Wants to Be a Millionaire?* was – you guessed it – already a millionaire: Judith Keppel, a distant cousin of Camilla Parker Bowles, Prince Charles's girlfriend.

For in the West too the gap between rich and poor is widening.[12] In America, the spoils of a long period of prolonged economic expansion and low unemployment have not been widely distributed: 97 per cent of the increase in income has gone to the top 20 per cent of families over the past twenty years. While the rich earn more – average earnings of the top fifth of male earners rose by 4 per cent between 1979 and 1996 – the bottom fifth saw a 44 per cent drop in earnings. Some 36.5 million Americans (13.7 per cent of the population) now live in poverty, while 40 per cent of the country's wealth is owned by the top 1 per cent, compared with 13 per cent less than twenty-five years ago. While the national unemployment rate in the USA is 4.1 per cent, on many of its Native American reservations the rate is as high as 70 per cent. In isolated rural areas in America, the unemployment rate is often two, sometimes four, times as high as the national average. In the US incomes are now less equal than at any time since the Great Depression.[13]

In the UK, after eighteen years of Conservative rule, the situation New Labour inherited was similar if less marked. The distribution of incomes in the UK is more unequal now than at any time since World War II. When Margaret Thatcher came into power in 1979, the richest fifth of the population accounted for 43 per cent of all earned income, and the poorest fifth 2.4 per cent. In 1996, the last year of the Conservative government, the figures were 50 per cent and 2.6 per cent respectively. Since in the same period Britain's GDP rose substantially, the poor are getting a smaller slice of a much bigger pie.[14] The number of families below the poverty line rose by 60 per cent in the 1980s, and by 1996 the UK had the highest proportion in Europe of children living in poverty, with 300,000 British children worse off in absolute terms in 1995–6 than in 1979.

The number of people living below the poverty line has continued to rise under New Labour, despite efforts to reverse the trend. The number of households existing on less than half the average weekly income of £278 after housing costs rose by 1.3 million to 14.25 million between 1994 and 2000, more than double the number in the early 1980s.[15] Some 500,000 of that increase occurred after Labour took power in 1997. Poverty is heavily concentrated among single-parent families (at least half the single-parent households with children have incomes below the poverty line) and in homes where nobody has a job. The proportion of pensioners living on less than 40 per cent of average income rose from 20 to 23 per cent between 1998 and 1999.

In this new competitive world of free market capitalism it is the unskilled that fare worst. They have become the Epsilons of our new Brave New World – effectively commodities, easily replaceable by an ever growing overseas supply; and, in our post-manufacturing era, in ever less demand.

Those who were already earning lower wages are earning even less: they have less and less political and economic clout, thanks to their diminishing attractiveness as a group now that technological advances have lowered the demand for the unskilled, the decline of union power, and the increased competition from lower-cost manufacturing outposts or migrant labour willing to work for significantly less. Jobs and incomes in rich and poor countries have become more precarious as the pressures of global competition have led countries and employers to adopt more flexible labour policies, and work arrangements that absolve employers from long-term commitment to employees. The Netherlands, Spain and the UK have all decentralised wage bargaining.[16] And even France and Germany have weakened their worker dismissal laws.

While those at the top of the food chain are being courted ever more assiduously – wages for top managers have been rising and perks for the 'right' hires have been becoming even more extravagant[17] – in the United States there has been a 28 per cent decline since 1973 in entry-level wages in real dollars for male high-school graduates, and a decline in wages and benefits for all unskilled labour.[18] A fifth of American employees work at rates below the official poverty level, making a mockery of the low official unemployment rates. Even workers carrying out hazardous jobs are being paid less. In the late 1980s the union wage for removing asbestos insulation from old buildings was $31 an hour, but by the 1990s the rate had collapsed, thanks to the rise in non-union removal companies and an influx of immigrants eager for work. 'Contractors had no trouble getting workers for $12 to $15 an hour – and workers willing to do the job without respirators,' said Pawel Kedizor, the business manager for Local 78 of the Asbestos, Lead and Hazardous Waste Laborers union.

Now increasingly able to operate globally, corporations 'bottom fish', moving to countries with low labour costs to produce their goods. Production continues to shift to lower-cost options: from US factories to the *maquiladora* plants on the Mexican border where nearly a million people are employed at wages of under $5 a day; from Israel to nearby Jordan, putting scores of Israeli Arabs and Druzes out of employment as a consequence; from Silicon Valley to India and the former Soviet Union, where software is developed for a fraction of the cost it would entail domestically, from unionised workplaces to regions or countries where unions are less militant or there are non-unionised labourers, just glad to get a job.

And these jobs, even at reduced rates and with their spartan packages, are not even secure. For many, job security has become increasingly rare. Jobs are increasingly part time, casual, contractual for those who still are in employment. In Latin America, for example, by 1996 the proportion of workers without contracts increased to 30 per cent in Chile, 36 per cent in Argentina, 39 per cent in Colombia and 41 per cent in Peru.[19]

Technological advances have allowed machines to replace people. The 'knowledge economy' requires less manpower. While the world's 500 largest multinational corporations have grown sevenfold in sales, the worldwide employment of these global firms has remained virtually flat since the early 1970s, hovering at around 26 million people.[20]

Increased competition due to liberalisation of trade policies has meant that inefficient industries have had to downsize or streamline (euphemisms, of course, for sacking staff) or be forced out of business altogether. Even companies that are performing at levels that in the past would have been considered acceptable, nowadays fire staff, not because they are struggling but because the pressure on companies to make high returns is unprecedented (in many industries returns of between 20 and 35 per cent are now excepted), competition for investment flows is ever greater, and corporations feel more vulnerable than ever to threats of takeover or acquisition. IBM fired 122,000 people between 1991 and 1995 and reduced total wages by a third in a bid to push up their dividends and share price. The return for such 'prudence'? In 1995 the company's share price and dividend beat all previous records. The announcement by the American food company ConAgra that it would lay off 6,500 employees and close down twenty-nine of its plants pushed the price of its shares up so steeply that the company's market capitalisation increased by 500 million dollars in twenty-four hours. 'For shareholders and managers downsizing does pay off. Wall Street now simply prefers a dollar saved in costs to an extra dollar earned.'[21]

Even those who have jobs are losing benefits. In the USA, where people are mostly dependent on corporations for health benefits and pensions, the consequences are particularly worrying. While 70 per cent of American workers have pension plans, less than 10 per cent of those in the bottom tenth can rely upon any employer-financed retirement benefits. And the 20 per cent of Americans now working on temporary contracts or part-time receive no benefits at all, or insignificant ones.

Add to this the problems engendered by the privatisation of fundamental public goods and the situation is even bleaker. In the US there have been numerous cases of HMOs (for-profit corporations that provide health care) having been exposed over the past decade as 'cherry picking', that is, making sure that they attract healthy people and avoiding those who will be heavy utilisers of services. And most HMOs that were set up to take care of Medicare patients (US Citizens over 65 years) are now going bankrupt and getting out of the business since they cannot keep up with escalating costs, especially prescription costs, of elderly patients.

But it is not just HMOs that are the problem. The ability to secure health insurance at all is proving elusive for significant numbers of Americans. Forty-five million Americans currently do not have health insurance, 25 per cent of the chronically ill do not have adequate coverage. Disqualified from some insurance plans because of pre-existing health conditions, viewed as high risk by others and facing premiums they cannot afford, millions of Americans are facing potential crises. James Huth, a 55-year-old with a heart condition and diabetes, on a monthly pension of $1,045, clearly cannot afford the coverage of $1,200 a month he has been offered. 'I have a choice,' he said. 'Do I want to eat and have a place to sleep, or pay for health insurance and sleep in the street?' With Britain looking to America for answers to its healthcare problems and private health insurance being proposed as a solution, the American experience needs to be taken heed of. Given the track record of one of Britain's largest health insurers, PPP, which has refused to provide long-term treatment to a number of patients with chronic illnesses such as Hepatitis C,[22] are society's needs and the individual's right to healthcare to be determined by some kind of actuarial process? Will people get cast on a scrap heap if companies deem their custom no longer worth it?

Even those succeeding well in this new world – those with good careers and prospects, health benefits and private insurance, those who fall into the top percentiles – are suffering. Stress-related illnesses, obesity and diabetes are on the rise. The antidepressant market grew 16 per cent per year in G7 countries between 1989 and 1999.[23] Sales of Prozac have eclipsed the GDP of small nations. Illness is now costing UK employers £11 billion a year. The seemingly unstoppable craving for wealth, for the trophies of capitalism displayed on every billboard but ever harder to bag, is destroying the very fabric of people's lives.

Those in work are working longer and longer hours. British men emulate their American peers and now work the longest hours in Europe: half of the UK's fathers spend less than five minutes a day in direct contact with their children. Having a life now is being traded off for the prospect of getting a significantly better life in the future. The Internet mogul wannabes who network in London at Home House, in Tel Aviv at Espresso Bar and in San Francisco at The Thirsty Bear, have ceded their relationships, their passions, and any semblance of a normal existence in the hope of becoming the next Tim Jackson or Jeff Bezos.

In 1991 Ichiro Oshima, a 24-year-old employee of Japan's Dentsu Inc., the world's biggest advertising agency, hanged himself after an eighteen-month career of eighty-hour weeks, days when he did not leave the office until 6 a.m. and then only to get changed before returning. Rare were the times that he managed to catch more than two hours' sleep. 'I cannot function any more as a human being,' he told his superior about a month before his death. Japan's Supreme Court ruled that the company was fully liable for working the young man so hard he killed himself, and for failing to prevent his death. And Ichiro's story was not an isolated incident: suicides from overwork are becoming more frequent in a country which now even has a word for the phenomenon of people who work until they drop – *karoshi*. It is thought that there are 10,000 such deaths a year. Some fifty similar lawsuits are before the courts.[24]

The West's booming economy in recent years has not ended homelessness, poverty, or inequity. Unchecked, the situation is only likely to get worse. Research has repeatedly shown that it is not those who live in the richest societies, but those who live in societies with the most egalitarian wealth distribution, that have the best health. It is relative income levels that matter, not as one might have thought, absolute ones. Death rates from some of the most significant diseases[25] are reduced when income differentials are lowered.

Similarly, higher crime rates, including murders and violent crime, are correlated with wider income differences,[26] both in the West and in developing nations, which make the statistics that 3 per cent of the American male workforce is in prison[27] and that America's gaol population has increased 800 per cent over the past thirty years[28] at least comprehensible, if no less shocking. So much for the land of the free.

The effects of a society that includes increasingly marginalised groups cannot be escaped by moving into a gated community, or merely stepping over the homeless person who begs in front of your local store. The costs of this breakdown in solidarity, of ignoring the predicament of others, of perpetuating the selfishness born of a feeling of abandonment by the state, are likely to be carried by all of us.

By making economic success an end rather than a means to other ends, governments and people have lost sight of the fact that economic growth was supposed to have a higher purpose – stability, increased standards of living, increased social cohesion for *all*, without exclusion.

Things are only getting harder . . .

The advocates of global capitalism would argue that this is a temporary situation, a consequence not of flaws in the system, but of the fact that this experiment has not been running for long enough, that wealth will ultimately trickle down to all, 'that by providing incentives to the rich, for example, through lower taxation, the rich will be spurred into entrepreneurial activity, which will in turn create jobs and boost growth', that free enterprise and free and open markets will ultimately deliver.

They might admit that the system is inherently ruthless, but would conclude that for societies as a whole, the costs of neo-liberalism are worth paying. Thomas Mayer, chief economist in the Frankfurt offices of investment bank Goldman Sachs, has said:

When I look out on to the trading floor, I see no need to get the wages of the traders down. That's besides the point. But the need is to get the cleaning workers' wages down and to widen the spread between them. If we do that, we get more employment, less tax burden on those who are financing the unemployment, and therefore, greater growth.[29]

But who will look after capitalism's initial losers while they are waiting for the benefits to trickle down?

Not, it appears, most governments. The Thatcher–Reagan ethos is widespread, regardless of party persuasion. New Labour's Stephen Byers, in his first speech as Trade and Industry Secretary in 1999 declared: 'Wealth creation is now more important than wealth distribution.[30] And George W. Bush's school of 'compassionate conservatism' emulated by British Conservative leader, William Hague, takes the enforcement of social justice out of the government's hands and puts it into those of the community.

But even if governments want to address these issues, can they really do anything significant? As the former president of the German Bundesbank, Hans Tietmeyer, has said, 'Politicians have to understand that they are now under the control of the financial markets and not, any longer, of national debates.'[31] And if the financial markets deem that a new national healthcare scheme or a massive education reform will prove too costly, they will respond with higher interest rates or a collapsing currency. In this way global market forces not only rule out the kind of compensation to losers that would reduce the social costs of globalisation, they also seem to challenge state sovereignty itself. The footloose, mobile nature of global capital increasingly dictates what governments can and cannot do.

Beggar thy neighbour

Pressure on governments comes not only from capital markets but also from corporations. The world of the twenty-first century is a seller's market for business. Advances in communications and technology and the deregulation of capital markets have meant that corporations are now increasingly portable, able to decamp and set up elsewhere with relative ease.

Recognising the power that they now wield, multinational corporations play countries and politicians off against each other, exacting for themselves ever better and more lenient terms. Corporations effectively auction off promises of new jobs, infrastructure investment and economic growth to the highest international bidder, declining to move to or threatening to pull out of countries whose employment costs and taxes are too high, or where standards are too stringent or subsidies and loans not forthcoming. Globally, dominant companies increasingly call the shots, able to move money freely, deciding for themselves where to invest and produce, where to pay taxes, and playing these potential sites off against one another.[32] Politicians are left trying to stem the flow, offering sweeteners to corporations to maintain factories so as to minimise the political and social costs of closure, but without any long-term guarantees that the firms will not eventually relocate. National governments appear increasingly impotent in the face of the giant corporations, who transcended national borders many years ago.[33]

The levying of taxes, arguably the most fundamental right of the nation state and a potential means of redressing social and economic inequality, is being squeezed by corporate pressure.[34] As capital and highly-paid labour are now able to move more freely from high-tax countries to low-tax ones, as the world becomes more integrated in the wake of globalisation and developments in communications, a nation's ability to set tax rates higher than other nations is being put in question. The resultant mindset is one of 'beggar thy neighbour'. Ireland opposes harmonising corporate tax rates across the EU because its low rates give it an advantage over other member-states in attracting multinational firms. Britain blocks an EU savings-tax directive because it might hurt the City of London. America might ask for a worldwide ban on new Internet taxes, because as a net exporter of e-commerce it would benefit.

In Germany, where revenue from corporate taxes has fallen by 50 per cent over the past twenty years, despite a rise in corporate profits of 90 per cent,[35] Finance Minister Oskar Lafontaine's attempt to raise the tax burden on German firms in 1999 was thwarted by a group of companies, including Deutsche Bank (assets over $400 billion), Dresdner Bank, the insurance conglomerate Allianz, BMW, Daimler-Benz and RWE, the German energy and industrial group, all of which threatened to move investment or factories to other countries if government policy did not suit them.

'It's a question of at least 14,000 jobs,' threatened Dieter Schweer, a RWE spokesman. 'If the investment position is no longer attractive, we will examine every possibility of switching our investments abroad.'[36] Daimler-Benz proposed relocating to the USA; other companies threatened to stop buying government bonds and investing in the German economy.

In view of the power these corporations wield, their threats were taken seriously. So seriously that they were undoubtedly a major cause of Lafontaine's resignation. He remained defiant to the end: 'The heart isn't traded on the stock market yet,' he said as he left.[37] 'Things will be different now,' Bobo Hombach, Chancellor Schröders's closet aide, commented in response. 'We have to move in a different direction. Gerhard Schröder will have different priorities, that's obvious'.[38] If Oskar Lafontaine's resignation proved anything, it was that Schröder was willing to take the pressure from business very seriously. Within a few months Germany was planning corporate tax cuts which would reduce tax on German companies below US rates.[39] As one of Schröder's senior advisers in Washington commented, 'Deutsche Bank and industrial giants such as Mercedes are too strong for the elected government in Berlin.'[40]

It is not just corporate tax that concerns corporations. Countries with high rates of personal taxation are coming under pressure from the international business community too. Several large Swedish companies, including Ericsson, have threatened to leave their home country because of high income tax which, they claimed, made it hard to recruit highly skilled employees.[41] (Ericsson actually did fulfil its threat, moving several corporate and production functions abroad and opening a big headquarters in London in 1999.) And in the UK, Internet companies are in conflict with the Treasury over national insurance charges on share options, which they claim will encourage highly skilled workers to move overseas.

In the twenty-first century, corporations are increasingly deciding how much tax to pay and where to pay it. The Internet is only likely to make it even harder for governments to collect taxes. A company can now locate in a low-tax haven, base its physical production facilities (where it may angle for subsidies) elsewhere, and sell to its customers from a virtual location – outside of the reach of governments.[42] And the greater the advances in communications, the more cases we are likely to see of corporations locating in one place, and paying tax in another or even nowhere at all. Companies like the banking firm BCCI, which through a complex web of aliases managed to be registered nowhere for tax purposes, and Rupert Murdoch's News Corporation, which has earned profits of over $2.3 billion in Britain since 1987 but as of 1999, paid no corporation tax there at all and no more than 6 per cent tax worldwide,[43] may well become the norm rather than then exception.

What is the impact of this non-collection of taxes from corporations? At worst, such damage to tax systems that governments could become unable to meet the legitimate demands of their citizens for public services. At best, the government's ability to spend is severely restricted, and an ever higher burden put on individual taxpayers' shoulders. If governments were willing to implement such a redistributive strategy, that is.

For despite polls that report a large majority of the British public as willing to pay higher levels of tax to improve public services (in a recent survey, Britain was unique in this among seventeen industrialised nations),[44] no British party would, these days, risk campaigning on a tax increase platform. Labour strategist Philip Gould has said, 'If the election campaign [in 1997] had one crucial battle, one defining fight, it was over tax. We lost the 1992 election and won the 1997 one in large part because of tax . . . It was impossible to compete and succeed if tax increased continually as a proportion of GNP.'[45]

Not only would such a policy be perceived as a vote loser, but the fear is that the rich or skilled would simply leave if they perceived the tax burden as too high. As able people of all kinds become increasingly migratory, it will be harder still to sustain heavy demands on them to bear the cost of social spending. Those with large incomes and capital resources are likely to follow the example of corporations, and locate themselves with low taxes in mind.

As has Laetitia Casta, the 21-year-old French actress, sometime Victoria's Secret lingerie model and latest incarnation of Marianne, the personification of France, whose face will adorn French coins and stamps for the next decade. In April 2000 she moved to London, a relocation that made the front pages of newspapers both sides of the Channel. Although Mlle Casta has denied that taxation is her reason for moving, the predominant feeling in France is, as one French deputé has put it, that Marianne has moved to *perfide Albion* to escape the punitive wealth taxes of *la belle France*. With upper level income tax rates of 47 per cent in France, compared to 35 per cent in the UK, it seems that she had a very good reason for moving. Many more of her well-heeled compatriots are reportedly crossing the Channel to establish fiscal residence in one of the EU's most lenient tax regimes.

Nevertheless, despite the substantial differences in taxation between the UK and, say, Germany and France, and despite the relocation of Laetitia Casta and others, we haven't yet seen significant levels of wealthy economic migrants to the UK. And William Hague's lower tax platform (in December 2000 he proposed that a future Conservative government would cut taxes by £8 billion), was met with marked indifference by the electorate. But the raising of taxes in lower-tax environments is still *perceived* by politicians as far too risky a strategy to openly endorse or execute, which threatens a growing gap between the demand for public services and the taxation available to pay for them.

Caring for the corporation

Not only are governments finding it harder to raise taxes, they are also finding themselves having to provide 'welfare' to a not terribly needy client – the private sector. In America direct subsidies to businesses total over $75 billion annually,[46] with the poorest states – those where the difference in income between rich and poor is greatest – offering the largest amounts.[47] In Ohio $2.1 billion in business property went untaxed in 1996 thanks to business assistance programmes. Beneficiaries of Ohio's 'corporate welfare' included Spiegel, Wal-Mart and Consolidated Stores Corporation, all of which were absolved from property taxes. In the US it is property taxes that fund public schools. As one school treasurer put it, 'Kids get hurt and stockholders get rich'.

Borden Chemicals has been excused approximately $15 million in tax over the past decade as part of Louisiana's corporate welfare programme. The same Borden Chemicals that in August 1996 released a dense grey cloud of toxic ethylene dichloride, vinyl chloride monomer and hydrogen chloride into the atmosphere; that in 1997 was responsible for the release of vinyl chloride monomer and ammonia into the atmosphere which forced the closing of Route 73; and in July 1998 released a cloud of hydrochloric acid fumes, shutting down roads in the area.

In Arkansas the state government spent over $10 million building new infrastructure to lure Frito-Lay to Jonesboro, Arkansas; while a neighbouring town plagued by dirty water supplies and in need of a new water infrastructure, waited for ten years for the $750,000 it needed to remedy the situation.[48]

This is by no means unique to the United States. The Taiwanese TV tube maker Chungwha generated a bidding war between Scotland and Wales at the end of 1995. General Motors touted the positioning of a $750 million car plant all across South-East Asia.[49] The pharmaceutical company Glaxo allegedly threatened to relocate its British research and production facilities if its new anti-influenza drug, Relenza, was not approved for sale in the UK.[50] And Tony Blair supported efforts to persuade BMW not to shut Rover's Longbridge plant, granting a £150 million subsidy in order to save 10,000 jobs at Rover. Within a year, however, BMW had pulled out of the UK, giving no notice of its plans. Although the granting of subsidies has become a vote-winning strategy, it is not always enough.

But when governments provide welfare handouts to corporations (sometimes even in defiance of their own regulations) and respond to the threats made by corporations to pull out and relocate, the rules of the game subtly change. It comes to make good business sense for corporations to turn their attention towards the political arena. Competitive advantage may be gained not only from lower costs, better service or differentiated products, but also by a company's political strategies and effective lobbying.

Ordinary citizens once again lose. Money spent on subsidising corporations is money that becomes unavailable for public services; the promised jobs and investment flows often do not materialise, or if they do, can swiftly vanish (as at Rover). Companies relocate with relative ease to places where the terms are sweeter, despite the damage they can wreak en route. In Germany workers would at least have to be consulted in such cases, but in the USA and UK they typically don't

As Ohio State Senator Charles Horn, has said,

We know companies are manipulative, but it's the nature of business to go after every dollar that's legally available. Don't place the blame on the company; place the blame on government. This is government's folly.

Quite.

Passing the buck

So governments are caught between a rock and a hard place; unwilling to risk losing the electorate's support by raising taxes, and unable to increase spending for fear of market censure. What will be the impact of the enforced capping of government's social spending? More inequity? A world in which the poor become ever more marginalised, and the rich even richer? A world in which the principal division is between those who are inside and those who are outside the global corporation? A world in which the consumer has some power, but those who cannot afford to be consumers have none?

Politicians who talk of a Third Way have over the past few years espoused noble aims of reconciling capitalism with humanity, social justice with economic success. In the USA such aims sound increasingly hollow. The country regularly stands last among developed nations in the proportion of its GNP devoted to social programmes or to redistribution. In the UK, New Labour has made some inroads into inequity while operating within the confines of the global capitalist system. Despite the discouraging results so far in tackling poverty, the poorest households have on average gained from recent budgets with the bottom tenth 9 per cent better off, against virtually no gain for the top tenth. More than £2.5 billion in spending has been shifted away from the top half of the income distribution to the bottom, and various national measures have been introduced to reduce inequality of opportunity. In July 2000 Chancellor Gordon Brown indicated his commitment to break what had almost become a taboo, increasing public spending with a £43 billion package which would put more money into education and employment, childcare, transport, poorer regions and inner cities over the next few years.

New Labour has not been honest, however, about the trade-offs that will undoubtedly have to be made if this goal is to be pursued in the long term. It is only thanks to the strong economy, which resulted in falling payments to the unemployed and booming tax receipts, to one-off moneyspinners such as the auction of mobile phone wavebands, and to money stored up from three lean years during which there had been a freeze on departmental spending, that the Labour government was able to allocate this extra money without raising taxes.

Indeed, this has been a key feature of the New Labour government's approach to tackling poverty. While it appears to deny the received wisdom that says governments are bullied out of redistributive spending by the dictates of global capital, in fact the Labour approach demonstrates precisely the limits of what governments can now achieve.

Increases in income tax and corporation tax have become politically and economically untenable, ensuring that governments must fund public services through a sleight of hand dependent on continued economic growth. If the economy is booming it is easier for politicians to improve the lot of the worse off without penalising the rich. Through techniques directed at improving the chances of those at the bottom, such as in-work benefits, tax credits such as the Working Families Tax Credit and the minimum wage, and by initiating moves to reduce benefits on groups least likely to be able to protest – single mothers, pensioners, the disabled – the British New Labour government was able to largely avoid unpopular tax hikes. There has been some redistribution, but it has been redistribution by stealth: taxes on pension funds and the utilities, for example, or increases in indirect taxes – which fall on all of us, not just the rich – or the restriction of benefits for the better off.[51]

Will I have enough to live on when I retire? Will I get proper health care when I am sick? Who will look after me if I am old? If I lose my job or become unable to work, will I end up in poverty or dependent on charity? These are significant questions for everyone, and across the world they are being asked with growing apprehension. For the burden on the state is only anticipated to get bigger. Growing elderly populations are already putting an ever increasing burden on government (China will provide the most dramatic example of this after 2040), and global labour market pressures resulting from the technological revolution will only lead to more unemployed. And without adequate funding, will even governments genuinely committed to social justice and welfare be able to deliver what their societies need?

Attempts to raise money at the margins without advancing a sustained argument for higher taxes encourage voters to believe in a politics without difficult choices, and reduces room for manoeuvre when the economic bubble of the current boom finally bursts, as it undoubtedly will.

Ignoring one of the fundamental dilemmas of the capitalist age will not make it go away. International forces are undermining government's ability to sustain the welfare state, and its ability to restrain economic forces so that society could be a more humane and equitable place.

Abstaining from a discussion of the limits of Anglo-American style capitalism, a system that favours the rich so blatantly, and puts the profit motive above all else is not a conscionable option. Suggesting an alternative way forward that apparently does not necessitate tough choices and is able to reconcile the goals of social justice and economic growth without asking the question of 'economic growth for whom?' is fundamentally misleading.

Governments need to address the underlying issues and not evade them. But has the pursuit of economic success become so overriding a goal that any discussion of cost has become untenable? How far is society willing to go to gain a few extra points of economic growth? Where do our true priorities lie?

MANNING THE DOOR AT
THE PRIVATE SECTOR HQ

Spies-R-US

In 1947, British and American spy chiefs banded together to share security information. It was decided to operate a joint surveillance system, codename Echelon. Later three other English-speaking nations, Canada, Australia and New Zealand, joined the project, although the USA remained the dominant partner.

The idea was sound: to renew the alliance that had successfully defeated Nazi Germany, in order to thwart a new threat, that of Soviet Russia. Moscow was on the verge of acquiring an enormous nuclear arsenal, and was trying as never before to spread her influence around the globe. The British and Americans concluded that they could better contain this new menace by working together. In America, military Sigint (signals intelligence) units were established at Sugar Grove in West Virginia. In Britain, a listening station at Menwith Hill, in Yorkshire in the north of England, far from London, became the most important international site for the group, and in particular for America's National Security Agency (NSA), the leading player in Echelon.

The history books have yet to detail just how significant a role the project played in countering the spread of Soviet communism. But no doubt it played a part, and in 1989 the Berlin Wall came down. By 1991, the whole Soviet bloc had crumbled, and the communist threat all but disappeared.

Echelon's electronic surveillance, however, did not; and a decade later, in February 2000, startling allegations emerged. Echelon was no longer being used for political and military espionage against dictatorships that threatened the free world. Instead it was being used to monitor everyday commercial activities of businesses belonging to some of America and Britain's closest allies.

Moreover, startling advances in technology during the 1990s meant that the system was now so powerful that it was reportedly capable of picking up every word of telephone, fax and e-mail communications relayed by satellite anywhere in the world. Frighteningly, it applied to us all. Our each and every phone call and e-mail could be monitored. The implications were enormous. In a massive abuse of its original purpose, senior US, and possibly British, espionage chiefs used Echelon to spy on individuals and to pass on commercial secrets to American businesses.

These startling revelations came to light in February 2000, when newly declassified American defence department documents were posted on the Internet, and for the first time provided official confirmation that such a global electronic eavesdropping operation existed at all. (The existence of Echelon had first been exposed in 1996 by a renegade agent in New Zealand, but had not previously been proved.)

Within days the European Parliament released a report containing serious allegations. American corporations had, it was said, 'stolen' contracts heading for European and Asian firms after the NSA intercepted conversations and data and then passed information to the US

Commerce Department for use by American firms. In Europe, the Airbus consortium and Thomson CSF of France were among the alleged losers. In Asia, the US used information gathered from its bases in Australia to win a half share of a significant Indonesian trade contract for AT&T that communication intercepts showed was initially going to NRC of Japan.

The European nations were furious, both with the Americans and with the British, their supposed partners in forging a new united Europe. In France, a lawsuit was launched against the US and Britain (on the grounds of breach of France's stringent privacy laws), in Italy and Denmark judicial and parliamentary investigations began, and in Germany members of the Bundestag demanded an inquiry. One Belgian member of the European Parliament summed up the feeling of many of his colleagues when he said that if the Americans and British had actually done this, it was 'an intolerable attack on human rights'. The Portuguese government – which at the time was chairing the European Union's rotating presidency – proposed establishing a European secretariat to monitor Echelon's activities.

The Europeans were stunned to discover that Big Brother was no longer communist Russia or Red China, but its supposed ally and partner, America, spying on European consumers and businesses for its own commercial gain.

The European Parliament's report stated that in 1995 the US National Security Agency tapped calls between Thomson-CSF and the Brazilian authorities relating to a lucrative $1.5 billion contract to create a satellite surveillance system for the Brazilian rainforest. The NSA gave details of Thomson's bid (and of the bribes the French had been offering to Brazilian officials) to an American rival, Raytheon Corporation, which later won the contract.

The report also disclosed that in 1993, the NSA intercepted calls between the European consortium Airbus, the national airline of Saudi Arabia, and the Saudi government. The contract, worth over $5 billion, later went to the American manufacturers Boeing and McDonnell Douglas.

Another target was the German wind generator manufacturer Enercon. In 1999, it developed what it thought was a secret invention enabling it to generate electricity from wind power at a far cheaper rate than had been achieved previously. However, when the company tried to market its invention in the United States, it was confronted by its American rival, Kenetech, which disclosed that it had already patented a virtually identical development. Kenetech subsequently filed a court order against Enercon banning the sale of its equipment in the US. The allegations were confirmed by an anonymous NSA employee, who agreed to appear in silhouette on German television to reveal how he had stolen Enercon's secrets. He claimed that he had used satellite information to tap the telephone and computer modem lines that linked Enercon's research laboratory with its production unit. Detailed plans of the company's secret invention were then passed on to Kenetech.

German scientists at Mannheim University, who were reported to be developing a system enabling computer data to be stored on household adhesive tape instead of conventional CDs, began to resort to the Cold War tactic of walking in the woods to discuss confidential subjects.

Security experts in Germany estimated that by the year 2000, American industrial espionage was costing German business annual losses of at least $10 billion through stolen inventions and development projects. Horst Teltschik, a senior BMW board member and a former security adviser to the former German Chancellor, Helmut Kohl, said, 'We have discovered that industrial secrets are being siphoned off to an extent never experienced until now.'

A Parisian lawyer, Jean-Pierre Millet, went further in the spring of 2000, claiming, 'You can bet that every time a French government minister makes a mobile telephone call, it is recorded.'

The orders, it seems, may have come from the very top. Early in his presidency, Bill Clinton decreed that industrial espionage should be one of the main tasks of the CIA. 'What is good for Boeing is good for America,' he was quoted as saying.

Was this the new world order we had hoped for in the days of the Cold War?

The new politics

In fairness to the US and Britain, virtually everyone was guilty of listening in on business. The European Union's report also revealed that France and Germany co-operate to eavesdrop on both North and South America, a claim backed up by insiders in Washington, who confirmed that European secret services pursue the same policy as the Americans.[1] China encourages its overseas students and scientists to pass commercial secrets back home; and the Japanese are known masters of commercial espionage.

In the post–Cold War era, in the age of international laissez-faire capitalism, commercial and economic interests have superseded all other national interests. Instead of acting as a check on corporations, governments are now doing all they can to romance them, acting less as night watchmen – the role Adam Smith said that they needed to play in order to ensure the success of free markets[2] – and more as round-the-clock doormen at the headquarters of Private Sector plc. The very same institutions that served a national purpose in the Cold War era, political and military intelligence, are now being tapped to service corporate interests. In the new state of security considerations, commercial interests have gained primacy.[3]

Economics is the new politics, and business is in the driving seat. Governments have redefined their role from that of rule maker to that of referee, from warden to corporate champion. Because of their dependence on the success of the private sector and exports for wealth, stability, rising aggregate standards of living, jobs – factors that can today be equated with political power – governments do not just sit back and let the market take its course. Instead they actively pursue policies that benefit business, giving up in the process their ability to set an independent agenda and favouring corporate Goliaths over individual Davids.

International politics in the twenty-first century is less and less about territorial gains, and more and more about increasing market share.[4] In advanced economies governments now act as salesmen, promoting the fortunes of their own corporations in the hope of providing a core prosperity for their state[5] and keeping themselves in power.

Tony Blair and Gerhard Schröder almost certainly spend more time on promoting the sales of British and German corporations than on foreign policy. Commercial success has become a primary criterion for the success of a country's ambassadors.

To quote Madeleine Albright, former US Secretary of State:

Competition for the world's markets is fierce. Often, our firms go head-to-head with foreign competitors who are receiving active support from their own governments. A principal responsibility of the Department of State is to see that the interests of American companies and workers receive fair treatment, and that inequitable barriers to competition are overcome. Accordingly, the doors to the Department of State and our embassies around the world are open – and will remain open – to US businesspeople seeking to share their ideas and to ask our help.[6]

Instead of fighting over territory, nations now battle over access to markets and economic freedoms. The great wars of the twenty-first century will be trade wars fought with the weapons of commerce.[7] Economic power has replaced military might as the key to international dominance. Investment capital provided by the state is the equivalent of firepower; state-subsidised R&D is the equivalent of weapons innovation; market pentration supported by the state has replaced military bases and garrisons on foreign soil; and trade barriers are now the most formidable of all artillery.[8] Who would have thought that eleven years after the fall of the Berlin Wall, major issues in European–American relations would be groceries[9] – rum, beef,[10] bananas[11] and peaches?[12] Or that the most critical issue in Sino-US relations would be China's admission to the WTO?[13] The overriding concern of governments in the free-trade, free-market world of the early twenty-first century is how to ensure their firms get a decent slice of the global economic pie.

The deal of the century

In Russia, after the collapse of the Soviet Union, commercial interests quickly gained primacy. On 20 September 1994 the Russian state-owned oil company Lukoil signed an oil exploration contract with the Republic of Azerbaijan and a consortium of Western oil companies including BP, Agip and Statoil, in what was billed as 'the deal of the century', a contract that was expected to generate £100 billion in profits from the realisation of Azerbaijan's vast oil reserves.

What made this deal particularly unusual was the fact that Russia's involvement went entirely against the country's nationalistic sentiment. Since 1991 one of the pillars of official foreign oil policy of the Russian Federation had been its non-recognition of the rights of other Caspian states to unilaterally exploit their offshore national resources.[14] Boris Yeltsin spoke on several occasions about the need to protect Russian strategic interests in the 'near-abroad' of the old Soviet Union, and Pavel Grachev, the former Russian Defence Minister, said on a visit to Turkey only a few months before the deal was signed that Turkey should keep out of 'our' Azerbaijan.[15]

It seems, however, that even after the Russians had denounced the proposed deal as implicitly recognising Azeri jurisdiction over the disputed waters, once they realised that they risked losing their share of the spoils, nationalistic foreign policy considerations were subordinated. At the very moment that the Russian Ambassador and representatives of the Russian Ministry of Fuel and Energy were celebrating at the official deal signing ceremony in Baku,[16] the Russian Ministry of Foreign Affairs was declaring that Russia 'will not recognise [the agreement], with all the ensuing consequences'.[17] Empty words from a ministry that in the post-Cold War era was clearly losing ground.

Not so ethical foreign policy

Elsewhere in the world commercial interests are also being given primacy. Shortly after the electoral victory of Britain's Labour Party in 1997, Robin Cook, the new Foreign Secretary, approved a pre-existing arms sale contract with the Republic of Indonesia. This was despite the official adoption of a government 'ethical foreign policy' which prohibited the sale of arms to regimes that might use them for internal repression, the abuse of human rights or external aggression, and despite growing concern for massive human rights violations and fears of genocide in Indonesia's forcefully annexed territory of East Timor[18] – fears which later events proved justified.

According to Labour ministers the contract (for an estimated £438 million[19]), which included sixteen Hawk fighter jets manufactured by Britain's largest defence company, British Aerospace, would be 'too hard to revoke'.[20] This statement was somewhat misleading. The government could in fact have revoked licences without having had to pay damages or compensation to the parties involved. It was not prepared to do so because of the impact such a decision would have had on the British defence industry, an industry which it is estimated has sales of over £5 billion a year and employs over 400,000 people. Mr Cook apparently had this clearly spelled out for him by both the Prime Minister's office[21] and BAE senior executives.

Nor was it only the British arms industry that stood to lose if the government blocked the arms sales to Indonesia. The UK, Indonesia's second largest investor, hoped that the deal would enhance the interests of other sections of the British industry. At this time bidding was under way for billions of pounds' worth of contracts related to the giant Natuna gas field project, 'one of the biggest investment opportunities in the world'.[22] The prevailing wisdom seems to have been that Britain could not afford to risk its special relationship with Indonesia, whose imports from the UK had risen by 150 per cent in less than five years.

Rather than discouraging sales to Indonesia for ethical reasons, the Labour government, since coming to power, has issued 125 export licences for arms to Indonesia for a wide range of products including machine-guns, military helmets and aircraft spares. As late as July 1999, when British Aerospace Hawks were flying over Dili strafing the East Timorese, the UK had still not suspended the export of all military equipment to Indonesia. Such delays led to Britain being condemned by the East Timor Independence Movement as having been 'the single worst obstructionist of any industrialised country'.

To be fair to Robin Cook, it appears that he had earlier tried to change British policy. But in October 1998, when he tried to implement tough disclosure rules on arms exports, he was thwarted by the then Industry Secretary Peter Mandelson, who put forward commercial objections, arguing that making licence applications public would identify companies' export plans and damage their competitiveness. More likely the true reason was to avoid political embarrassment for potential overseas customers or for Britain's massive arms export industry (the world's second largest after the USA).[23] As one of Robin Cook's aides commented, demands from the Department of Trade and Industry, which was bowing to 'merciless' business pressures, had compromised Cook's ability to act.[24] Ethical considerations had little weight when pitted against a possible loss in sales and an erosion of market share.

The Indonesian case provides a clear example of the way that individual companies' interests and the aggregate interests of industry can now dictate foreign policy and override moral, humanitarian and even legal considerations – Indonesia was violating international law in annexing and forcefully occupying East Timor. What is particularly noteworthy in this case is that the sales were not approved by a Conservative government but by a Labour one, by a party traditionally associated with a social conscience. In fact Tapol, the Indonesian human rights group, claims that the list of export licenses for Indonesia approved since Labour came into power bore a marked resemblance to the supply deals done under the Conservatives.[25]

Not only the Indonesians have benefited from Britain's trade policy. In Labour's first year of office, numerous arms licences to ethically dubious regimes were approved: eighty-four to Pakistan, forty-two to Sri Lanka and 105 to Turkey.

The British public had come to expect this kind of behaviour under previous Conservative governments. Conservative scandals had included Mrs Thatcher's son Mark's alleged receipt of a multi-million pound commission on the £20 billion Al Yamamah arms contract, which his mother signed with Saudi Arabia in 1985; and the £1.3 billion defence deal with Malaysia in 1988, later found to have been illegally and expensively linked with British aid. But Labour in opposition had always been a vocal critic of such deals. In fact Robin Cook, while he was shadow defence secretary, was the most vehement critic of the 'Arms to Iraq' scandal in which a number of Conservative ministers were found to have sanctioned breaches in an embargo on the sale of arms to Iraq.

In the quest for market share, the traditional lines separating left and right are disappearing. In the name of competitive markets, private interests are being served with little regard for ethics.

What about human rights?

It is not just that arms are being sold to repressive regimes; the whole idea of safeguarding human rights, a concept that was imbued with real meaning after World War II, has also fallen by the wayside as Western governments perceive only their need to promote trade and champion their firms' interests worldwide.[26]

The European Union agreed a customs union agreement with Turkey at the same time that the European Parliament was voicing concern on human rights violations and fears of genocide of the Kurds in Turkey's eastern territories. It did little for years about Nigeria's human rights violations under the regime of General Sani Abacha, apart from routinely condemning them. Trade and oil interests prevailed.

The US backed the dictatorial Taliban regime in Afghanistan until 1997, despite its terrible record on human rights, its severe oppression of women, public executions, and intransigent Islamic fundamentalism. In large part, this was because the American oil company Unocal had signed a deal with the Taliban to build a $2 billion gas line and $2.5 billion oil line to transport oil and gas from Turkmenistan to Pakistan via Afghanistan. Washington eventually got tough with the Taliban – but only after immense pressure from the US feminist movement and because of the Taliban's support for the Saudi terrorist Osama Bin Laden.[27]

Saudi Arabia's human rights record is almost as bad, but foreign governments unwilling to jeopardise their relationship with the oil-rich sheikdom continue to supply the country with equipment that can be used to torture or ill-treat prisoners. Between 1980 and 1993, the US government authorised export licences worth $5 million under the category OA82C, which includes thumb cuffs, leg irons, and shackles.[28]

The West continues to woo China despite its continuing poor record on human rights – its jailing of followers of the Falun Gong spiritual and exercise group, underground Christians and dissidents; its ignoring of the internationally recognised rights of workers spelled out in the UN Convention on Human Rights; its use of forced prison labour – because of the huge market opportunity that China presents to Western firms. China has a good fifth of the world's population, and Hong Kong and Shanghai (with Singapore) lead economic and financial revitalisation in the post-crisis East Asian economies[29] and are becoming the main 'business hubs' of the region. It is not difficult to understand the attraction.

Bill Clinton, as a presidential candidate in the 1992 election, criticised then President George Bush for promising to renew China's Most Favored Nation trading status, because of China's human rights abuses. But once he was in office he personally undertook the business of admitting China as a full partner in the WTO,[30] and by May 2000 he had succeeded in normalising trade relations with China.

Clinton explained his about-face on China with the 'trade encourages democracy' line, which claims that the greater the access to foreign business and influence the Chinese have, the quicker the communist grip on the country will be loosened and the faster its attitude on human rights reformed – a view endorsed by various academic findings correlating investment by multinational firms with increasing levels of GDP, and correlating growing GDP over time with greater respect for human rights, freer markets and even democratisation.[31] Or at least that was the justification he used in 1994 when he took the radical step of uncoupling trade and human rights, so that he no longer considered the illiberal nature of the Chinese regime in his annual executive order extending Most Favored Nation trading status to Beijing.

A correlation between foreign investment and democratisation does not of course necessarily imply that foreign investment causes an improvement in local conditions. It is equally possible that foreign investment is attracted by an already improving political situation.[32] Furthermore, other academic studies dispute such findings, finding no meaningful relationship between levels of foreign investment and improvements in a country's human rights performance. One study carried out by the OECD[33] found that a country's desire to increase trade and investment could lead to a deterioration rather than an improvement in human rights, since, as we saw in the previous chapter, some governments feel that by failing to impose basic labour standards they can help attract inward investment.

Clearly the evidence is inconclusive. Yet it is not in question that countries such as the USA, which wield huge economic purchasing and investment potential, are in extremely strong bargaining positions. Surely if they were to make better human rights a condition of strong trade ties, developing countries would have to listen?[34] In the global economy, could any country really afford to refuse these terms and turn their backs on trade with the West? Are Western governments not giving up the human rights issue unnecessarily, and failing to extract promises that they almost certainly could successfully demand?

If dangling the carrot of investment is considered an acceptable strategy, what about wielding the stick of sanctions? Shouldn't democratic governments dealing with repressive regimes at least consider the possibility of actively preventing trade and investment inflows?

Sanctions are gaining favour: between 1945 and 1990 only two UN sanctions were imposed, on South Africa and Rhodesia, but over the past decade they have been used 13 times. It remains unclear, however, whether they ultimately help or harm. Archbishop Desmond Tutu stated during South Africa's apartheid era:

> I have no hope of real change from this government unless they are forced. We face a catastrophe in this land, and only the action of the international community can save us . . . I call upon the international community to apply punitive sanctions against this government to help us establish a new South Africa – non-racial, democratic, participatory and just. This is a non-violent strategy to help us do so . . .
>
> You hear so many extraordinary arguments. Sanctions don't work. Sanctions hurt those most of all you want to help. That is interesting . . . I have to say that I find this new upsurge of altruism from those who suddenly discover they feel sorry for blacks very touching, though it's strange coming from those who have benefited from cheap black labour for many years. Spare us your crocodile tears, for your massive profits have been gained on the basis of black suffering and misery.[35]

The Burmese dissident Aung San Suu Kyi echoed Tutu's sentiments when she said in 1994:

> If material betterment . . . is sought in ways that wound the human spirit, it can in the long run only lead to greater human suffering. The vast possibilities that a market economy can open up to developing countries can be realised only if economic reforms are undertaken within a framework that recognises human needs.
>
> There are those who claim that the people of Burma are suffering as a consequence of sanctions, but that is not true. We want investments to be at the right time – when the benefits will go to the people of Burma, not just to a small, select elite connected to the government.[36]

Yet it is not clear that in all cases sanctions are the best option. Much criticism has been attached to the use of sanctions against Saddam Hussein's Iraq, for example.

> The economy has been shattered and agricultural output badly disrupted. Malnutrition is endemic and medical services have been eroded. The UN's own agencies admit that up to 5,300 children are dying every month from disease, malnutrition and related conditions. All told, it is believed that 500,000 Iraqis have died since 1991 as an indirect result of sanctions. Baghdad puts the figure at 1.5m, or roughly 7.5% of the entire population.[37]

More understanding is needed before we can determine those cases where sanctions will be most likely to lead to the desired results, and those in which they will make the situation worse. Clearly the context in which they are imposed is important. What was appropriate in the case of South Africa, where it was essentially the white middle class who were most hurt by them, appears to be wrong in the case of Iraq where it is the poor who are most affected and where the sanctions are serving to keep Saddam Hussein in power.

A framework is needed for determining the most apt response to a particular situation. But at present the only single unifying principle that seems to determine whether or not sanctions are imposed is whether or not they will harm the corporate interests of the country that is considering imposing them. How else could America's willingness to ban new investment in Burma by US companies, where US business interests are virtually non-existent, be reconciled with its failure to impose sanctions on China? Why wouldn't the 'trade encourages democracy' line work there too? Perhaps it is too much to expect consistency from a country that preaches human rights on the international stage, yet ignores reports of rights violations in its own prisons, is the only advanced Western country that maintains the death penalty, and along with Saudi Arabia, Iran, Libya and China is one of a handful of countries that still executes adolescents, the mentally ill and the mentally retarded.

Cloaked in America's concern for human rights is a clear economic agenda. So the protests from human rights activists against Chinese policies towards Tibet and Taiwan that met China's Premier Zhu Rongji when he visited the United States[38] in 1999[39] fell on deaf ears in government. The dominant view was that 'the bilateral relation with China is the most important that the US now has',[40] and that the US 'needs to improve relations with China and the best way to achieve this is to keep out of its domestic politics, in particular human rights and Taiwan'.[41]

Cynics have long noted that American foreign policy is not driven by a concern for the greater good. US government policy has long been dictated by corporate interests. But whereas during the Cold War corporate interests masqueraded as military interests, this rationale is no longer convincing or relevant. In an ideal world a superpower like the US, now that the Soviet military threat has disappeared, would concentrate on important issues like human rights. Instead, despite a growing rhetoric on human rights, we see little willingness to make any sacrifice to guarantee them; purely commercial interests are allowed to dwarf all others. The spy satellites that are being used to pass on corporate secrets to American companies could be being used to monitor human rights abuses in, say, Burma instead.

When governments evaluate trade, sanctions and human rights on purely economic rather than ethical grounds, they do not only fail the people in the countries in question. They also fail to respect the wishes of many of their own citizens. Choice is restricted to what business or the markets want rather than the traditional democratic notion of what the people want.[42]

The Western public, to varying degrees, wants politicians to be more proactive in this area. For example, according to a recent opinion poll, 69 per cent of British people either strongly agree or tend to agree with the statement that 'The British government should do more to implement its human rights policies abroad.'[43] In Denmark and Sweden over 40 per cent of people want the European Parliament to make human rights a priority.[44] The human rights organisation Amnesty International now has over one million members in over 170 countries.[45] In the UK membership has doubled since 1990, suggesting that the human rights issues are of increasing public concern. And 62 per cent of Americans believe that America should not increase trade with China until it gives more economic, political, and religious freedom to its citizens.[46]

However, the problem facing politicians is that despite these espoused progressive beliefs, when faced with the realities that prioritising human rights in foreign policy would entail, it is unclear whether Western electorates would favour action (which may incur personal costs) over doing nothing. How likely is it really that people would be willing to risk their own comforts, much less their own lives, to protect the lives of strangers in faraway places? Until the public's rhetoric on human rights can be taken to be a reality, until the public cries out for governments to balance economic aims with other goals, corporate interests with concrete aims and vote-winning outcomes (jobs, lower prices and so forth) will prevail at the expense of what is perceived to be and perhaps is an ambivalent public.

Confusing democracy with capitalism

But it is not just human rights that have been relegated; democracy has also lost out to trade interests for much of the past century. This is nowhere more striking than in the case of the United States of America, the world's loudest proponent of democracy, which has regularly allowed democracy to take a back seat to capitalism, despite its claims that it is its main priority.

When the tanks carried Yeltsin into Red Square in August 1991, Clinton said that democracy must prevail. What he probably didn't mean was a system in which people had the vote. It is unlikely that he really cared whether Russia was democratic; what he did care about was that a system should emerge in Russia that was favourable to US interests, and shared its economic values. A Singaporesque authoritarian system would have been just fine. Among potential investors in America and elsewhere in the West, the prevailing view was that 'What

Russia needs is a benevolent dictator' – that is, a dictator sympathetic to the American capitalist system.

America's official line during the Cold War was: 'The overreaching aim of our foreign policy is to spread democratic values'. The truth, however, seems to be that foreign policy decisions were and are driven by a belief that the American system and its values are best protected by 'a global system based on the needs of private capital, including the protection of private property and open access to markets'.[47]

In Iran in 1953 the CIA backed the fall of the popular government of prime minister Mohammed Mosaddeq, who had been demanding that the Anglo-Iranian Oil company (the antecedent of BP) share more of its profits with Iran. Once the rule of Shah Mohammed Reza Pahlavi was restored, the returning ruler renegotiated his country's oil arrangements so that for the first time American oil companies were able to operate there, taking a 40 per cent stake in the international consortium of private oil companies that were now to own and operate Iran's oil assets.[48]

In 1954 the US helped overthrow the elected government of Guatelmala's President Jacobo Arbenz after he had expropriated 80 per cent of the Tiquisate and Bananera plantations then the American-owned United Fruit Company. US State department interest in the affair was intense, since the former law firm of the secretary of state, John Foster Dulles, represented United Fruit, and the head of the CIA, Allen Dulles, had been a member of the company's board of trustees.[49] Furthermore, Washington officials viewed this behaviour as a serious threat to American investors' interests, and thus to American security. Arbenz's reformist government – which had undoubtedly made these expropriations in retaliation for the fact that none of United Fruit's profits had been reinvested or redistributed in Guatemala itself – was replaced by a CIA-backed military dictatorship in 1954. 'Over the next forty years the military built the worst human-rights record in the Western Hemisphere.'[50]

In 1964 the USA encouraged the pro-military politicians José de Magalhães Pinto and

Humberto de Alencar Castelo Branco in their successful attempt to overthrow Brazil's democratically elected government, a government whose espoused economic policies were again unacceptable to Washington owing to its leftist learnings. 'The new regime imposed military rule on Brazil for the next twenty years. During those two decades, the US was the regime's best trading partner, while Brazil attracted more US investment than any [other] Latin American country.'[51]

Reagan took up the battle cry for democracy in the mid-1980s. The views of Jeanne Kirkpatrick, his ambassador to the UN, were central in reconciling the apparent paradox between actively supporting non-democratic regimes such as those of President Marcos of the Philippines, General Pinochet of Chile, and South Africa's pro-apartheid government, while continuing to demonise those in Cuba, the USSR and China. According to Kirkpatrick there was no paradox once a distinction was made between authoritarianism and totalitarianism. Authoritarian regimes such as those in the Philippines, South Africa and Chile were not democratic, often violently oppressed their peoples and were usually corrupt but, because they shared American beliefs in open economic systems, it was acceptable for America to work with them. Totalitarian regimes, on the other hand, 'were evil because they controlled every part of society especially the economy which was closed to private enterprise and foreign access'.[52] If freedoms were ranked in order of priority, the first seemed to be freedom for American corporations to make money.

As we saw in the case of China, the Clinton administration continued to support the view (although not overtly) that the spread of capitalism was more important than the expansion of democracy. Again party politics seem to create few differences of opinion in a world in which economic interests are paramount. As Jacques Attali, former president of the European Bank for Reconstruction and Development, has put it: 'The main mission of American diplomacy seems to be the "export" of Western values including democracy – as long as doing so serves American interests.'[53] Rather than democracy being inexorably linked to markets – as the

Democrats suggested with the term they coined 'democratic markets' – wherever the two ideals clashed, America favoured the market over democracy.

Woodrow Wilson's proclamation that 'the world must be made safe for democracy' has been presented as the driving ideology behind US foreign policy for most of the last century. This is clearly misleading. When the American government talks about spreading democracy, what it really means is spreading its own flavour of liberal democracy. In fact its policies suggest that what it cares most about is just the 'liberal' element or, even more narrowly, just the economic element of liberalism. It will encourage liberal attitudes to human rights only to the extent that they favour the development of a market economy – but in practice, as we have seen, it often prefers authoritarian regimes. Other elements of liberal democracy that it might value are the rule of law and the protection of private property, since investors need to feel secure from arbitrary seizures of their assets. But the 'democratic' elements of liberal democracy – mass participation, an active civil society, regular elections – have proved much more expendable.

Throughout the last century, the United States has cloaked a foreign policy based on trade considerations, and centred on safeguarding private economic interests in a veil of a concern for democracy. The leading US diplomat in Asia in the early part of the twentieth century, Willard Straight, was probably closer to the truth when he observed that Americans make 'politics out of money'.[54]

WTO – whose trade organisation?

Nearly all capitalist countries do the same today. Competing economic interests have replaced ideological differences as the most divisive force in world politics. But whose interests are being fought over: corporations' or nations'? The answer today must be corporations, although nations consistently support them in fostering their interests overseas. Multinationals, many now as large and as powerful as many nation states, have a larger stake in the new world order than do many individual governments. And where the interests of corporations and states come into conflict, it is increasingly the corporate agenda that prevails.

Nowhere is this new imbalance of power between corporations and the state clearer than in an imposing 1930s building beside Lake Geneva. Here, at the headquarters of the World Trade Organisation (WTO), rulings are made in the name of free markets that limit states' abilities to safeguard their peoples' interests, even in cases where states wish to do so.

In 1996, for example, the US state of Massachusetts resolved not to award public contracts to companies that do business with or in Burma, because of the country's appalling human rights record. Unilever, Siemens and the Dutch banks ING and ABN-Amro were among a number of European companies that stood to lose out in consequence and they lobbied Brussels in an attempt to thwart the decision. Thanks to their efforts, the European Union threatened to take the case to the WTO, arguing that the proposed ban was an unfair barrier to trade.[55] A British government spokeswoman said at the time: 'This is not about Burma, it's about the United States and the application of international trade rules.' Lawyers representing Massachusetts argued that had current trade rules been in force during the 1980s Nelson Mandela would still be in prison.[56]

Once it complies with the Association of South-East Asian Nations' (ASEAN) trade rules that will govern the South-East Asian bloc from 2006, the Vietnamese government is unlikely to be able to maintain its ban on cigarette imports. Free trade policies would consider such a ban unfair, as indeed they did when China attempted to ban the importing of opium in the 1830s!

In 1996, the European Parliament voted 366 to 0 to ban synthetic hormones from beef, on the basis of strong evidence that they could cause cancer, reduce male fertility, and in some cases result in the premature onset of puberty in young children. Three months after the ban the US government, responding to pressure from the agrochemical company Monsanto, the

US National Cattlemen's Association, the US Dairy Export Council, the National Milk Producers' Federation and other interest groups, complained to the WTO, arguing that the ban created a barrier to imports. In 1997 the WTO ruled in favour of the USA. The EU appealed but its appeal was rejected. In July 1999 the WTO authorised the US and Canada to impose retaliatory trade sanctions worth over $125 million. European exports such as fruit juice, mustard and Roquefort cheese were suddenly subject to massive tariffs.[57]

> In 1997, the European Union dropped its proposed bans on cosmetics which had been tested on animals and on fur from animals caught in leghole traps, for fear that the legislation would conflict with WTO rules. WTO guidelines will prevent it from banning imports of eggs from battery chickens, which means that US producers will be able to undercut our farmers when battery cages are proscribed in Europe. The European Union . . . will probably have to drop its plans to make electronics manufacturers responsible for recycling their products. [In 1999] the UK forbade the sale of asbestos. Canada, which mines asbestos, will use the WTO to force [it] to lift the ban.[58]

Time and time again the WTO has intervened to prevent governments from using boycotts or punitive tariffs against companies that they have found to be acting in ethically unacceptable or environmentally unsound ways. In fact, in all environmental cases it has so far considered, the WTO has ruled in favour of corporate interests against the wishes of democratically elected governments.[59] Accountable to no one, it has restricted our choice over what we can eat, overridden laws passed by our democratically elected governments, started or sanctioned trade wars, and put our health at risk.[60]

Various aspects of the WTO have proved constructive; prior to its existence, trade disputes often led to prolonged, entrenched and damaging economic warfare – in the 1930s, for example, the average world rate of tariffs was 45 per cent, and wealthy countries had become protectionist and autarkic. Nevertheless, in imposing free trade doctrines upon states, the WTO makes it increasingly difficult for countries *not* to put trade interests first even on occasions when their electorates or governments wish to give other interests primacy. National sovereignty is thereby weakened, not for a holistic greater global good, but for a very particular one – that of American and European multinationals.

Behind closed doors

The WTO settles disputes in private. 'When a challenge to a national or local law is brought before the WTO, the contending parties present their case in a secret hearing before a panel of three to five people who review written submissions and consider expert opinions.'[61] The composition of the panel is determined by the Dispute Settlement Body, which almost always selects panel members and experts for their trade expertise. While many corporations advance their interests by participating in the expert meetings that are integral to negotiations, other input, such as testimonies, technical advice, and guidance on the environment or human rights, is purely discretionary and depends on whether a panel chooses to solicit them.[62] In contrast to the UN, environmental and other public interest groups are not allowed to observe WTO discussions, even when commercially valuable secrets are not at stake.

The burden is on the defendant to prove that the law in question is not a restriction of trade. Once a panel has decided that a domestic law does violate WTO rules, it may recommend that the offending country changes it. Countries that fail to make the change within a prescribed period face financial penalties, trade sanctions or both. Panel reports become final in sixty days unless there is a unanimous consensus of the Dispute Settlement Body – all 139 member countries – to reject the report (highly unlikely), or the decision is appealed.

Developed and developing countries alike have been ruled against – both the EU and the US have faced the WTO's censure, but developing countries often feel that they are treated as second-class citizens within the organisation. At the Uruguay Round trade negotiations in 1993, the trade ministers of most Third World countries were excluded from the final phase despite the fact that the developing countries account for 80 per cent of the WTO's membership. Stories of developing countries' trade ministers being 'forced to wait for hours on end in the coffee bar, begging the emerging journalists to tell them the latest developments in the negotiations' later emerged in the international press.[63] In Seattle in 1999, African nations were understandably angered by the US decision to deprive their scheduled internal meeting of both translators and microphones.

Some thirty of the organisation's 139 members cannot afford to base even a single representative at its Geneva headquarters. Switzerland promised in 1993 to finance a low-rent centre to house representatives of developing countries, but the centre has still not materialised. And when a developing country runs into a trade dispute with a rich nation, the huge disadvantage under which they are operating is made even clearer. Most cannot afford the legal costs involved in a long-running dispute,[64] while rich nations can afford to fly in teams of highly-paid lawyers. Third world nations are being forced to play a game in which the ante is unacceptably high and the openness of the forum is in question.

'I recommend that the system undergo some fundamental change,' Panitchpakdi Supachia, Thailand's deputy prime minister, said in 1999. 'It's high time we made it serve our development goals'. Not surprisingly, Supachia's candidature for the top WTO job of Director-General was opposed by the USA.[65]

While developing countries have far too little influence in the WTO, corporations have far too much, despite the fact that the WTO is ostensibly an organisation of states. The very rules of the system have been established with corporate interests in mind and corporations themselves have played an increasingly significant part in shaping them. As James Enyart, a senior employee at Monsanto, has put it, 'Industry has identified a major problem in international trade. It crafted a solution, reduced it to a concrete proposal and sold it to our own and other governments . . . The industries and traders of world commerce have simultaneously played the role of patients, diagnosticians and the physicians.'[66]

Corporations safeguard their interests by attending WTO ministerial conferences as members of national delegations. Preparations for the Seattle round were financed by soliciting large contributions from the private sector, in return for which business leaders were promised frequent access to the world leaders attending the conference.[67]

Helmet Maucher, the president of the International Chamber of Commerce (ICC) – an organisation comprising 7,000 member companies and representing the world's largest transnational corporations, including General Motors, Novartis, Bayer and Nestlé – is pushing for his organisation to be granted formal status within the WTO, despite the fact that at the moment only nation states are WTO members. 'We want neither to be the secret girlfriend of the WTO,' Maucher said in an interview, 'nor should the ICC have to enter the World Trade Organization through the servants' entrance.'[68] To pursue this more intimate relationship with the WTO, Maucher has made former GATT General Director Arthur Dunkel chairman of the ICC's commission on trade. Dunkel is also on the board of Nestlé.

But while the ICC waits for formal WTO status, the ability of big business and its representatives to sidestep the controls imposed by elected governments is already apparent, as evidenced by the growing dominance of free trade interests in international decision making.[69] In ancient Rome, gladiators owned by the rich would fight to the death in the Colosseum. In Geneva, nations more or less owned by corporations are pitted against each other in the WTO arena, unable to decide for themselves how they and their citizens would like to live and trade.

Chiquita la Bamba

Take the case of the US multinational Chiquita. When the EU decided to award a quota of less than 10 per cent of European banana imports to the company in order to protect small producers in former British and French Caribbean and African colonies, countries that rely on banana exports for survival, Chiquita persuaded US trade representatives that the policy was unfair and harmful to the interests of the USA, claiming that the three largest US fruit multinationals – Chiquita, Dole and Delmonte – would lose $520 million per year were this allowed to go ahead.[70]

Doubtless encouraged by the money donated by the corporation to both major political parties, the US administration protested on Chiquita's behalf, lodging a formal complaint about the quota with the WTO and charging the EU with having a 'discriminatory' approach to importing bananas. The US government also threatened to impose a new 100 per cent duty on a range of European products, from Walker's Shortbread and Scottish cashmere sweaters to Italian light fittings, if the EU was not able to negotiate an agreeable settlement on banana imports. The negotiations, causing intense friction between the EU and United States, continued until June 1999 when the WTO ordered the EU to amend its quotas to allow more Central American bananas into Europe. The EU did not comply and the US instigated retaliatory sanctions in the form of punitive duties worth $191 million on such unrelated EU goods as bath salts, handbags and bed linens.

Whether Carl Lindner, owner of the Chiquita fruit company, would have been able to put enough pressure on the US administration to influence the international trade negotiations in the banana war case had he not been such a massive donor to the Republican and Democratic parties is debatable, especially as the Clinton administration's decision to pursue a trade war over bananas was sharply at odds with the way it had dealt with other comparable agricultural issues.[71] Lindner was undoubtedly a major contributor to party funds. Just before the USA had threatened to impose the tariffs on European imports, he had donated $200,000 to the Democratic National Committee. And only hours before the USA lodged the formal complaint with the WTO, Chiquita had given $415,000 to state

Democratic parties throughout the country. In fact it has been estimated that in all during the 'Great Banana War', Lindner gave $4.2 million to Republicans and $1.4 million to Democrats.[72,73,74]

The acknowledged fact that in 1996 an entire village of 600 people in Honduras, one of the Caribbean countries in which Chiquita operates, was bulldozed by government troops allegedly provided with food and fuel by Chiquita, seems to have been deemed irrelevant by the national and supranational decision makers; as was the fact that Chiquita had been involved in legal cases brought about by male workers who had allegedly been rendered sterile by frequent exposure to the pesticide DBCP (banned in the countries which produced it) on the plantations on which they worked – more than 20,000 cases of sterility have been reported.[75] Objections to the USA's demands on the grounds that without access to European markets the economics of Caribbean islands would be devastated, increasing the economic pressures to produce drugs, and that for many Caribbean countries preferential access to EU markets is critical because small island producers cannot hope to compete on cost with the vast Central American plantations, were also set aside. Its protecting of the interests of Chiquita is typical of Washington's current policies towards Europe.

Puppets on a string

The Chiquita story exemplifies two major features of our new world order: the increasing degree to which governments and supposedly neutral global governance systems are dancing to the corporate tune; and the fact that global capitalism can often be a zero-sum game, with a gain by one side matched by a loss of another.

Once again we see that a world in which economic considerations are not balanced by other interests can be a grim one. In the global context, the situation is particularly worrying. While in a national context, a finance ministry is typically only one ministry among others and decisions are reached collectively after different ministers have stated their case, international organisations such as the IMF and WTO, which shape and constrain the behaviour of nation states, base their decisions purely on economic criteria, despite the fact that the implications of their decisions reach far beyond the domain of economics.

It is not that national statesmen and elected officials should not seek to bring prosperity and jobs to their own countries and act to ensure the robustness of their economies. It is that by giving corporate wishes such priority, by defining themselves solely in terms of economic success, by supporting international institutions that value economic interests above all else, governments are in danger of becoming the puppets of business. By defining political power in terms of economic power, democratic politicians lose sight of the reason they are elected – to serve all their constituents' needs, not solely the needs of big business. By determining foreign policy solely on the basis of commercial interests, governments forsake the opportunity to pursue other goals. Instead of creating a better world for people, governments work to create a better environment for business, under the mistaken belief that one will always lead to another, seemingly oblivious to the fact that in the age of globalisation multinational corporations lack national loyalties and cannot be relied upon to serve governments or national populations by delivering on either taxes or jobs.[76]

The needs of capital are not always the same as the needs of society. We, the people, are displaced – and in the one-ideology world of the twenty-first century, if things start going wrong, where can the global citizen go to be granted asylum? Is there a place where the sweeteners offered by the Chiquitas of this world are not accepted? Is there a place where these often conflicting priorities are better reconciled? Is there a place where governments can afford to remain impartial, or where politicians are not so dependent upon business? Can those of us living in the developed world at least draw comfort from the fact that, within the constraints imposed by globalisation, democracy is working well enough for us?

POLITICS FOR SALE

Grandmother's footsteps

Doris Haddock celebrated her 90th birthday on 24 January 2000 in Cumberland, Maryland. It was not a quiet affair. She had walked over 3,000 miles across America to be there, and celebrated by delivering a heartfelt speech on electoral reform to a large crowd. She then shared a birthday cake with local activists and, sent on her way by thirty local people singing 'This Land is Your Land', set off again for Washington DC. There, she gave three rousing speeches outside the Capitol, and was arrested twice.

It is fair to say that Doris, known to her thousands of supporters as Granny D, is no ordinary nonagenarian.

When her husband Jim, a life-long grassroots political activist in Dublin, New Hampshire, died after sixty-two years of marriage, Granny D decided to overcome her grief by acting upon her and her husband's shared ideals in the most visible possible way. Five foot tall, with eleven grandchildren, she set off from Pasadena, California, on 1 January 1999 and walked the 3,200 miles to Washington to protest about the growing corruption of America's political system by the vast donations made to the party machines by corporations and unions.

Supported financially and practically by the Fogies (Friends of Granny) she stayed with like-minded people, spoke to crowds and individuals, and gave interviews to the media as she went. Despite arthritis and emphysema she covered an average of ten miles a day, mostly on foot but, where there was snow, on skis.

In little over a year she trekked through California, Arizona, New Mexico, Texas, Arkansas, Tennessee, Kentucky, Ohio, West Virginia, Maryland and Virginia to Washington, DC. Early on much of her journey was through empty desert, hundreds of miles from supporters and with scant media coverage, walking either alone or joined by one or two volunteers. 'That never mattered,' Granny D said at the time. 'I had decided that I would go as a pilgrim.'

But by the time she arrived at the Capitol in February 2000, over 2,000 people were walking with her. She even made the pages of the political magazine *George,* appearing behind Hillary Clinton but ahead of Tipper Gore in its list of the Twenty Most Fascinating Women In Politics.

'It is, of course, a fool's errand,' she said of her trek. 'It is just an old woman walking across the land . . . talking about the kind of political reforms most people don't believe can really happen. But there are two things I would like you to understand about impossible missions. One is the fact that, sometimes, all you can do is put your body in front of a problem and stand there as witness to it . . . The second is that there are no impossible causes on this earth if they are good causes. My dream of political reform will come true. I may live to see it from this side of life, or I will smile to see it from the other side.'

Electoral campaign finance reform is not a subject that garners much support from within mainstream US politics, but at grassroots level Granny D's fear that politicians are being corrupted by the donations made to their campaign funds has struck a very real chord. As she said at her birthday party in Cumberland, 'A flood of special interest money has carried away our own representatives and our own senators, and all that is left of them — at least for those of us who do not write $100,000 cheques – are the shadows of their cardboard cutouts.'

On her website – www.grannyd.com – hundreds of people shared their experiences of joining her on her walk; the site still receives 20,000 hits a day. Beth Kanter remembers 'hanging out of the window at work, waving energetically and displaying homemade "Go Granny Go!" posters.' John Parker caught up with her in Washington at the end of her trek: 'To me, Granny D's speech was absolutely incredible. We had heard a number of other senators extol on how their brethren needed to change the laws. But when she took the microphone, she blistered everyone for having neglected their responsibilities. She must have spent 3,200 miles composing that speech, and she delivered it with some of the best oratory that I've ever heard. Despite her age, if she ran for office, I would vote for her.'

Granny D's first arrest, in April 2000, was for attempting to read aloud the Declaration of Independence in the Rotunda of the Capitol. She was arrested again at the same place in July 2000 for trying, unsuccessfully, to read out the Bill of Rights. Manacled by the police, she was reportedly brought to tears when an officer tried unsuccessfully to wrest her wedding ring off her arthritic finger.

One of Granny D's particular targets is so-called 'soft money' – donations originally meant for incidental office expenses – which has become a major factor in American electioneering. Although direct campaign contributions have been banned in America since the Watergate scandal, a regulatory loophole means that soft money is most commonly used for television advertising. In the 1992 campaign the two main parties raised $86 million in 'soft' donations. By 1996 the figure had jumped to $260m and analysts estimate that the 2000 election was financed to the tune of $393 million in soft money alone.[1]

Granny D's walk was initially aimed at supporting Wisconsin liberal Democrat senator Russ Feingold, whose bill, co-authored by populist Republican John McCain, condemned the soft money system as 'legalised bribery'. The pair called for a voluntary ceiling on campaign finance, but in October 1999 failed to gain enough Senate support to carry the bill forward to a vote. Granny D was however, undaunted. In speeches she quotes the council of the five Nations of the Iroquois: 'Cast all self-interest into oblivion . . . You heart shall be filled with peace and good will and your mind filled with a yearning for the welfare of the people.'

Unashamedly nostalgic, she has no qualms about wishing Teddy Roosevelt were still alive. Her campaign poster features her arm-in-arm with the former president: 'I think I know what the great Republican would say to these dangerously overlarge monsters [large corporations] and I think I know what he would say about their trained monkeys in Congress,' she said in Austin, Texas, in June 1999.

The court case following her Capitol demonstration sent out signals that at least parts of the US establishment may be coming round to her point of view. In sentencing, Chief Judge Hamilton of DC federal district court said to her and her fellow demonstrators: 'As you know, the strength of our great country lies in its Constitution and her laws and in her courts. But more fundamentally, the strength of our great country lies in the resolve of her citizens to stand up for what is right when the masses are silent. And, unfortunately, sometimes it becomes the lot of the few, sometimes like yourselves, to stand up for what's right when the masses are silent, because not always does the law move so fast and so judiciously as to always be right. But given the resolve of the citizens of this great country, in time, however, slowly, the law will catch up eventually.'

Facing a six-month sentence and a $500 fine, Granny D was instead let off with a $10 administration charge and time served. She then went straight to picket a $26 million dollar Democratic Party fundraiser at the Washington MCI Arena, where what she described as '$500,000 fatcats' sat at tables on the arena floor eating barbecue, while 'regular people – $50 contributors – paid $3 per bottle of water to watch them eat'.

She continues to campaign from her home in New Hampshire, and went on shorter protest walks in Oregon, Missouri and Arizona. As she said in Pecos, Texas, in a speech delivered to

400 people who had joined her for an all-night rally: 'I do it for you as your political granny, if you will have me be that.'

The price of politics

But why do political parties in a democracy need to raise so much money in the first place? Because in the absence of clear ideological distinctions, parties can most effectively differentiate themselves in terms of marketing strategy and spend. Not only do politicians now defer to big business, politics itself emulates corporate tactics. Door-to-door canvassing, leafleting and local meetings were the politics of yesteryear: low-cost, low-tech, and labour-intensive. The politics of today is expensive, businesslike and capital-intensive, and relies to a greater extent than ever before on mass communication via the media and advertising. Newspaper and magazine advertisements; terrestrial, cable, and satellite television commercials (where these are permitted); and Internet spots[2] are today's methods of reaching what we will see to be an ever more elusive electorate. Twenty-second ads are countered by twenty-second ads; the Conservative Party's 'demon eyes' poster campaign was countered with a major Labour advertising campaign with promises about the National Health Service. No party or politician can afford to be outspent by its rivals.[3,4]

In the United States a phalanx of political consultants leads the way, seeking to engage voters with new and bolder ploys, from hard-hitting TV ads to direct mail campaigns. In Britain, by the 1990s advertising and public relations were already fully established as a part of political campaigning. 'When the Conservative Party hired Saatchis in 1978, it was headline news. By the end of the 1980s it would have been just as big news if a major party had chosen not to use professional marketing expertise in an election.'[5] Political media advisers, advertisers and image makers have become minor celebrities, their names probably as widely recognised as those of many cabinet ministers or congressmen.[6]

The cost of the new media circus is truly astronomical, especially in the United States. In the run-up to the 2000 US presidential elections the candidates seeking nomination raised and spent over $1 billion – the most in US history – following the $651 million spent on campaigning in the 1996 congressional elections; and the 1998 House and Senate midterm elections in which more than $1 billion was spent, seven times the total for the 1978 election, and almost double the 1992. On average an individual Senate campaign now costs $6 million, meaning that each senator, as well as each defeated candidate, must raise an average of $2,750 every single day of his or her six-year term to pay for it.[7] Access to elected political office in the US is now almost exclusively the privilege of the seriously rich. In his first four months of campaigning for the 2000 election, George W. Bush raised $37 million, more than either Bill Clinton or Bob Dole raised during the entire campaign in 1996.[8] Jon Corzine, the former chairman of Goldman Sachs, spent $36 million of his own money to win a Senate seat. Defeated candidate Michael Huffington laid out as much as $30m when he stood for the Senate in California.[9] It is not possible to raise that kind of money from raffle tickets or barbecues. How can elections be free and fair when only the bankrolled can participate?

These developments are not unique to the USA. Although the figures are smaller, similar trends can be observed elsewhere. In an increasingly global political environment in which politicians are less able to deliver on actual policy and content, they need more money to capture their audience's attention. The 1997 general election was the most expensive British campaign to date, with the Labour Party spending just under £27 million and the Conservatives £28.5 million, double the amount spent in the 1992 election.[10] Although under new legislation enacted under Blair, party campaign spending in an election year will now be capped at £20 million. In Taiwan the world's wealthiest political party, the Kuomintang (KMT), paid voters between £10 and £30 to turn up at campaign rallies for the 2000 presidential election. In Russia, the Our Home is Russia party hired the German supermodel Claudia Schiffer and rap artist MC Hammer to provide support in the 1993 parliamentary elections.

Quid pro quo

This level of campaign spending is inherently problematic. The escalating costs of running campaigns and supporting political parties can no longer be met by membership contributions, union funds (where they are given) or personal donations. Even in countries that provide some degree of direct state funding to political parties, the funds provided by the state are nowhere near enough for today's political extravaganzas. 'The democratic political process costs money – in ever increasing amounts.'[11] So who do politicians turn to, to meet the shortfall? As grandma would say, the private sector, of course.

All over the world from Moscow to Paris, from Washington to London, corporations and business people are bankrolling politicians and political parties. Parties and candidates are given support; money is contributed to campaigns; political rhetoric is publicly endorsed; unwritten IOUs are registered.

Such funding comes from a small elite. In the US, for example, 'only one-quarter of one per cent of the population gave $200 or more to congressional candidates or the political parties in the 1995–6 election cycle and ninety-six per cent of the American people [didn't] give a dime to any politician or party at the federal level.'[12] America's largest 500 corporations, on the other hand, gave over $260 million to the Democrats and Republicans from 1987 through 1996.

Of course, corporations are not in the business of giving something for nothing. Money buys action and influence.[13] In exchange for amounts of money, that are often quite small from their point of view, they expect a significant return. As US Supreme Court Justice David Souter has said, 'There is certainly an appearance . . . that large contributors are simply going to get a better service, whatever that service may be, from a politician than the average contributor, let alone no contributor.'[14] So when Charles Keating, the boss of an American thrift company, Lincoln Savings and Loan that later defaulted and cost the US government and taxpayer hundreds of billions of dollars,[15] was asked whether the $1.3m he had donated to five senators' campaigns had influenced their behaviour, he replied, 'I certainly hope so.'[16] Mr Keating could afford to be frank, because his contributions were above board and entirely legal.

Despite their legality, such donations undoubtedly create an undesirable opaqueness. It is always difficult to prove a link between corporate funding and policy changes that favour a donor company, but the string of unproven connections and unlikely coincidences that link financial contributions and favourable policy changes is becoming just too long to explain away. Chiquita was no anomaly.

In the USA, where the problem is probably more widespread and of a greater magnitude than elsewhere in the developed Western world, we see countless examples of probable cause-and-effect. For example, the Center for Public Integrity draws attention to the 1994 Fair Trade in Financial Services Act, which had been lobbied for by NationsBank, for whom the legislation would mean savings of $50 million a year. 'Two weeks later, the cash-strapped Democratic National Committee (DNC) received a $3.5 million line of credit from the NationsBank at a favourable interest rate.'[17]

There are many similar examples. In 1993 Al Gore broke his public pledge to support the creation of a publicly funded information superhighway, advocating private funding in its place. Within a couple of days, the DNC received $132,000 from major telecommunications companies.[18] Other generous donors to the DNC were given seats on a diplomatic trade mission with the former Commerce Secretary, the late Ron Brown, where companies subsequently garnered international contracts worth billions.[19]

Many prominent American politicians have been tainted by allegations that they have given preferential access to their corporate backers. In 1992, for example, House Democratic leader Richard Gephardt of Missouri persuaded President Clinton not to tax beer as a means of financing his proposed health care plan; since 1988 Gephardt has received over $300,000 in campaign contributions from the Anheuser-Busch Company, the country's largest brewer.[20] Even Bill Bradley and John McCain, who both stood on campaign finance reform tickets in last year's presidential primaries, seem tainted. Mr Bradley, while senator for New Jersey, apparently supported forty-five special bills aimed at offering tariff reductions and export aid to companies producing highly toxic chemicals. During that same period, chemical firms were among the biggest donors to his election fund.[21] Senator McCain was accused of intervening with the Federal Communications Commission on behalf of a major contribution to his campaign, Paxson Communications, and of trying to stop the expansion of a national park in Nevada – a move which would have benefited the property development company Del Webb, his seventh biggest sponsor.[22]

The protection given to tobacco interests in the United States, although recently undermined by product liability litigation in some states, further illustrates the influence that money can buy. 'From 1987 through 1996, the tobacco companies have contributed more than $30 million in contributions to members of Congress and the two major political parties. In 1997, a single sentence added to a mammoth tax bill by Republic House and Senate leaders Newt Gingrich and Trent Lott, gave a $50 billion tax credit to the tobacco industry.'

The list of links between campaign donations and votes in Congress is almost endless. Jennifer Shecter of the Center for Responsive Politics collates campaign contributions and the resultant votes by legislators who receive them. She notes that 'The ten House and ten Senate members who received the largest contributions from the American sugar industry all voted to preserve a sugar quota that keeps prices high for consumers. Similar matchups are made for the timber industry, the B-2 bomber, the gambling industry, and even drunk-driving legislation, among others.'[23] In fact it has been argued that the very reason why Microsoft's monopoly was ever addressed by the US government was that Bill Gates did not join the campaign and lobbying bandwagon soon enough – Microsoft had, as recently as 1995, no Washington office.[24] It is unfortunate for Gates that George W. Bush was not then president, for in his attempts to woo Silicon Valley prior to the 2000 election, Bush promised to support 'innovation over litigation every time'.

Politics has been on sale even in issues with potential national security implications. In 1997, for example, President Clinton overrode the objections of the Justice Department, and permitted an American company, Loral Space and Communications, to export technology to China that would allow it to improve its nuclear missile capabilities, granting a waiver to sanctions that had been imposed after the 1989 massacre of hundreds of pro-democracy protesters in Tiananmen Square.[25] Bernard Schwartz, chairman of Loral, was the largest personal donor to the Democrats that year. President Clinton of course denied any quid pro quo. 'The decisions we made were made because we thought they were in the interests of the American people,' he later said. Which American people was that, exactly?

And across the ocean . . .

In the United States, where the level of funds needed to finance political campaigns is particularly excessive, at least all sides seem to be operating within the confines of the law. In many other countries, however, money has been shown to turn the wheels of policy-making in contexts whose legality is frequently in question.

In fact in almost all advanced democracies in recent years, major political parties and senior statesmen have been implicated in covert deals, many of which are related to issues of access for large corporations. In Belgium, for example, a scandal was uncovered in 1993 involving the payment of more than £2 million in bribes by the Italian helicopter firm Agusta and the French aerospace manufacturer Dassault in exchange for the securing of orders for equipment from the Belgian armed forces.[26] Senior politicians in Spain have been convicted of channelling money into secret funds and their own bank accounts. France has been plagued by a series of substantial illegal payments by companies to all the leading domestic political parties, which led to an outright ban on corporate donations in 1993 and a reform of party funding rules.[27] In 1999, the French Finance Minister Dominique Strauss-Kahn resigned, following moves by examining magistrates to investigate a payment of about £60,000 from a left-wing students' health insurance fund.[28]

Revelations in Germany surrounding former Chancellor Helmut Kohl have exposed the venality of a system that formerly had a reputation for cleanliness. A major part of the corruption scandals engulfing Germany's Christian Democrats revolve around Helmut Kohl's alleged offers to companies in exchange for significant donations. A parliamentary committee is currently investigating claims that the Kohl government took millions in bribes from the French oil giant Elf Aquitane during the early 1990s, in payment for the company's takeover of the East German Luena oil refinery and a chain of petrol stations in the former communist east. The German chancellery has disclosed that all documents relating to the debacle have gone missing. The committee is due to issue its final report in December 2001. In Italy the entire political system has come under suspicion; in the early 1990s 40 per cent of members of parliament were under investigation for corruption.[29] It is hardly surprising that only 19 per cent of Italians say they are fairly or very satisfied with their country's democratic performance in the 1990s.[30] The ability of business to use donations as a way of buying influence or securing lucrative contracts is also substantial in Japan, where in 1991, despite the reform of campaign-finance rules, a steel frame maker was found to have given Y80 million (£600,000) to a former minister in return for government contracts.[31] Endemic corruption brought to the end the thirty-eight year rule of the Japanese Liberal Democratic Party in 1993.

In Britain the former Conservative government was brought down at least in part by its association with financial 'sleaze', prompting a government inquiry into the funding of political parties. In 1989, for example, John Major, then Britain's Chancellor of the Exchequer, refused to even consider a bill that would have required foreigners doing business in Britain to pay taxes on their earnings there. There may have been no connection, but it is undoubtedly true that a number of those who would have been hit were significant donors to the Tory party.[32] By 1994, a Gallup poll found that nearly two thirds of the British public believed that 'most MPs make a lot of money by using public office improperly.'[33]

That belief seemed verified by subsequent events. Before the 1997 general election, a number of Tory MPs were found guilty of receiving cash for asking parliamentary questions from lobbyist Ian Greer, who represented private business interests. Businessman and owner of the prestigious Harrods store Mohamed Al Fayed recalls hiring Greer after being told by him at their first meeting, 'You can rent them [Members of Parliament], you can do what you want, you can rent them exactly like taxi drivers. They will do anything for you and I can handle this for you.'[34] Further revelations from the Neil Hamilton–Al Fayed libel trial revealed the truth of Greer's claim. Hamilton, a former Tory minister, was found to have accepted envelopes stuffed with £50 notes, Christmas hampers, Harrods gift vouchers, and a family holiday at the Ritz Hotel in Paris in exchange for asking specific parliamentary questions, signing early-day motions, and meeting ministers, all on Al Fayed's behalf.

The new Labour government did not escape the taint of sleaze. In 1998, soon after its election victory, controversy erupted over the issue of a political donation. Before the election, Labour had received £1 million from Bernie Ecclestone, the man behind Formula One motor racing. Once in office, the party dropped its stated opposition to tobacco sponsorship of motor racing. When the story came out, the potential link between the donation and the policy shift clearly made the payment suspect. And Peter Mandelson, the Northern Ireland secretary, was forced to resign in the 'cash for passports' debacle of January 2001 when it was suggested that he had inappropriately intervened in the application for British citizenship by S. P. Hinduja, who had given £1 million to New Labour's ill-fated Millennium Dome.

The connection between corporate donations and policy decisions is of course not always clear-cut. While the US gun lobby is a large contributor to political campaigns – in 2000 it hosted the biggest fundraiser ever in American politics, raising $21.3 million for the

Republicans in one night – it also has genuine mass support. And many politicians support local industries not only because they donate money to campaigns, but because jobs, and therefore votes, are tied up in these industries. 'Dairy-state representatives like Senator Pat Leahy, a Vermont Democrat, will vote to protect dairy interests whether or not they receive cash contributions from dairymen.'[35]

Whether or not definite causal links can be found, what is clear is that by making money available to politicians, or bankrolling the armies of lobbyists that now fill the corridors of power, corporations and business people are at least ensuring that politicians listen to their demands and consider what they want. After all, why would business bother if they didn't think donations were likely to serve their interests generally, if not specifically through bills or policy decisions? But by permitting a system that allows such transfers to take place, politicians are essentially admitting their inability to control 'corporate creep' – their willingness to rate the interests of certain groups higher than those of others.

Read it in the papers

Even if comprehensive limits on campaign spending and the financial involvement of corporate interests were introduced, as is happening in the UK, political playing fields would probably never be entirely level. For it is not just money that politicians need from business. Given a diminishing interest in politics, an increasing distrust of politicians, and the limited loyalty people now feel for particular parties (discussed later in this chapter) politicians more than ever need the endorsement of influential external forces to either gain or retain the electorate's support. And no external factor has more influence than the media. A favourable editorial, or an item on the evening news, allows a politician to communicate with thousands or millions of people, for free, via a medium that many voters are likely to trust more than paid-for political advertising. And the more limits that are put on financial support, the greater the extent to which media influence becomes important, and the greater the incentive for parties to seek other means of support of a non-financial kind.

In Britain it is the print media that wields immense political power. The extent to which the owner of the *Sun* and *The Times,* media baron Rupert Murdoch, whose News Corporation owns 30 per cent of British newspaper circulation[36] and whose papers span the social spectrum, has been wooed by first Conservative and then Labour leaders in Britain as well as by politicians in other countries where he has media interests, attests to his enormous influence.

In fact Tony Blair's wooing of Murdoch before the 1997 general election has been seen by many as a crucial element in Labour's winning strategy. Rumour has it that in 1994 Alastair Campbell would take the offered job of press secretary to new party leader Tony Blair only if Blair would look through some 'documents'. The documents were front pages of the *Sun* from around the times of the previous two (lost) elections, all of which endorsed the Conservatives including the one with the now famous headline 'It Was the *Sun* Wot Won It!' published the day after Neil Kinnock's 1992 defeat. Campbell's message was clear – if we don't get Murdoch on our side, we won't win.

Blair agreed, Campbell came on board, and New Labour's campaign to win over the newspaper magnate began. In 1995 Blair was invited by Murdoch to address his annual News International conference at Hayman Island, a resort off Australia's Queensland coast. No deal was struck at the conference, although it is believed that Murdoch was told that his empire would be safe under New Labour.[37] Six weeks before the 1997 election, the *Sun* made a historic shift away from the Conservative Party, telling its 4 million readers that 'The *Sun* Backs Blair',[38] assuring them, a week before the election, that 'there is no doubting his conviction.' Blair's courting of Murdoch seemed to have paid off.

Although Blair denies paying a price to Murdoch for the *Sun's* election support, the latter was no doubt delighted by the Labour leader's confirmation that he would not impose new restrictions on cross-media ownership,[39] as well as by the Blair government's refusal to back a

House of Lords initiative to introduce legislation to curb 'predatory pricing' of newspapers, the practice of taking a loss on the cover price which enabled *The Times* to double its circulation over a five-year period to the detriment of its competitors.

Arguably, the Conservatives had repaid Murdoch rather more substantially for his previous staunch support. Murdoch's 1981 acquisition of *The Times* and *Sunday Times,* for example, was never referred to the Monopolies Commission, despite the fact that it gave him the control of four national newspapers.

For many years before the Murdoch-Blair rapport, Murdoch had been, in the words of Charles Douglas-Hume, a former editor of *The Times,* one of 'the main powers behind the Thatcher throne'.[40]

Rupert and Mrs Thatcher consult regularly on every important matter of policy, especially as they relate to his economic and political interests. Around here he's often jokingly referred to as 'Mr Prime Minister', except that it's no longer all that much of a joke. In many respects he *is* the phantom Prime Minister of the country.

Somewhat ironic, then, that by 1997 Murdoch was supporting Blair's New Labour. But given Murdoch's response when asked whether he intended to live up to the promises he had made in connection with his battle for control of *The Times,* his switch of sides should not perhaps be too much of a surprise:

One thing you must understand. You tell these bloody politicians whatever they want to hear, and once the deal is done you don't worry about it. They're not going to chase after you later if they suddenly decide what you said was not what they wanted to hear. Otherwise they're made to look bad, and they can't abide that. So they just stick their heads up their arses and wait for the blow to pass.[41]

Which might help explain the fact that by 1 May 2000, the front page of the *Sun* under the headline 'Mayday, Mayday' was warning its readers that the Blair administration was beginning to lose the next election. Blair had not fulfilled expectations, the newspaper claimed, the people were feeling let down. The Conservatives' William Hague was a real threat.

Blair, on holiday at the time, sent the newspaper a 975-word handwritten defence. The three-page letter made the front page the following day, under the headline 'Rattled'.

A hundred years on . . .

In the twenty-first-century world of global capitalism, in which economic power has replaced military might, while nations compete for investment flows and the jobs and growth that corporations can provide, and politicians need ever greater funds to compete with their rivals to win over the electorate, governments actively do what they can to promote the interests of business. They court corporations, sponsor their causes, pander to their needs. Rather than keeping them in check, governments are providing them with countless alibis. Rather than aiming to control and limit their activities, governments are allowing business to help shape them and their policies.

In 1876 US President Rutherford B. Hayes remarked of his government, 'It is a government of corporations, by corporations and for corporations.'[42] In the chaotic and blatantly corrupt environment of late nineteenth-century America large companies were virtually able to buy legislation. As Matthew Josephson put it in his classic study of early American capitalism, *The Robber Barons*, 'The halls of legislation were transformed into a mart where the price of votes was haggled over, and laws made to order were bought and sold.'[43]

Over a hundred years later the situation seems broadly similar, not only in the US, which has a well-charted history of corruption and pork-barrel politics, but elsewhere too. As we enter the new millennium, arguably the entire world is *of* (international) corporations, *by* (international) corporations and *for* (international) corporations. The problem is the same, its geographical extent significantly worse. Corporations have, in effect, begun to lay down with force what is and what is not permissible for politicians all over the world to do.

The end of politics

With governments, regardless of their political persuasion, increasingly impotent, unwilling or unable to intervene on their citizens' behalf, and seemingly having lost any sense of moral purpose, it is hardly surprising that the electorate is turning its back on conventional politics, even in countries that proclaim democracy as one of their greatest achievements. No wonder that their citizens are ignoring the ballot box, and parliament itself, as a means of registering their demands and protests. People are growing more distant from political parties, and more critical of political institutions.[44] Never since the development of the mass franchise has there been such disengagement from politics.

The soundbite culture in which politics now operates has debased political rhetoric and helps to make voters feel that political institutions are increasingly irrelevant to their lives. The issues discussed in parliaments rarely have much to do with their concerns. In the UK, Gallup polling since 1991 has consistently shown that people see the most urgent problems facing Britain as health, education, the cost of living and unemployment.[45] Yet debates in the House of Commons are dominated by controversies over the European Union – of little interest to most voters – or legalistic debates that seem to fail to engage the interest of many MPs, let alone the general public.[46]

Politicians are increasingly seen as impotent, irrelevant and dishonest. People see their governments as unable to deliver what they promise, obsessed with unimportant issues and internal politicking, riddled with corruption, clinging to outmoded notions of authority, and increasingly in the pockets of business people. The distinction between incompetence and dishonesty is becoming blurred as, in country after country, senior politicians are discovered to have engaged in corrupt practices.

In today's 'one-ideology' world, where parties have such similar policies on key issues such as taxation and welfare that it is almost impossible to differentiate clearly between them, voters are failing to develop an enduring sense of party identity and are increasingly unwilling to offer long-term loyalty to any political party. If current trends continue, less than half the American population will identify with *any* political party, making election results increasingly volatile and unpredictable.

Many people have simply lost faith in politics. According to polls in the UK, the percentage of the electorate who had 'great confidence' or 'quite a lot of confidence' in parliament dropped from 54 per cent to 10 per cent between 1983 and 1996.[47] A survey of British 16-to 21-year-olds carried out in 1998 found that 71 per cent believed the way they vote will make little or no difference to their lives. In a 1990 poll, 60 per cent of French respondents expressed 'no confidence' in political parties. In the United States, a 1997 poll showed only 14 per cent rating the honesty and ethical standards of congressmen as 'high' or 'very high' – only narrowly beating car salesmen and advertising executives.[48]

All over the world, from the developed democracies of the United States and Western Europe to Latin America and the Far Eastern countries, poll respondents have less confidence in their institutions of government than they had a decade earlier.[49] In all advanced industrial democracies the public is effectively detaching itself from party loyalty and disengaging from politics. Most people, wherever they live, seem to believe that elected officials don't care about their concerns.[50]

Boycotting politics

Alienated, dissatisfied and sceptical voters are boycotting politics, even in countries where democracy has a long history. The 'landslide' victory for Labour in the UK general election of 1997 was achieved on a turnout of 69 per cent of the voting-age population, down six points from 1992 and the lowest turnout since World War II. In the United States only 51 per cent of voters turned out in the 2000 presidential election despite the knowledge that it would be close run; 55 per cent had voted in 1992.[51] More than 90 million Americans today do not participate in elections at all. The public's sense of resigned alienation manifests itself in other ways, such as tuning out of public affairs altogether. For example, 40 per cent of the American people did not know the name of the Vice-President of the United States.[52] The elections for the European Parliament in 1999 saw less than 50 per cent of the EU's 297 million electorate bothering to vote, down from 57 per cent in 1994. In the UK the turnout was only 24 per cent of registered voters[53] – in the same week that one million British people bothered to vote to change the Choco Krispies brand name back to Coco Pops. Even in eastern European countries that only finally managed to become democracies in 1989–91, turnout has been falling. In Poland turnout started out at 64 per cent in 1989 but had fallen to 49 per cent by 1997. In the Czech Republic, turnout in 1990 was 93 per cent but it has fallen at every election since then, and stood at 77 per cent in 1998. In Hungary turnout fell from a high of 76 per cent in 1990 to 60 per cent in the 1998 election.

Membership of political parties in Germany,[54] France,[55] the United States, in fact pretty much anywhere in the developed world, is lower than at any time since the war. In 1950s Britain, for example, the Labour Party claimed a membership of about a million; today that is down to 360,000. Over the same period membership of the Conservative Party declined from some 2.8 million to less than half a million.[56] By comparison, the Royal Society for the Protection of Birds currently has over one million members.

How are the politicians responding? Desperate to woo those who will vote, and to re-assert their legitimacy, politicians and political parties are turning to business to provide them with the tools. Pollsters, image consultants and advertising specialists, such as James Carville, Stanley Greenberg and Philip Gould – the team who helped Clinton to victory in 1992 and have subsequently been active in Britain, Germany and Israel – are being brought in to advise politicians on how to project themselves to increasingly less interested electorates. 'From Latin America, through Europe to India and Australia . . . professional media consultants have swelled in number and increased in influence. Where once electoral strategy was determined by party leaders it is now increasingly influenced by the media professionals, relying on in-depth focus group surveys . . . direct mail and market research.'

What influence do politicians really have in a world of global capitalism? Single-handedly, not much, as we have seen. Governments are now like flies caught in the intricate web of the market. And voters see their powerlessness. They sense that politicians' hands are tied and that their promises are increasingly empty. They watch politicians dancing to corporations' tunes. They are aware that the political rhetoric they hear is not being translated into any sort of actual reality; they feel that in many cases politicians have entered into a covert pact with business. And so, increasingly, they are turning their backs on politics.

As the political class clamours ever more loudly to be heard, and goes to ever greater financial lengths to be noticed, evidence suggests that voters have stopped listening. In this ideologically singular world, where democratic parties and politicians are becoming increasingly homogeneous, and in which the people's interests are being usurped by those of business, the people are registering their discontent by not voting. After all the long fight for universal franchise, the great-granddaughters of women who chained themselves to railings for the vote are now making their political statement by refusing to buy politics.

SHOP, DON'T VOTE

Eco-shoppers save butterflies

In the autumn of 1999 there was little doubt about which topic environmental pressure group Greenpeace should choose for its annual conference. Fears about genetically modified food crops, dubbed 'Frankenstein foods' by the media, had dominated British headlines throughout the summer, and footage of eco-warrior activists with scythes and billhooks destroying fields of GM crops had become a familiar sight on news bulletins.

Scheduled to appear were, in the green corner, Lord Melchett, organic farmer and former Labour minister; and against him Robert Shapiro, the chairman and CEO of Monsanto, the world's leading producer of GM seed.

Lord Melchett, executive director of Greenpeace, was at the time facing criminal charges for tearing up a test crop of GM maize on a farm in Norfolk in July that summer. But where once Shapiro would have appeared in person at the conference and evangelised about the cleaner, healthier future offered by GM, he changed his mind at the last minute and instead spoke by satellite link from America. Onlookers found him grim, defensive and defeated. He as good as apologised to Lord Melchett and Greenpeace's 2.5 million members. 'Our confidence in this technology and our enthusiasm for it has, I think, been seen widely, and understandably so, as condescension and indeed arrogance,' he said. 'Because we thought it was our job to persuade, too often we forgot to listen.'

After a bruising year of protests, campaigns and consumer revolt, Shapiro was facing up to the fact that Europe, and particularly Britain, were rejecting Monsanto's biotechnology. And things were to get much worse for the American company, which had invested $8 billion in its attempt to dominate global GM biotechnology. Its mission statement, to help people 'lead longer, healthier lives, at costs that they and their nations can afford and without continued environmental degradation', had done little to convince a British public once-bitten by the BSE scandal and deeply mistrustful of further scientific 'improvements' to agriculture. Furthermore, opposition to GM had spread rapidly through Europe and beyond, to Japan, Mexico and Brazil, finally provoking outcry back in the USA.

Shapiro was right to be downbeat. The company's share price had fallen steadily from £31.80 in May to a low of £22.80 in December 1999, at which stage the drug manufacturers Pharmacia and Upjohn announced a merger with Monsanto, attracted not by its GM interests but by its highly profitable pharmaceutical arm. Agribusiness, once the jewel in Monsanto's crown, was spun off into a much smaller stand-alone company accountable to its own shareholders. Robert Shapiro was to remain as Monsanto's CEO only until the merger was complete.

Monsanto's GM soya beans, potatoes and cotton were first launched in the US in 1995 and had provoked only the mildest of protests from America's environmentalists. Despite the premium cost, sales increased rapidly and within three years 25 per cent of corn, 38 per cent of soya beans and 45 per cent of cotton grown in the USA was GM, almost all from Monsanto seeds, altered to make them resistant to its bestselling herbicide, Roundup.

In Britain, however, the response was very different. The European Commission approved

European imports of GM products in 1996 but withheld permission for GM seeds to be planted commercially. Even this was enough to provoke alarm. At first the opposition was sporadic, with letters to *The Times* in 1997 from sources as diverse as the National Union of Farmers and the National Council of Women.

Monsanto then made perhaps its biggest mistake, launching a heavy-handed £1 million advertising campaign which only served to focus opposition. The GM issue moved from the letters pages to the front pages, and was soon dominating British news bulletins and headlines. Protests against the ill-advised campaign were upheld by the Advertising Standards Authority, which criticised the company for misleading the public and presenting opinions as fact.

Middle England was, for once, wholly in agreement with the eco-warriors. In April 1999 the *Daily Mail* launched 'Gene Food Watch', a major campaign highlighting the use of GM ingredients – mostly, at this stage, processed food 'tainted' by American imports of Monsanto's soya and maize. Consumer fears translated into falling sales, and that spring Marks & Spencer became the first UK high street retailer to remove all GM foods from its shelves. By the end of May 1999 Tesco, Sainsbury's, Safeway and Asda had followed suit, as had most of the country's major food producers. The chairman of Birds Eye Walls, Iain Ferguson, said, 'We have taken this decision in direct response to the wishes of a growing number of consumers in the UK.'

In the summer of 1999 America's (and the world's) largest miller, Archer Daniels Midland, bowed to European consumer pressure and instructed its farmers to separate GM from non-GM export crops. British alarm began to filter back to America, especially after a huge public outcry in May 1999. Researchers at Cornell University had revealed that pollen from GM corn (soon known as 'Killer Corn') could prove deadly to the endangered monarch butterfly. Monsanto was suddenly under attack from all sides.

Back in Europe, Deutsche Bank issued a stark warning to would-be investors in GM companies. 'Genetically modified organisms have crossed the line. Today the term GM becomes a liability,' said its analysts in August 1999. As a final indignity, in October that year the US Food and Drug Administration reacted to the outcry by announcing plans to hold public hearings into the long-term effects of GM products.

In November 1999 Shapiro admitted publicly that Monsanto had 'hopelessly underestimated' European consumer fears. The company then tried hard to promote its 'skylark-friendly' sugar beet in an attempt to convince environmentalists; but it was a case of too little, too late.

In February 2000 Tony Blair finally backtracked, having only a year earlier dismissed the public's concern with the claim that 'there [was] no scientific evidence on which to justify a ban on GM foods and crops', admitting there was indeed 'potential for harm' to health and the environment. He announced a three-year moratorium on commercial planting of GM crops, hailed by campaigners as a U-turn. Scientific tests of GM plants, however, continued to be given the green light, with twenty-five new trial sites announced in August 2000. In the long term, it may prove more difficult to resist the spread of GM foods than protesters hope, but that is scant comfort for Robert Shapiro and Monsanto.

Supermarket activism

In the world of the Silent Takeover, many citizens of democratic societies feel that their governments are no longer looking out for them, so many of them are increasingly looking out for themselves. If the state is perceived as no longer to be relied upon to ensure the quality and safety of the food we eat, the air we breathe, the environment, a growing number of people are beginning to bypass traditional political channels and express concerns and demands directly to the bodies that can, the corporations.

Cases like that of Monsanto have taught us that, just as we once possessed political power by the combined impact of our votes, today we can wield real power over corporations by combining with other consumers. The outcome of the UK public's reaction to GM foods – the near collapse of Monsanto, and the banning of GM products by most UK food manufacturers and retailers – happened not because politicians willed it, but because consumers, aided by the media, did.

The Monsanto case is not unique. On both sides of the Atlantic, people are banding together and using the threat of boycott and negative publicity not only to pressurise corporations into changing the way that they do business, but also to address the flaws of the system itself. If governments, pleading the constraints of globalisation and the need to pursue economic growth, and taking corporate PR at face value, are perceived as failing to monitor how corporations are making money and to put limits on their activities, people increasingly will. In Roswell, a suburban community of Atlanta, Georgia, local residents have been protesting against advertising billboards. 'It's a visual pollution,' says Jay Litton, a resident of six years. 'They are destroying Roswell.' The residents have launched a successful campaign against the companies who advertise on and own the billboards. 'These companies are making money out of us by polluting the air . . . Those companies are making millions of dollars in profit from advertising here. Everyone is profiting but the taxpayer.'[1]

Litton's words echo the feelings of a growing number of people who are beginning to ask who exactly is profiting from the capitalist dream. The increased indifference to party politics seems not to be matched by a growing lack of interest in a wider world. A lack of faith in traditional politics should not be confused with apathy or disengagement from society. Thatcher was wrong when she said there was no such thing as society; society has in fact proved remarkably durable. During the same period that trust in political authority has been fading, membership of grassroots movements has been on the rise – a rise due to individuals' inability to gain recognition in the public arena by conventional means, and to loss of faith in politicians' ability to champion their interests, or make any difference to their lot. They no longer believe that politicians can resist the force of non-elected organisations. They have lost faith in politicians' ability to put the people's interests first.'

Believing that their governments are weakening in the face of multinational hegemony, seeing that the nation state is no longer the focus of power in the world, sensing that politicians are no longer leading business but that business is telling the politicians what they can and cannot do, we no longer concentrate our efforts on politicians.[2,3] Instead, more of us are going straight to the new political power – business.

Increasingly the most effective way to be political is not to register one's demands and wants at the ballot box, where one's vote depends on the process of representation, but to do so at the supermarket where a dollar spent or withheld can, cumulatively, lead to the desired end, or vocally at a shareholders' meeting. These forms of direct action are replacing rather than complementing conventional forms of political expression. All over the developed, democratic world, people are shopping rather than voting.

I am what I buy

The use of consumer pressure to keep corporations in check is not new. For as long as there has been a market in commodities, there have been champions of the interests of those who consume. From the Co-operative Movement in nineteenth-century Britain, via the American Progressives at the turn of the century, to Ralph Nader and the US National Consumer Council, producer interests have been called to account for the price exacted for their goods, whether in terms of money or in their effects on safety, health or human rights.

In the past, however, it was usually only a small minority who engaged in consumer boycotts and political shopping, and then only on isolated occasions. Today there is a sense that consumer activism is beginning to enter the mainstream, that because of the increased visibility of corporate actions and the corresponding invisibility of political will, and because of recent major popular successes, there is an increasing realisation that tarnishing the corporate image of unethical companies, or leaving their products on the shelves, are powerful weapons. In an era of political apathy and disengagement, consumerism is beginning to replace citizenship as the tool through which ordinary people gain identity and recognition in the public arena.

We took decisions, which in retrospect were mistakes. We now realise that alone we could never have hoped to reach the right approach – that we should have discussed them in a more open and frank way with others in order to reach acceptable solutions . . . In essence we were somewhat slow in understanding that environmentalist groups, consumer groups and so on were tending to acquire authority. Meanwhile those groups we were used to dealing with [e.g. government and industry organisations] were tending to lose authority.

So said Shell's President C.A.J. Herkstroter in late 1995, after the Brent Spar oil storage structure, which the company had planned to dump at sea, had instead been moved to a Norwegian fjord for dismantling,[4]

The year 1995 was seminal for consumer activism, and Shell was the company under the spotlight. Setting a pattern that would later be mirrored in most of the later consumer victories, the media played an active role. In this case Greenpeace, a central player in the new consumerism, masterfully engineered a media campaign to protest against Shell's decision to sink the redundant Brent Spar in the deep Atlantic. The Greenpeace–media alliance was extremely effective, buoying up public resistance. German consumers boycotted Shell petrol stations – on one day in the summer of 1995 sales fell by 50 per cent – creating a serious concern for senior management and damaging the company's image. Britain's Conservative government, as might be expected, backed the company, assuring the public that Shell's solution was the least environmentally damaging one. In this instance, their claim proved to be true, but too late to prevent the damage to Shell.

It was not only over environment issues that consumers were beginning to act without reference to their elected politicians. While politics was becoming further removed from ethical issues, shopping was becoming imbued with a sense of morality. The new cathedrals of the middle classes are shopping malls with parking for thousands. And the new religion practised by a growing number of these shoppers is consumerism with an ethical slant, a stance actually endorsed by the church. The Church of England-approved prayer book for the millennium, *New Start Worship,* counsels the faithful that

Where we shop, how we shop and what we buy is a living statement of what we believe . . . Shopping which involves the shopper in making ethical and religious judgements may be nearer to the worship God requires than any number of pious prayers in church . . . If we take our roles as God's stewards seriously, shoppers collectively are a very powerful group . . .

The liturgy then goes on to say:

If, when we ourselves are not on the poverty line, we always go for the cheapest price, without considering that this price is achieved through ethically unacceptable working conditions somewhere in the world, we are making a statement about our understanding of the word neighbour.[5]

The consideration of how a product is made soon became the next manifestation of enlightened consumerism. In April 1996, the American public was shaken to discover that Wal-Mart's Kathee Lee collection of clothing – endorsed by their favourite chat show host Kathee Lee Gifford, who was paid $5 million a year to do so – was being stitched by teams of Honduran children, some as young as 13, working twenty-hour days for wages as low as 31 cents an hour.

Gifford burst into tears on national television when confronted with the evidence, and quickly became an active campaigner against sweatshops. Over the next few months she set up a charity; talked Wal-Mart into changing its policies; personally went to the factories to ensure that they were no longer hiring children; gave $300 to each of the rather bewildered factory workers at Seo Fashions in New York's Chinatown, who it emerged had also been making blouses for her line under sweatshop conditions; and testified before Congress at a subcommittee hearing on child labour. The conference on sweatshops the following day was attended by supermodel Cheryl Tiegs, the heads of Levi Strauss, Wal-Mart, K-Mart and dozens of other corporate chains who were there largely in response to Kathee Lee's public plea that they 'do the right thing', as well as the then Labor Secretary, Robert Reich, who said, 'We will look back to today, years from now, and say that this was a major turning point in our collective commitment to rid the nation – and also even the world – of sweatshops.'

Kathee Lee Gifford in tears on national TV was a turning point. Corporations began to realise that they could no longer use their distant suppliers as scapegoats: Western consumers were demanding that similar rights be extended to overseas workers as to those at home. But on the whole, the corporate response was reactive. Following the Wal-Mart saga came exposure of the practices of Nike, Gap and Disney, among others. Each case provoked similar consumer actions and only then damage control reactions from the firms. Five years on, the issue still makes the front pages, but this time the target is university-endorsed clothing and sportswear, not high street brand names, and the protesters are not A-list celebrities but 18- to 22-year-olds. Protests, described as the biggest act of student unrest since the anti-Vietnam campaign of the 1960s, are taking place on university campuses throughout the United States with students objecting to factory conditions in Guatemala, Nicaragua and Bangladesh where, they claim, exploitation is commonplace in the garment industry. In the first six months of 2000 alone, college students led sixteen sit-ins at university buildings in protest. And their demands are being heard. The Universities of Oregon and Michigan, and Brown University, all withdrew their membership of the industry-backed 'Fair Labor Association' which the students claimed to be ineffective, and instead signed up with the Workers' Rights Consortium, a body made up of students, university officials, and labour and human rights campaigners – but not government officials – that will monitor how the clothes are made.

The globalisation of production over the past years has been matched by an increasing globalisation of information and concern, although a clear information asymmetry exists between corporation and consumer, with consumers unable to react until a story breaks. But each time a company *is* exposed, we see images of 6-year-old children bowed over workbenches, or adults crammed thirty at a time into squalid dormitories in the brief intervals from stitching the trainers, footballs and sweatshirts that we wear and play with. These images in themselves seem to create an upsurge of a sense of responsibility. Molly McGrath from the University of Wisconsin sweatshop campaign has said, 'A lot of the students involved in the campaign are generally like me, white kids who've never been involved in political or social justice activity before, but who recognise that our clothes shouldn't be made by people who are treated like slaves – it's an easy thing to understand.' Easy because, unlike traditional political concerns such as healthcare or defence which are complex, multidimensional and require sophisticated analyses of multiple trade-offs, a single issue like this is easy to grasp.

While politicians are allowing corporations increasingly free rein, and while traditional voting is seen to be increasingly ineffective as a means of political expression, shopping has been imbued with a new political significance. It is the most effective weapon in the armoury of ordinary citizens, enabling people to press for some degree of accountability in governments, international organisations and multinational corporations. In the world of the Silent Takeover, in which the social contract between government and the people is increasingly meaningless, popular pressure is doing something that governments can't or won't: demanding that corporations be judged by non-economic criteria, holding them accountable in a way that we cannot hold our elected representatives.

The new consumerism

Consumer politics offers us a chance as individuals to make a difference, a chance to exercise direct power in a way denied to us by contemporary representative democracy.

But how significant is this trend? Are a growing proportion of us political shoppers paying the premium for Fairtrade coffee, and 'child labour free' footballs? Or are we merely paying lip service to good causes, and willing to revolt only from the comfort of our own armchairs? Is serious activism, as it was in the 1960s, 70s and 80s, still a minority cause?

Sunday morning. Central London, home. I wake up to the excesses of the night before. Washing up in piles. Open my bottle of Ecover and squeeze biodegradable liquid on to yesterday's plates crusted with residues of GM-free organic pizza. Fill a cafetière with Fairtrade coffee and boil a free-range egg. Take a 'not tested on animals' Lush bubble bath. Pull on my 'child labour free' Reeboks, 'made by 100% union labor' Levis, and 'never use furs' Chloe T-shirt. Spray my hair with a Wella non-CFC canister. Read the papers and learn about the latest McDonald's boycott. Remind myself to pick up a leaflet from the protesters on my next outing by jotting down a note on my pad of recycled paper.

Nip down to the Body Shop to get my 'fairly traded' moisturiser, read in-store leaflet on globalisation while paying for it with my 'investments only in ethical companies' Co-Operative Bank credit card. Stop to fill up with unleaded petrol on way home. Two petrol stations on either side of road. Same prices, same petrol. Remember that the one on the left has been involved in an oil spill in Nigeria. Turn right with no second thought. Come home and log on. Check mail on 'we put social issues first' AOL. Send off a standard form e-mail to McDonalds, protesting at their activities in Argentina. Enter the UN hunger site,[6] click my mouse, and silently thank American Express for donating that day's bowl of rice and mealies. All the while snacking on Ben & Jerry's 'we don't cut down trees in the Amazon' ice cream.

And I am not alone. A Gallup poll in Britain in 1995 found that three out of five UK consumers are prepared to boycott stores or products because they are concerned about their ethical standards, or have already done so.[7] A survey in the US at the same time revealed very similar results: over 75 per cent of Americans would boycott stores selling goods produced in sweatshops. Almost 85 per cent said they would be willing to pay up to $1 more on a $20 garment if it carried a label guaranteeing that it had been made under humane conditions.[8]

More recent polls have confirmed these earlier findings. A Mintel poll in the UK in 1999 found that three quarters of respondents would make their choice of products on a green or ethical basis.[9] And a MORI poll carried out in 1998, which measured the percentage of Britons who said they had chosen – or boycotted – a product or company for ethical reasons in the last twelve months found that 28 per cent of respondents said that they had done so. A study carried out in the States that same year[10] showed that between 40 and 50 million Americans, about 25 per cent of the adult population, are beginning to make these value-based choices in more and more product categories. When price and quality are comparable, socially responsible businesses have the advantage.

A survey carried out at the end of 1999 of 25,000 people in twenty-three countries confirmed these earlier findings. Consumers worldwide are more likely to base their impressions of a company on its labour practices and ethical conduct than on the quality of its product or service or its finances. Asked to say in their own words what formed their impressions, those surveyed put issues related to corporate social responsibility at the top of their lists. And 20 per cent of consumers worldwide – 40 per cent in North America – said they had acted on their perceptions. They told pollsters they had avoided the products or services of companies they saw as socially irresponsible or had spoken negatively about those companies.

Once the preserve of left-wing activists who drank low-grade coffee because it was co-operatively produced, ethical and political values are now being factored into the buying decisions of a significant proportion of the population. In a world in which people no longer feel that their elected representatives will do the right things on their behalf, they are increasingly asking this of corporations; and it appears that, when confronted, corporations are prepared to deliver. The business world is much more responsive than the political one. Consumers in the private sphere constantly make decisions about how and where to buy, and businesses – at least successful ones – have learnt to react swiftly to their consumers' desires.

But why have we seen such an increase in consumer activism since 1995? Why are we seeing a burgeoning of activity on the part of consumers now?

Timing undoubtedly plays a part in the explanation. By the mid-1990s the Western middle classes were in financial terms doing better than ever before. In the developed world at least, their material needs were well sated and they felt physically safe now that the threat of Soviet attack had been laid to rest. This 'feel-good factor' lessened their need to focus on themselves, and allowed for a shift in emphasis towards other issues such as quality of life, and care for others – distant strangers and future generations too, not only people in their own neighbourhood: concerns that seemingly no longer troubled the state.

Another factor was the strategic decision taken by pressure groups and non-governmental organisations to shift away from government-focused campaigns, and co-opt the media in an attempt to mould public sentiment and thus force accountability from corporations.

Shrewd pressure groups have realised that global companies can be used as a lever to influence the actions of their host countries. Campaigners against the regime in Burma in 1997, for example, saw that while their own governments were unresponsive, they were able to have a significant impact by identifying corporations with major operations there, and threatening a worldwide consumer boycott.[11] When in the summer of 1995 Australians sought to protest against French nuclear testing in the South Pacific, environmental groups, in contrast to earlier campaigns, didn't ask their government to get involved. They called for a consumer boycott of French products. A national free telephone service was run by Consumer Power, a group formed solely to campaign on this issue, offering advice to consumers on what products to avoid.

This new consumerism focuses on the corporations themselves, rather than using governments as a conduit. Human Rights Watch published in 1999 a damning report not on a government, but on a corporation, Enron, and its activities in India.[12] And increasingly activists are redirecting resources away from lobbying and government-oriented campaigns, and using the mass media and advertising campaigns to appeal directly to consumers. By generating negative publicity against target corporations, they can create public support for boycotts or other forms of consumer protest.

Lord Melchett highlights the need for business-focused campaigning:

A lot of international regulation arises out of what business will deliver – it's not politicians leading business, it's business telling the politicians what they can do. If you're campaigning for change, you have to get business to change, and then the politicians will follow.[13]

The best way of getting business to change is by getting consumers on board, which is a much easier prospect than ever before. Satellite, digital, cable and the 500-channel universe have shortened the distance between the child labourer in Saipan, the domestic retailer and the individual shopper. Images of seals being clubbed to death for the sake of a fur coat, misery inside factories in faraway places, and computer simulations of 'Frankenfoods' graphically depict to consumers the result of inactivity.

Each successful campaign encourages others. People are more likely to demand of companies that they reform the way they are doing business because of the success of similar campaigns. The students protesting on American campuses have seen previous similar protests deliver results. And people have learnt that corporations, unlike politicians, nowadays respond quickly to their demands and seem to take them seriously. It took twenty years of consumer pressure for Barclays bank to pull out of apartheid South Africa, but Shell moved the Brent Spar platform within months, and Marks & Spencer removed GM foods from its shelves overnight.

Making use of the Internet, the speed with which consumers can now communicate with each other or with pressure groups and with which corporations can get things done makes a mockery of the time taken by governments to effect any changes in policy. Unlike politicians, corporations cannot afford not to keep their customer base happy, let alone make them actively unhappy. They don't have the luxury of guaranteed stays in office.

Shareholder activism

It is not only consumers that are steering corporations in new directions. A growing number of individual investors and, more importantly, financial institutions, are choosing to use their power as shareholders to 'regulate' corporate manoeuvres.

Over $1 trillion is currently invested in the United States in managed portfolios that use at least one social investment strategy, a thirty-fold increase since 1984. One dollar of every eight invested in the US is now invested in ethical funds. Ethical investments by the British public have exploded from almost nothing in 1980 to more than £2.8 billion today, with new launches of ethical funds almost monthly. Projections are that they will triple again within the next five years.[14] In Australia ethical investment is the fastest growing sector in the managed fund market, with major companies joining the trend. In Germany, the influx of money into ethical and environmental funds has risen 36-fold over the past two years.[15]

While ethical funds vary from the palest to the deepest of green, most avoid investing in companies involved in tobacco, arms, nuclear power and animal experiments, and many will reject companies which are active in or linked to oppressive regimes that do not respect human rights. All these, of course, are issues that our governments have failed to address adequately.

How ironic that *Homo economicus,* who was only ever supposed to be interested in maximising his own self-interest, has turned out to be so interested in investing in the common good.

And how depressing that politicians, who were expected to focus on realising the public's needs, in the world of the Silent Takeover have so often remained mute.

Individuals' investments in ethical funds are still small compared to the total investment funds in Britain, accounting for only about 1 per cent of the total UK market, so their impact is small. But pension funds wielding huge amounts of money look likely to have an increasing impact on how companies do business – over 50 per cent of American investment funds are managed by pension funds, and between 70 and 80 per cent in the UK. Investments made by these institutions are so large that they have to view them in the long term. Research findings over the past few years have positively correlated social and environmental performance with financial performance over time, so that a corporation's commitment to these values is increasingly being factored into the fund manager's purchasing decisions.[16] Not so politicians who, as we saw in the cases of the UK government and Monsanto and Brent Spar, were still regarding as top dollar stocks those that the market and any reputable fund manager had already heavily discounted.

Despite its reluctance to champion social and environmental matters too openly, Britain's New Labour government introduced legislation in July 2000 whereby British pension fund trustees now have to report on whether they take account of social and environmental matters. Although it is not mandatory for them to adopt green or ethical criteria, they will have to justify their decisions if they do not. Several of the UK's leading pension funds, in light of this new act, stated a clear commitment to factoring in social and ethical issues when considering which companies to invest in. 'We are taking this approach for financial reasons, not moral ones. We believe that environmentally sound companies are better run and will make good investments in the long run,' said a spokesman from Prudential Portfolio Managers, which manages £150 billion worldwide.[17] By changing the pay-off structure, has the British government acted by stealth to curb the behaviour of corporations?

Institutional investors now wield power over companies, not only by boycotting them if their activities do not please, but in subtler and more powerful ways. In the same way that corporations are 'buying' stakes in political parties and 'hiring' politicians to champion their causes, shareholder activists – whether pension funds, environmental groups, pressure groups, or activist funds – are using their power as shareholders to buy holdings in companies with weak ethical records specifically so that they can effect real change from within.

In the US the Interfaith Center on Corporate Responsibility is a shareholder advocacy organisation that counts among its members more than 275 institutional investors of the Jewish, Catholic and Protestant communities, whose combined assets are in excess of $110 billion. Members buy shares in target companies and then use shareholder resolutions to force votes on social issues at shareholder meetings. Hot issues include promoting equal employment practices, dogging the tobacco industry, and challenging US corporations to improve working conditions in factories outside the country. In this way, 78-year-old Sister Patricia Marshall of the Sisters of the Blessed Sacrament managed to get Anheuser Busch to drop several of its images of Native Americans from its advertising for Miller Beer in the USA. Other successes have included getting PepsiCo to sell its bottling plant in Burma; Kimberley Clark, makers of Kleenex, to sell off their tobacco operations, and 3M, America's third largest billboard company, to phase out tobacco advertising.

Not only nuns and rabbis are standing up to protest in shareholder meetings. Other activist pension funds, investment funds, and environmental groups are also adopting this strategy. 'Corporations often ignore stakeholders, but they listen to shareholders,' said Brent Blackwelder, President of Friends of the Earth. 'By aligning ourselves with investors . . . we can greatly increase our chances of being heard and heeded by belligerent companies.'

Often, the purpose of, for example, turning up at shareholder meetings dressed as polar bears – as a coalition of environmentalists, investment groups and pension funds did at BP's annual meeting in April 2000, to protest against the company's exploration activities in the Arctic Ocean – is not to get a resolution passed, but to generate publicity and so shame and pressurise the company into action. In this case the motion gained the support of only 13 per cent of voting shareholders; but since BP was just about to relaunch its company brand as environmentally minded and careful of natural resources, the protest couldn't have come at a worse time. As a survey of Canada's top 100 CEOs revealed in 1996, 'Shareholder activism and unpredictable questions top the list of "worst nightmares" at annual meetings.'

At a time when the threat of hostile takeover is ever present, and competitive pressures are ever greater, corporations must handle their shareholders' concerns and demands carefully. Politics is buffered by its monopoly status, but business is increasingly vulnerable to the vagaries of the market.

Beautifying the brand

In the age of the logo, reputation is paramount. Corporations are increasingly realising that there are new expectations of them. As their actions become more and more public, they are expected to justify their policies and actions, and address their consumers' and shareholders' concerns, to a hitherto unprecedented degree. Does the company mistreat its employees? Is the company damaging the environment? Is the company backing a repressive regime? Can the company be trusted? These are increasingly questions asked by their key stakeholders rather than by politicians.

No wonder, when such priorities are stated, that many corporations are professing great concern. CEOs of several leading brand-name companies confess to the vulnerability that they feel under the media spotlight. 'What we fear most,' says one, 'is not new legislation, but consumer revolt.' Another speaks of a feeling of powerlessness: 'If people think corporations are powerful, they haven't been in a corporation. We are by no means powerful – we are confined and restricted in what we do. Consumer choice doesn't allow us to have unfettered power.'[18]

Although still a relatively new phenomenon, the forcefulness of today's consumer and shareholder activist movement, and the breadth of its 'church', have triggered a response from corporations or, at least, from those who are caught. While governments have allowed the interests of corporations increasingly to take precedence over the public interest, the public, through the marketplace, is reclaiming its interest for itself.

It is too early in this process to gauge the size of the impact. Only a few corporations have been actively targeted; corporations that do not sell consumer goods are to a large extent shielded from activist action, for highly visible brand names obviously provide a better target for smear campaigns and other public attacks;[19] and instances of active protest are still relatively few, so that each gains significant media interest.

However, in the same way that governments are now unwilling to risk raising taxes because of the backlash from voters, many captains of industry have a fear of adverse publicity.[20] The cost of rebuilding a negative reputation is high; in fact, once lost, a reputation may be impossible to regain. Memories of the GM debacle, Brent Spar and Kathee Lee Gifford have left their mark.

Increasingly, the cost advantages of cheaper labour or cheaper inputs from suppliers dismissive of human rights, or actuarial calculations of the risks of retroactive environmental rulings, must be weighed against the damage from negative publicity, the cost of poor public relations, and the possibility of consumer protest. 'The spotlight does not change the morality of multinational managers; it changes the bottom-line interests of multinational corporations.'[21] Bottom-line interests that politicians seem increasingly unable to meet.

Many corporations are now concerned to ensure that they are well thought of by the public and the media. In practical terms this has meant a substantial increase not only in the number of multinationals that now have codes of conduct (*all* Fortune 500 companies in the US do), but also in those now willing to undergo an audit of their environmental, and to a lesser extent social, policies. Whereas in 1993 only 15 per cent of Europe's largest companies had carried out environmental audits, and social audits were the domain of the ethical brands like Ben & Jerry's and the Body Shop, by 2000 more and more companies were taking this tack, with over half carrying out environmental audits and a number of significant players such as Shell, BP, GrandMet and BT now carrying out social audits too.[22]

While the independence of the auditors remains in some cases questionable, and companies' willingness or indeed ability to respond to findings is still unproven, what is clear is that corporations are acting more transparently than before. The rhetoric of business, at least, is changing as many of the biggest brand names seem to have realised that while they do not always have to be seen to do right, a pre-emptive admission of culpability is probably a better PR strategy than a denial or even a valid explanation, once they have been exposed in unethical practices.

Unlike parties or politicians that have been 'outed', most of the companies and industries that have been singled out by activists have made changes in their way of doing business. Nike initially adopted a very defensive posture in late 1997 when environmental researcher Dara O'Rourke revealed that poor ventilation, exposure to hazardous chemicals and inadequate safety equipment and training at a plant in Indonesia were putting the health of workers at risk. But a year later Nike allowed O'Rourke back into the plant to establish, and presumably publicly report, that changes promised by the company had actually been made. Global Exchange, a human rights organisation dedicated to promoting social justice around the world described this as 'an astounding transformation for a company that once treated independent monitoring as a public relations exercise'. Furthermore, the company claims to have severed contracts with plants that paid below minimum wage levels, promised free after-hours education for all its Third World factory workers, and raised the minimum age of footwear factory workers to 18 and the minimum age for all other light manufacturing workers to 16. If Jeff Ballinger of Press for Change, a group which monitors workers' rights in Asia, was right when he said that market research revealed that 12-year-old girls in focus groups back in the

States were talking about Nike's labour abuses, it is not surprising that the company acted in this way.

Thanks to the boycotts of sporting goods in the mid-1990s and resultant negative publicity, many footballs in America now carry a label declaring 'No child or slave labour used on this ball'. Only a few years ago, Disney wouldn't have considered children in Indonesia to be important stakeholders in their business; now they have no choice but to do so. The diamond industry, chastened by the experiences of the anti-fur lobby during most of the 1990s and alerted to the threat of a consumer boycott, finally woke up to the fact that consumers might not want to wear gems that were funding the apparatus of war; diamonds are a girl's best friend no longer unless they are seen to be 'blood free'.

Nearly all the companies targeted by the joint action of the Free Burma Coalition and associated consumers and shareholders pulled out of Burma. Before governments and state authorities proved willing to take action against the repressive regime, consumers themselves applied sanctions with some success. Siding with Aung San Suu Kyi rather than politicians or corporations on the question of the effectiveness of such action, Generation X turned their back on the 'Choice of a New Generation', joined forces with the Baby Boomers and marched with the Free Burma Coalition in rallies that targeted well known brands. Philips, Heineken, C&A, Ralph Lauren, Motorola, Carlsberg and Kodak were just some of the multinationals who decided that the potential attractions of the Burmese market were not nearly great enough, and left the country, fearing a damaging boycott were they to remain.

These are just a few examples of real changes that corporations have made over recent years in direct response to actual or threatened consumer or shareholder revolt. The corporations did far more than merely comply with their legal obligations. Neither legislation nor regulation drove these firms to change the way they did business – in most of these cases government or regulatory demands have been weak or absent – but consumers, who by boycotting products or exerting pressure at shareholders' meetings are beginning to make companies realise that responsible behaviour is increasingly less of an option; rather it is a necessity if a company means to continue to safeguard its commercial interests. Many of these consumers are largely uninterested in politics, believing that politicians do not listen to them and court only the private sector. Until politicians learn to respect and trust the electorate, voters will not be inclined to reciprocate.

The impotence of politicians

So while consumers are beginning to play the role of global policemen, what are politicians doing? Afraid to resist corporations directly, they are tacitly endorsing consumer activism. Politicians are stepping aside so that consumers and shareholders can become, to an ever greater extent, the watchmen over corporations' activities.

It is increasingly evident that concerns are being inadequately represented in the traditional political sphere, and cannot be met through public-sector provision. The growth of the ecology movement in the 1980s, for example, was a response to the failure of political parties to take seriously the environmental costs of industrial production.

Environmentalism has now moved into the mainstream, but despite the 'greening' of politics few governments have succeeded in challenging the vested interests of the business community and imposing a reduction of carbon fuel emissions or the safeguarding of natural resources. Environmentalists' response has been to target multinational corporations and international organisations directly. In a dual strategy, they have fought a PR battle against big business, exposing its record of destruction, while battling at local level to prevent environmentally damaging developments. In the midst of confrontations and protest, national governments have been marginalised, alienating both sides by endorsing pro-environment rhetoric while using the coercive power of the state against protesters – or, as in the case of Monsanto, actively coming out on the side of the corporation.

Politicians, unable and unwilling to take corporations to task for fear of jeopardising their relationship with them, and recognising their own inability to effect change on a global stage that lies outside their jurisdiction, are furtively supporting consumer vigilantism and imitating its language and demands. In the UK, Trade and Industry Secretary Stephen Byers endorsed the new culture of consumer power, calling on individuals to use their wallets and voices to protest against high prices and end the image of 'Rip-off Britain'.[23] In the United States, President Clinton urged companies to be 'good corporate citizens' by monitoring working conditions at manufacturers who produce their goods.[24] Clare Short's Department for International Development is encouraging British retailers to adopt buying policies that would satisfy non-governmental organisations (NGOs) such as Greenpeace and Amnesty International.

But these requests and urgings are rarely backed up by the muscle of the law. The British government asked Premier Oil to pull out of Burma but did not *make* it do so (it did not) by imposing economic sanctions on Burma. Companies are not compelled to enforce labour standards in their overseas operations, under threat of penalties at home, despite politicians' rhetoric. External verification of environmental programmes and reports is not required either in the US or in most of Europe. Governments issue ethical declarations but fail to back them up with legislation. For all the British government's talk of an ethical foreign policy and Clinton's insistence that America's trading partners improve their record on human rights, these have proved to be empty promises in the face of possible loss of trade. The only financial penalties faced by companies that trade with countries such as Indonesia, China and Burma are the consumer boycotts imposed by Western shoppers.

Many politicians recognise their own impotence. Edward McMillan Scott, leader of the Conservatives in the European Parliament, tells a story that clearly illustrates the helplessness that many politicians feel. In November 1996 he organised a rally with Ken Wiwa, the son of Nigerian activist and critic of Shell's operations in Ogoniland Ken Saro-Wiwa, to commemorate his father's execution. Crowds gathered and someone asked him, 'Mr McMillan Scott, what are you going to do about this injustice?'

McMillan Scott replied, 'I'm going to stop putting Shell petrol in my car.' Taking action as a consumer was, in his opinion, more effective than anything that he could do as a politician.

ALL THAT GLITTERS . . .

Outfoxing the fox

At first it all looked so promising. Husband-and-wife team Steve Wilson and Jane Akre joined Robert Murdoch's Fox 13 TV station in Florida trailing clouds of glory. She was a former CNN anchorwoman, he had won four Emmy awards for investigative journalism. His documentaries on Chrysler's faulty door locks, corrupt senators and Ford's fire-hazard ignition had made him one of the most famous and feared journalists in America. They had been hired to beef up the Tampa Bay station's serious news coverage.

Yet within a year both had been fired. Their only crime, they claimed, was their refusal to broadcast untruths about agrochemical company Monsanto, a major Fox advertiser.

The couple decided to fight Fox in the courts under Florida's whistleblower legislation, alleging that they had been sacked for simply trying to tell the truth. And, in August 2000, they won.

The David and Goliath nature of the court case afforded a disturbing insight into the complicated relationship between major advertisers and media moguls in the USA. 'We were telling the secrets the supermarkets didn't want aired, the dairy farmers didn't want and Monsanto didn't want,' says Wilson of the trial. 'When you put those advertisers together, you're talking about a lot of advertising dollars, both in Tampa and at Fox's other stations across the country . . . When media managers who are not journalists have so little regard for the public trust that they actually order reporters to broadcast false information and slant the truth to curry the favour or avoid the wrath of special interests, as happened here, that is the day any responsible reporter has to stand up and say, "No way!"'

The story begins in 1996, when Rupert Murdoch bought thirteen major TV stations in America to add to his Fox cable network. This brought his holdings of US TV stations to twenty-two, reaching more than half the nation's viewers. Tampa Bay's WTVT, a former CBS station known for in-depth reporting, was one of the new acquisitions. High-profile duo Akre and Wilson were brought in to boost ratings; initially it looked as though the station would maintain its high journalistic standards,

The pair were quick to uncover a major story. They discovered that Florida's milk supply came from cows injected with a substance called bovine growth hormone, or BGH. Sold under the brand name Posilac, it can boost a cow's milk yield by as much as a third. It is made by US agrochemical giant Monsanto, and was approved by America's Food and Drug Administration in 1993. However, BGH was, at the time, banned in Canada, Britain, New Zealand and most of Europe. Scientific research has suggested that the hormone could be linked to cancer, a theory strongly disputed by Monsanto. In response to consumer fears in Florida about BGH, the state's giant supermarket wholesaler of milk and dairy products announced in February 1994 that it would not buy milk from treated cows 'until there was widespread acceptance' of the hormone. But in 1996 Akre photographed cows receiving Posilac injections at all of seven randomly selected Florida dairy farms, challenging the milk supplier's claims.

WTVT, by then known as Fox 13, was enthusiastic about the story. The station booked several thousand dollars' worth of radio advertising to promote the documentary, scheduled for broadcast on 24 February 1997. But days before transmission Monsanto's lawyers contacted Fox's head office in New York, claiming that the documentary was inaccurate. The Monsanto letter of complaint included a sentence which Akre and Wilson – and, eventually, the Florida state jury – found particularly disturbing. It read: 'There is a lot at stake in what is going on in Florida, not only for Monsanto, but also for Fox News and its owner.' The documentary was pulled 'for further review'.

Initially Fox 13 refused to back down: the news manager examined the film and, according to Akre and Wilson, found no reason to doubt their claims. A new date was set for a broadcast the following week. But then Monsanto's lawyers again wrote to the Fox head office saying that the reporters were biased and that the story would damage the country. The station pulled the BGH broadcast again. It was never to be shown.

Shortly afterwards, Fox 13's news manager was fired. According to the journalists' affidavit the new management offered Akre and Wilson 'large cash settlements' in exchange for their resignations and a promise not to publish details about Posilac or how Fox had handled the story. They refused. Over the following six months they rewrote the story seventy-three times, at Fox's insistence, but consistently refused to include an assertion that they strongly believed to be false: that BGH milk is as safe as milk from untreated cows. Finally, in December 1997, the pair were dismissed for 'insubordination'. Six months later the station broadcast its version of the story, including the statement that BGH milk was safe.

Akre and Wilson decided to sue Fox for violating Florida's 'whistleblower' act. 'We are parents ourselves,' Akre said at the time. 'It is not right for the station to withhold this important health information. Solely as a matter of conscience we will not aid and abet their effort to cover this up any longer. Every parent and every consumer has the right to know what they're pouring on their children's morning cereal.'

In court, Fox insisted the dismissal had 'nothing to do' with the BGH story or with letters from Monsanto. David Boylan, Fox 13's general manager, said the pair were fired for 'contentious, argumentative, *ad hominem* and vituperative conduct and for refusal to abide by [Fox 13's] established policies and procedures'.

Wilson would agree that he can be difficult. He is part of the generation of American journalists who cut their teeth in the Watergate era and freely admits he cares more about nailing the bad guys than pleasing his bosses. But his claims were vindicated in court. On 18 August 2000, after a five-week trial and six hours of deliberation, a Florida state court jury unanimously determined that Fox 'acted intentionally and deliberately to falsify or distort the plaintiffs' news reporting on BGH'. The jury also found that Jane Akre's threat to blow the whistle on Fox's misconduct to the Federal Communications Commission (FCC) was the sole reason for the termination of their contracts, and awarded damages of $425,000.

'We set out to tell Florida consumers the truth about a giant chemical company, and a powerful dairy lobby clearly doesn't want them to know,' Wilson said. 'That used to be something investigative reporters won awards for. As we've learned the hard way, it's something you can be fired for these days whenever a news organization places more value on its bottom line than on delivering the news to its viewers honestly.'

The truth will not be televised

In the previous chapter I may have risked giving the impression that consumer politics operates in some approximation of a perfect information environment. The Fox story shows that this is not the case. Consumers and shareholders are often left to operate blind. Their inability to get full and accurate information is a major handicap for activists.

News broadcasting is becoming increasingly commercialised as the pressure on broadcasters to make profits continues to increase, creating an overriding focus on ratings and advertising revenues. Once again, the pressures are greatest in the US, but other countries are following fast. Belgium is the only European country where television still remains free of commercials.

In the UK, as David Liddiment, Director of Programmes ITV Network has put it, 'We are less able to ignore the commercial imperative than ever before, although we're not running an audience delivery service for advertisers. Our job is to provide a service for viewers that serves the advertisers at the same time.'[1]

Of course, serving the best interests of the advertisers may not be in the best interests of viewers. Fox's story dilemma is faced by an increasing number of broadcasters: whether to run a story, even if it risks jeopardising crucial advertising dollars.

Recognising the explicit corporate agenda we tend to be sceptical of the claims of product labels and advertising copy but are less likely to scrutinise the traditional sources of our news, which we assume are free from external influence. But for every Brent Spar, child labour or GM disclosure that gets on the air, how many others, like the BGH story, are being suppressed?

Rupert Murdoch is, of course, notorious for using his control of information to support his business interests. As is by now well known, in his quest to capture a substantial slice of the Chinese media pie Murdoch worked hard to gain the favour of the Chinese authorities. In 1994 he dropped the BBC World Service from his Asian Star TV satellite after it criticised Chinese leaders for the Tiananmen Square killings – the BBC's independence and impartially were potentially damaging Murdoch's prospects in the Chinese market. And in 1998 HarperCollins, a Murdoch-owned publisher, cancelled publication of *East and West,* a book by Hong Kong's last British governor, Chris Patten. It was clear that publication risked aggravating the Chinese authorities given that Patten's recollections of his time as Governor of Hong Kong were highly critical of the Chinese government.

The suppression of stories that may harm corporate interests is hardly unique to Murdoch's media empire. A segment that was aired on NBC's *Today* show about defective bolts in nuclear plants reportedly omitted the following lines: 'Recently General Electric engineers discovered that they had a big problem. One out of every three bolts from one of the major suppliers was bad. Even more alarming, GE accepted the bad bolts without any certification of compliance for eight years.'[2] General Electric owns the network. Disney-owned ABC dropped a report which alleged that paedophiles had been employed at a Disney theme park.[3]

When tobacco advertising was still allowed on US television, a clear correlation was found between the amounts of money the networks derived from tobacco advertising revenues and their willingness to enter the debate on the health effects of smoking.[4] In Italy, where two influential newspapers, *Il Messaggero* and *Il Tempo*, are owned by construction companies, 'there is plenty of auto-censorship by journalists keen not to upset their bosses.'[5] Liza Brinkworth, the British investigative journalist who exposed tales of under-age sex and drug abuse at the Elite model agency, failed to sell her story to numerous women's magazines – they were clearly not prepared to risk fashion-related advertising. It was the publicly funded BBC that eventually broke the story.

Either to avoid jeopardising relationships with advertisers or to safeguard their wider interests – increasingly these media organisations form parts of larger groups of companies, with business interests outside the media – news reporting has frequently been found to be skewed in recent years. This is not, of course, a new phenomenon. 'A study of women's magazines in the period 1983 to 1987 revealed that not one magazine that carried cigarette advertising published any full length feature, column, review or editorial on any aspect of the dangers of smoking. During the same period lung cancer was determined to be the number one killer of women surpassing even breast cancer. Not one of the magazines surveyed mentioned this fact.'[6]

What is new, however, is that there has been a consolidation of the media industry over the past few years, and as few as ten global media players now wield immense power. As a result, the regulation of broadcasting has been much weakened, particularly in the United States where, for example, in August 1999 the FCC did away with longstanding media ownership rules that forbade the largest television companies and networks to own more than one station in the nation's largest cities. What we do or do not learn, at least through traditional channels, will increasingly depend on the decisions of a very few.

Aidan Whilee, general secretary of the International Federation of Journalists, the world's largest organisation of journalists representing more than 45,000 members in 103 countries, said when the $160 billion Time Warner–AOL merger was announced:

> We are now seeing the dominance of a handful of companies controlling information and how that information reaches people. Unless action is taken to ensure journalistic independence we face a dangerous threat to media diversity . . . Otherwise we will have corporate gatekeepers to the flow of information who will define content to suit their market strategies.[7]

As consumers of news, we are unable to police the news providers in the way we police other corporations. Unless the media are held accountable to an external and independent force, our independent press, one of the vital components of democracy, may be in danger.

Seeing the unseen

In a world in which governments are increasingly unable to keep corporations in check, and consumers and shareholders have to take on this role, loss of a free press is devastating. For if a story is not told, if a problem is not seen to exist, people have no reason to protest.

Ignorance is impotence. While it is likely that such scandals still usually – and eventually – come to light, not least given the media's attraction to David and Goliath stories which also appeal to the public, even when they do come out consumers, faced with the subsequent public relations onslaught, find it increasingly hard to gauge which sources of information can be relied on.

Consumers who sought a realistic assessment of the risks of genetically modified food, for example, were left to piece together the evidence on the basis of hard-sell from the agrochemical companies, half-hearted reassurances from governments, hysterical press reporting, and passionate denunciations by environmental groups. The findings of scientists who claimed to have rigorously tested the effect of GM foods were disputed by other scientists. In this, as in many other cases, it became impossible for consumers to act on the basis of objective evidence. They simply did not know whom to believe.

Even for those who wish to actively seek out the truth, dealing with the range of potentially conflicting information, not to mention misinformation, is both time-consuming and confusing. Whom to believe? Whom to trust? Which issues to champion? Is it Nike, Reebok or Adidas that I shouldn't be buying? With so many contradictory stimuli, and so many brands, even the most concerned consumers face information overload and compassion fatigue. Simply increasing the amount of information does not solve the problem, especially if the sources are tainted. Without a reliable source, the big consumer battles are likely to be won by those who shout the loudest.

When stories break, the media's interest is fleeting. Consumer campaigns are highly dependent on media coverage, but the media are by nature short-termist in their outlook. Their intense but brief attention to most political protests rarely reflects the longer-term nature of the issues. Like pressure groups, they have a vested interest in creating a hysteria that stimulates interest and sells more newspapers. During 1999 the campaign against GM foods went from being the preserve of left-wing environmentalists to a tabloid crusade and has now fallen back to relative obscurity.

Once something is no longer reported, people inevitably start to think the issue has gone away. For all except the most committed, boycotting of products tends to be short-lived, and once the issue is less newsworthy consumers generally revert to their original preferences, unless their chosen substitute has actually turned out to be as good or better.[8] The issue of the safety of British beef has been in and out of the news over the last few years, although it appears British beef is no safer now than it was when concern over BSE began, while cases of human CJD have yet to peak.

Although consumer activism is undoubtedly entering the mainstream, campaigns which are high profile, intense and fashionable are understandably more attractive and successful than those that are more routine and prosaic, however worthy of support. In recent years it has been possible to witness the fashion trends of consumer protest: from Nestlé boycotts in the late 1970s, through anti-apartheid protests in the early 1980s, global warming and rainforest depletion later in that decade, live animal exports in the early 1990s, then the rights of workers in developing countries, and most recently food safety. At each stage protesters secured small victories and corporations changed tack, but with the exception of apartheid in no case was the war won so conclusively that further protest was unnecessary, as we saw with the repeated denunciations of sweatshop labour. Consumer activism seems most effective when consumers remain active.

Rhetoric or reality

The haphazard information provided by the media is contrasted by the stream of information produced by companies. Corporations are spending more than ever before in marketing positive images of themselves. Of course company-provided information is usually treated with at least a degree of scepticism; it is only to be expected that a company will trumpet its successes and try to cover up its wrongs, and will typically tell only one side of the story, the side it wants its customers to hear.

Sainsbury's, for example, runs advertising campaigns claiming that it is pro-organic and anti-GM, in order to appeal to the prevailing public mood, while at the same time it is quietly involved in the development of new genetically modified strains of vegetables that will have a longer shelf life and reduce wastage. Dr Philip Dix, from the National University of Ireland in Maynooth near Dublin where the research is being carried out, has said '[Sainsbury's] is taking a passive role because of the climate [towards GM foods]. It prefers not to be too closely associated with the project.'[9]

As we saw in the case of Monsanto in the previous chapter, marketing spend is not always the solution. The firm misguidedly attempted to counter European consumer fears in 1999 with a $1.6 million advertising campaign proclaiming the merits of genetically modified foods. The slogan on its website just before the crisis was 'Food, Health and Hope'. Hope it's right? Hope it works? Hope the public buys it? In this case the public didn't. The campaign backfired, and European consumers and green lobbies created enough pressure to ensure that grocery retailers and restaurants were cautious about stocking and using GM products. The public is increasingly unlikely to take such platitudes at face value when they are posted on company websites or found in the companies' promotional materials.

What the public is less immediately able to write off as mere marketing, however, is the vogue for codes of conduct and environmental audits to which, as we saw, most leading companies now subscribe. All Fortune 500 US companies and over half the UK's top 500 companies, for example, now have codes of conduct.[10] In some cases they clearly have real significance: according to Sir Martin Sorrell, CEO of WPP, one of the world's largest communications groups, managers throughout his 33,000-employee organisation who are found not to be adhering to the code are fired. However, a survey from the Institute of Business Ethics reveals that such codes are often not 'active documents', but lie dormant in company filing cabinets.[11]

Although over half of FTSE and Fortune 500 companies now carry out environmental audits, a study of environmental reporting by the oil industry concluded that it remains 'virtually impossible' for stakeholders to draw meaningful comparisons between firms.[12] Only 18 per cent of the environmental reports of the top 100 firms in Australia, Belgium, Denmark,

Finland, France, Germany, The Netherlands, Norway, Sweden, the UK and the USA surveyed by KPMG were found to have been independently verified. Even then the study concluded that 'verification is a long way from a standard which readers can rely on to guarantee the reliability of the reported data and information', and 'users still have to read between the lines in order to interpret the report and the verification statement.'[13]

With no external means of verification or political or legal enforcement (though some Scandinavian countries, The Netherlands and Australia have introduced limited reporting requirements under 'green accounts legislation'), the accuracy of company reporting will continue to be difficult to ensure, a problem which will stand firmly in the way of consumer empowerment. In October 2000 the BBC current affairs programme *Panorama* revealed that Nike and Gap were still using suppliers who were employing underage labour despite their claims to the contrary. Even the trailblazing ethical retailer the Body Shop was accused of inaccuracy over its initial pledge that its products were not tested on animals, and subsequently substituted the watered-down slogan 'Against animal testing.'[14] Sheila McKechnie, director of Britain's Consumers Association, was among those pressing for a Freedom of Information Act that would give customers better access to the information they need to wield their power as consumers more effectively and appropriately. Unfortunately the version of the act that was ultimately passed was so weak that it barely affected the information asymmetry between consumer and corporation.

It is even more confusing when claims are made or endorsements provided by supposedly neutral third parties, who then turn out to have hidden corporate interests. An extreme case of this was Nestlé, which in the late 1970s employed marketing representatives to dress up like doctors in order to sell the company's baby milk to mothers in Africa as the healthiest alternative for their children. While deceptions such as these remain thankfully rare, what is increasingly commonplace is a blurring of the boundaries between independent research and the corporate agenda.

In the USA, corporate funding of academic scientific labs more than doubled over the ten years to 1997, when it stood at $2 billion.[15] In Britain scientific public research money fell by 20 per cent between 1983 and 1999, leaving a deficit that corporate funds were more than prepared not only to fill but also to augment. Although these boosts to research budgets can clearly be beneficial, conflicts of interest can, unsurprisingly, arise. Samuel Cohen, a University of Nebraska researcher on saccharin, whose findings were heavily relied on by the US government in justifying its decision to take saccharin off the list of cancer-causing chemicals, was revealed to have been funded in part by an industry group whose members included Cumberland Packing, the makers of Sweet-N-Low saccharin products. Steven Rosenberg, an oncologist at the National Cancer Institute, said that 'some colleagues now request confidentiality before discussing their work with [him]; one refuses to reveal the sequence of a protein fragment that could be useful in studying tumours.'

'I feel academia is becoming tainted in this,' says Drew Pardoll, an oncologist at Johns Hopkins University School of Medicine, 'it's an issue of public trust.'[16] If scientists will not publish in medical journals, for fear of losing out financially, or if findings are suspect because of potentially divided loyalties, our ability to access impartial scientific research in many areas will be lost.

It is not just the impartiality of scientific research that is being questioned. University centres, think-tanks,[17] public interest organisations and even consumer organisation are now funded by corporations. Nottingham University announced in December 2000 that it had accepted £3.8 million from British American Tobacco, which at the time was under investigation over smuggling allegations, to finance a new school of, most ironically, 'corporate social responsibility'.[18] The US National Consumers' League, which describes itself as 'America's pioneer consumer advocacy organisation', got 39 per cent of its income in 1997 from corporations and industry associations. 'Almost every current project, seminar, brochure, newsletter and fundraising dinner is sponsored in large part by major corporations or industry associations.'[19] These donations clearly risk jeopardising impartiality.

Even the allegiance of regulatory agencies has been questioned. Three of the key figures in the US Food and Drug Administration who were responsible for approving the BGH hormone had ties to Monsanto. One was a former Monsanto research scientist who had worked on BGH while at the company, another had been a lawyer with King & Spalding, a firm that represented Monsanto, and had helped draft regulations to be used by local governments to fight labelling of milk from BGH-treated cows, and the third had worked on Monsanto-funded studies at Cornell University.[20]

Although a subsequent investigation found no impropriety, Bernie Sanders, the Independent congressman who requested the investigation, remained adamant that corporate interests had been at play. 'The FDA allowed corporate influence to run rampant in its approval of the drug. The ethics rules were often stretched to the breaking point and broken on a number of occasions,' he said.

E-activism

In this confusion of information and misinformation from the traditional media, governments, corporations, think-tanks and research institutes, new sources of information have become essential to activists. We saw in the previous chapter the effort NGOs and pressure groups are now putting into getting their point of view across – with real success. In a 1996 survey of public confidence in various sources of information about modern biotechnology, respondents trusted consumer and environmental organisations most, by 30.5 per cent and 22.4 per cent respectively. Only 7.8 per cent put their trust in public authorities, and 1.6 per cent in the industry itself.

But what has really revolutionised information over the past few years, and has opened up completely new sources of information for all of us, is of course the Internet. Most of this information, at least at present, is out of the control of corporations or large organisations. Information provision is no longer the domain of the media giant. Any individual or organisation, with a minimum of technical know-how and equipment, can tell the world whatever they want it to hear by creating their own website.

Those who are looking to monitor corporate activity have never had an easier time of it. Type 'McDonalds' into any search engine and you will quickly be directed to the 'I hate McDonald's' site – the voice of a single disgruntled customer – and the McSpotlight site at www.mcspotlight.org, which gets over one million hits a month. This site not only provides full background on the infamous 'McLibel' trial, at the end of which in March 1999 three British Lord Justices ruled that it was 'fair comment' to say McDonalds workers worldwide suffer poor pay and conditions, but also accuses the company of doing all kinds of harm, from environmental destruction to the 'McExploitation' of kids.

Go to the Corporate Watch site at www.corpwatch.org, and you can 'find resources designed to help you find out more than you probably wanted to know about transnational corporations' and obtain advice on how to 'dig up the dirt on your favourite corporation'. On its Nike page, for example, you can read Ernst and Young's confidential November 1997 labour and environmental audit of Nike's facility in Vietnam, examine the lawsuit brought against Nike for presenting an allegedly false picture of their working conditions, peruse a collection of news articles on Nike's operations, and look at photos taken inside a Nike plant in Vietnam – including pictures of workers using dangerous materials, such as glue and solvents, without appropriate protective gear.

Don't like Bill Gates? There are numerous sites, including Corporate Watch, a research organisation that provides materials for activist or campaign groups, that have taken up the battle against Microsoft. NetAction, a US-based non-profit organisation, features reports and activist resources for 'fighting the Microsoft Monopoly' and provides a digest of anti-Microsoft websites. Under www.usdoj.gov you can find the United States Department of Justice's legal documents for its anti-trust case against Microsoft. Elsewhere you can find a memo leaked by a Microsoft whistleblower, describing an internal management plan to prevent consumer groups and state attorney generals from pursuing anti-trust action against the company.

The range and quality of such sites is immense. And as quickly as companies try to close them down, they reappear in other guises. A recent development has been that of corporations buying the domain names of oppositional sites. Domino Pizza bought 'ihatedominopizza.com'; and Chase Manhattan Bank has acquired the rights to 'ihatechase', 'chasestinks' and 'chasesucks'. But this strategy seldom works; there are just too many permutations. Scott Harrison, a 23-year-old New Yorker, launched a site against Chase in protest of an erroneous bill of $650 that it took him seven months and thirty phone calls to correct, and called it 'chasebanksucks.com'. Hardly activism at its most noble.

But the Internet does not only provide information passively. What most differentiates the Internet from traditional media is that it is an interactive medium. Community boards and newsgroups allow members to share stories and complaints. Wal-Mart Watch (www.walmart.watch.com) actively solicits personal stories relating to Wal-Mart's impact on local business, employees and consumers which are then posted on its site. Wal-Martyrs (www.walmartyrs.com) asks Wal-Mart employees, or former employees, to share their experiences and post their stories. And chatrooms provide live forums for discussing companies.

The Internet is like a game of Chinese whispers multiplied and magnified. It provides the ultimate medium for conspiracy theories; rumours pass across borders and time zones almost instantaneously. Messages appear on screen promiscuously, and there is no easy way to separate the truth from lies. From companies' point of view, this aspect of the Internet is chipping away at the significant benefits they are deriving from the dot-com revolution. It is proving to be a corporate nightmare, a medium which, to quote the CEO of one of the world's largest car manufacturers, 'promotes half truths and irresponsible representations of their companies that cannot be controlled or influenced'[21] – although they are of course trying to do so where possible. Many corporations are now hiring third parties such as e-watch to monitor anti-corporate sites for libel and to help with damage control when criticism of their companies is posted on the Net.

From the consumer's point of view, however, the Internet provides a means to scrutinise corporations more directly than ever before and unprecedentedly easy ways of taking action against them. There are sites that provide information on boycotts,[22] sites that give standard form letters of protest to CEOs, sites encouraging people to write to corporate moguls, and sites telling which stores to picket.[23] The Essential Action site (www.essential.org) was, in its own words, 'created to alert activists to current international campaigns and activities'. Current campaigns include an onslaught on the tobacco industry; race discrimination lawsuits against Coca-Cola; and 'Boycott Shell/Free Nigeria'. The Boycott Board's stated purpose is 'to provide the socially conscious consumer with a means of learning about various boycotts in progress'.

Search under 'child labour' on www.directhit.com, and the seventh site that you are urged to visit recommends that you:

Ask the right questions

By making store managers and corporate officers aware that you have concerns, you encourage them to take action. Does their company guarantee products being sold are made under humane conditions? Can you get a list of names and addresses of contractors and subcontractors? Does the company have a code of conduct? Can you have a copy?

Visit stores

Retailers have a saying that 'The customer is always right.' They may not actually believe that, but it does point out the importance of customers' opinions. After all, without customers, there's no store! Ask your store manager questions, and make sure they know you want honest answers. Often, organised visits by groups of customers can produce immediate results as chain store managers will call head office to get the answers.

This site it not that of a radical fringe organisation, but of the UCLWA, one of America's largest trade unions.

It is uncertain how long the Internet will be able to retain its irreverent and anti-establishment leanings. Takeovers, corporate influence and control and commercialisation are all likely in time to threaten its democratic and egalitarian spirit. Microsoft already steers net users to its own websites and those of its commercial partners although if the US anti-trust ruling currently under appeal is ultimately upheld it will no longer be able to do so.[24] Time Warner can now direct a torrent of information to AOL's 22 million subscribers.

But that does not mean that the traditional media will ever be able to rule cyberspace. Despite the head start that traditional media companies have in terms of available funds and avenues to promote their websites, the explosion in socially responsible sites, portals and public forums over such a short period means that in all likelihood many of these alternative news sites will not only remain intact, but will actually become larger and more powerful. Disinfo.com receives 11,000 visits a day and indymedia.net gets more than 1 million hits a month. Type in 'Nike boycott' on a typical search engine and you get a list of over 200 sites.[25] E-activism on the net continues to rise.

The number of people who actively seek out this kind of information may be relatively small, but once their findings are passed on to others the numbers grow exponentially. E-mail allows people to send news to hundreds of others almost effortlessly. Each of these, in the same way, can pass the story to hundreds of people on their address lists. Add this to the increasing ease of communication all over the world with mobile telephones, satellite pagers and so forth, and the virus-like infectivity of today's news is clear, not to mention the impossibility of containing it. Where governments have started to crack down and regulate the Internet, as has happened in Vietnam and Burma, ways have been found to bypass attempts at controls; for instance, accessing the Internet illegally by dialling out of the country using a mobile phone. 'By jumping over borders, by opening cheap access to information, and by providing forums for debate in countries where the media are monopolised, the Internet offers the disenfranchised a chance to participate.'[26]

The pervasive urban myths of the 1980s and 1990s – the rat found in the Kentucky Fried Chicken carton, Marlboro's relationship with the Ku Klux Klan (the secret sign was revealed by folding a Marlboro cigarette pack in a certain way) – miraculously managed to circle the globe even in the pre-Internet era. Now such things are commonplace. Truths, half-truths and blatant lies cross national borders with ever increasing speed.

. . . is not gold

Of course we should be extremely cautious in assuming that alternative sources of information are necessarily any more socially responsible than the traditional media. Pressure groups, aware of the importance of co-opting consumers in their battle against the corporations, have been found on several occasions to exaggerate risks. In 1995 the Advertising Standards Authority, the UK's advertising watchdog, accused pressure groups – including Friends of the Earth, Greenpeace and the International Fund for Animal Welfare – of exaggerating claims, exploiting public trust and damaging 'the credibility of the advertising industry as a whole.'[27] All of these groups had used shocking or misleading advertisements. Greenpeace overestimated by a factor of 37 the amount of hydrocarbons the Brent Spar oil platform might leak into the sea. And 'when the Braer oil tanker went aground off Shetland in 1993 and spilled tens of thousands of tonnes of crude oil into the sea, wildlife groups predicted catastrophic effects on marine life which were never borne out.'[28] Pressure groups' need to influence public debate often provokes them into the creation of unwarranted public anxiety.[29]

The drive to win media attention may also reduce the ability of groups to focus their campaigns effectively. Many environmental groups have been found to be 'keener on getting the attention of the media than on devising a sophisticated political strategy.'[30]

Raising popular awareness and support must be a fundamental part of all consumer campaigns, but it remains true that successful protests usually also require political strategies directed at policy makers or senior politicians. Neglect of these aspects of a campaign decreases its effectiveness.

And of course consumer pressure groups have their own agendas and priorities. What determines the malpractices on which they choose to focus? What motivates them to protest? Can we assume that they are any more high-minded than corporate executives? Whose interests are they really safeguarding? For just as corporations usually only promote ethical causes when it is in their interests to do so, the same is often true of consumer groups. This self-interest may be narrowly conceived as the interests of the group members – for example, an unwillingness to eat genetically modified food because of concerns that it may be unsafe – or it may reflect the values of the group, values which may not necessarily reflect those of a wider public, such as opposition to cosmetic testing on animals. In both cases there may be knock-on social benefits, such as safer food and less abuse of animals. But pressure groups do not necessarily exist to reflect the interests of society at large, and social benefits are often indirect and sporadic.

Focus groups among shoppers who described themselves as 'concerned about ethical issues', people who either had boycotted or would consider boycotting a shop or product because of ethical concerns, revealed that:

Only a small minority of ethical shoppers were purchasing ethical foodstuffs purely because of their ethical beliefs. A majority of respondents believed that these products were healthier and sometimes tasted better . . . Ethical issues such as pollution of the environment, political oppression or exploitation of the Third World were 'back in mind' worries which rarely altered food-purchasing habits.[31]

In the case of foodstuffs the interests of environmental campaigners and individual shoppers often coincide, since both share an interest in safe, high-quality products. However, in many other cases different consumer groups have divergent and conflicting interests, undermining their effectiveness as a bloc. According to Britain's National Consumer Council, 'Consumers often find it hard to reconcile their concerns for the environment with their day-to-day needs as consumers.'[32] In 1995, for example, Tesco bowed to consumer pressure by dropping cardboard milk cartons in flavour of plastic bottles. The company claimed that research had shown a 92 per cent preference for plastic. Yet the environmental costs associated with using plastic, which is energy intensive to make and more difficult to recycle, led to the move being criticised by green pressure groups.[33]

Shades of grey

Perhaps the greatest flaws of consumer activism are its inability to deal with uncertainty or risk, and its need to reduce all argument to black and white, good and bad. Is GM food necessarily always bad for consumers or the environment? Or could this technology be harnessed for good, as Robert Shapiro, the chairman and CEO of Monsanto, initially seemed to have hoped, with his plans to eradicate famines in the developing world? Child labour may be distasteful to western expectations, but does boycotting goods made with child labour improve or exacerbate the lot of Third World children?

The inability of consumers – at least *en masse* – to see things in shades of grey is due partly to a media and NGO culture that thrives on headlines and soundbites, partly to instinctive Luddism (motor cars and frozen foods were both initially widely resisted), and partly to a general fear of change, be it beneficial or harmful. Monsanto now treads with such caution that when it was approached last year by Dr Andrew Bamford, a genetic scientist at the University of Cambridge, to sponsor his work on using a rat gene to introduce iodine into rice, a development that could improve health in much of the Third World, the company rejected his proposal for fear of consumer backlash. Consumer boycotts of goods produced by child labour may well succeed only in driving the practice underground and force vulnerable children into more degrading or dangerous work.[34,35] 'Dismissing children (or not employing them in the first place) is tantamount to sentencing them to starvation.'[36] And not only children, but their entire families too: children in Third World countries are often their families' primary wage earners.

The world cannot be simplified to the extent that consumer politics tends to demand. Trusting the market to regulate may not ultimately be in our best interest. Such *de facto* populist politics can easily result in tyranny, not necessarily of the majority, but by those who can for whatever reason protest most effectively.

Rather than empowering all, consumer and shareholder activism empowers those with greater purchasing power and those with an ability to change their patterns of consumption with relative ease. It is a form of protest that favours the middle-class – an expression of the dissatisfactions of the bourgeoisie. For the poor and socially excluded, those excluded from a wider range of goods and services by their low incomes and poor credit ratings, this form of protest is rarely an option.[37] Would the GM campaign in Britain have been so great if Prince Charles and the Women's Institute had not joined forces with Greenpeace and the Consumers Association?[38]

Governments cannot leave by the back door

In democratic states, voting is premised on political equality: each citizen has an equal opportunity to shape the political agenda. Consumer activism, however, is skewed towards those with superior resources and organisational abilities. If we neglect our right as citizens we risk being marginalised as consumers. In turning away from traditional forms of expression, and embracing consumer direct action, protesters risk replacing representative democracy with a non-representative alternative.

The emergence of consumer activism as a significant force clearly has political ramifications. Citizens can directly exercise power through bringing pressure to bear on corporations in a way that is increasingly denied to them through traditional political channels. Individual forms of protest such as complaint and litigation are increasingly replacing rather than complementing conventional forms of political expression. It is frequently the lack of trust in the honesty and competence of professional politicians that leads consumers to pursue direct action. The relative success of such protests, in comparison to the perceived ineffectiveness of politicians, further confirms the widespread belief that conventional politics is no longer relevant to most people's lives.

In a deregulated global market, where national governments are becoming spectators rather than actors, we see the consumer emerge as a powerful figure, bringing multinationals to heel through their decisions about where and how to shop. But, just as consumer choice is premised on high-quality information, so also it is dependent on a framework of rights and regulations to protect the customer from unscrupulous vendors.

Because consumer power is market-based, it is effective only where consumers can convince a company that it is in its financial interest to comply. But consumer campaigns lack the legitimacy of democratically mandated protests, and so they are in this respect easier for powerful corporations to resist. Without the official weapons of sanctions, regulation and restrictive laws, consumers are obliged to organise protests as best they can. Lacking the resources offered by the backing of democratic institutions, they can be ill equipped to take on vested and powerful corporate interests.

Rather than providing an alternative to governmental action, the rise in consumer activism ironically makes it even more essential for governments to take an active role by providing the necessary information, or by enforcing standards of transparency and accountability in business. Yet they have been extremely reluctant to do so. When the British government passed new legislation on consumer protection in 2000, the *Daily Telegraph* commented that it 'places overwhelming emphasis on the power of informed customers to force down prices, while there are few solid plans for government action to force the pace'.[39] The maxim of *caveat emptor* prevails.

But the Silent Takeover is not only about governance. It is not only about governments' unwillingness and inability to check corporate power. It is also about governments that are no longer able to deliver what their 'customers' need. Is it possible that corporations will not only see the value in reacting to market pressure and deflecting criticism, but may also find a virtue in playing a proactively constructive role in society too? Or that consumer politics is not only a stick, but a carrot that can lure corporations and business people into redefining their roles in society? Is it possible that while governments are allowing corporate interests to take precedence over those of the public, corporations and business people may decide to put the public's needs first?

EVANGELICAL ENTREPRENEURS

The man who broke the Bank of England

Until Wednesday 16 September 1992, few people outside the world of high finance had ever heard of George Soros, the Hungarian-American currency trader who had made a fortune in high-risk hedge funds on Wall Street. But on that day Soros, then 62, made $1 billion profit, effectively by betting against the pound's ability to stay in the European Exchange Rate Mechanism. As a result Britain was forced to devalue the pound and crash spectacularly out of the ERM. Suddenly, Soros was a household name.

It was estimated at the time that Soros's winning gamble had cost every Briton £12 in currency reserves lost by the Bank of England's increasingly desperate attempts to shore up sterling. With hindsight, most commentators believe Soros did Britain a favour by freeing it from the ERM, giving the country a chance to recover from recession far more quickly than the rest of Europe. Either way, 16 September – dubbed Black Wednesday – made both headlines and history, and Soros has subsequently been known as The Man Who Broke the Bank of England.

Yet his is by no means a straightforward story of the naked power of pure capitalism. Soros the financier is also one of the world's most generous philanthropists, a billionaire who in many respects, simply wants to make the world a better place. Since the 1980s he has donated more than $1.5 billion to charitable causes, several times exceeding $350 million in a single year. And his high-risk approach to making money has spilled over into his charitable donations rather than into the concert halls and art galleries of traditional wealthy benefactors. Soros has consistently taken a punt on high-minded, edgy projects in areas where governments fear to tread, from the legalisation of drugs to the defence of Sarajevo against the Serbs. He has said, 'When I was offered an honorary degree at Oxford, they asked me how I wanted to be described, and I said I would like to be called a financial, philanthropic and philosophical speculator.' Not surprisingly, his idiosyncratic approach to giving has attracted both admiration and disapproval.

Soros grew up in Hungary, the son of a Jewish lawyer who managed by pretending that his family were Christians to save them from the concentration camps. The young George, or Gyuri as he then was, was 15 when the war ended. He subsequently lived under Communist rule in Hungary until, at 17, he travelled to London via Switzerland, where he worked in kitchens and studied at the London School of Economics. There he was influenced by Karl Popper, the philosopher who coined the term 'open society' – a society in which argument and debate are encouraged, in other words, the opposite of a dictatorship. Soros has said that Popper's views have influenced him enormously throughout his career. In the late 1950s the young Soros moved into banking and from London to the US, where he soon became an expert in arbitrage, the art of skimming off profits from buying and selling securities in different markets. He specialised in hedge funds, the high-risk investment vehicles which have the potential to make money whether securities or currencies rise or fall, by gambling on their future worth. Both he and his investors made huge profits. An investment of $100,000 in Soros's Quantum Fund in 1969 was worth $300 million by 1996.

But since the late 1970s his focus had been not simply on moneymaking. It was then that his first marriage broke up and he realised that he had neglected his relationship with his three children, something he later described as the biggest regret of his life. 'I underwent a serious change in my personality during that period. There was a large element of guilt and shame in my emotional make-up.' Soon afterwards he started giving money away. In the 1980s he supplied the whole of Hungary with photocopiers, inspired by a desire to support the democracy movement in a direct way that would foster communication and make censorship difficult. He then approached both the US and European governments with a seventy-year plan to assist the former Eastern bloc countries through the transition from communism to democracy. It fell on deaf ears. Frustrated, his stated aim in the Black Wednesday episode was to move himself from the City pages on to the front pages of the newspapers. 'I had no platform,' he explained at the time. 'So I deliberately [did] the sterling thing to create a platform.' Obviously people care about the man who made a lot of money.

Since then, governments have had to take Soros seriously. His initial charitable focus was on the former Eastern bloc. As a survivor of both Nazi and Communist regimes, he is passionate about supporting democracy in the former totalitarian states. He has spent $100 million to help post-Soviet science, given $50 million to support the beseiged city of Sarajevo from Serb attacks, provided $13 million to aid projects in Belarus, plus millions more funding Open Society foundations (named after Popper's famous thesis) to finance educational and humanitarian projects around the world.

In the US, however, he has attracted controversy for his opposition to what he calls 'excessive individualism'. In 1997 he warned that unfettered market capitalism could be as damaging to an open society as communism, prompting *Forbes* magazine to accuse him of talking 'nonsense'. His belief that drug addiction should be treated as a disease, not a crime, has led to him giving $1 million for a needle exchange project in the US and being branded by the US Secretary of Health as 'the Daddy Warbucks of drug legalisation'. He has also attracted criticism for giving $50 million to help legal immigrants apply for full citizenship in the US, and for sponsoring research on welfare and prison reform.

His touch on the markets has seemed a little less sure in recent years. His 1998 book *The Crisis of Global Capitalism* predicted a prolonged worldwide bear market following the Asian financial crisis, which has failed to materialise. He also failed to foresee the fall in technology stocks in the first months of 2000, with the result that his funds lost about a third of their value. But he is still branching further out into the worlds of politics and policy. He now runs his Open Society Institute from an office a couple of floors down from the Quantum Fund headquarters in New York, and leaves most of the hands-on trading to his employees and his son Robert, devoting much of his time to philosophy and contemplation instead. He says, 'I spend about a third of my day just thinking, and trying to clarify my own thinking about where I should be going, and where the world is going.'

Despite all his philanthropy and recent misjudgement of the market, in 2000 the *Sunday Times* listed Soros's personal fortune at £2.4 billion. At least for the foreseeable future, Soros still clearly has the power to turn thought into action.

Political philanthropy

George Soros is unusual, but by no means unique. Many of today's corporate legends, presumably motivated by thoughts of the judgement of posterity, with their resources exceeding any imaginable desire for consumer goods and property and wanting to leave their mark, are deciding to assume a political and social role.

In a world in which governments seem increasingly unable to deliver, an increasing number of business leaders see it as their responsibility to do so. In the absence of forceful political leadership, many CEOs and company chairmen are choosing to involve themselves in wider debates. As economics has become the new politics, the tendency is for the purveyors of wealth to take over politicians' traditional roles. Why? It is not just another means of pursuing the bottom line; as Sir John Browne, CEO of BP, has said, 'We are not put on this earth to facilitate easier driving to a video store.'

In the competitive world of twenty-first-century business, mega-entrepreneurs also compete with each other to make the biggest social and political impact. As media billionaire Ted Turner told the American chat show host, Larry King, 'I'm putting every rich person in the world on notice. They're going to be hearing from me about giving more money away.'

We are witnessing a new golden age of philanthropy, where the enormously wealthy are funding education programmes and health initiatives, as well as more traditional donations to the arts and cultural institutions. While governments are facing stiff voter opposition to high personal tax rates and opposition from business to increases in corporate taxation, some of the rich are in effect taxing themselves. They are playing Robin Hood: taking from the state and giving to . . . well, whichever cause they deem worthy. A not insignificant number of men who have benefited so greatly from a system that is loaded in their favour are now turning to help those against whom the odds are stacked.

The founder of the Domino Pizza chain, Tom Monaghan, is devoting almost his entire $1 billion fortune to a nationwide school-building programme in the US, and has also paid for a hydroelectic dam in Honduras. Mike Milken, the symbol of 1980s financial lawlessness and amorality, now spends most of his time working to restructure society rather than companies. One of his foundations has awarded nearly $30 million to individual teachers, another funds cancer research. Michael Saylor, the 35-year-old chief executive of the MicroStrategy software company, whose estimated[1] personal wealth at the height of the Wall Street Internet boom was $8.25 billion, is donating $100 million to start the first free Internet university, which, in his rather extravagant words, aims to provide 'free education for everyone on earth, for ever'. Peter Lampl, the British investment banker, is ploughing £40 million of his money into schemes to help children from deprived backgrounds benefit from private education. Bill

Gates, the world's wealthiest businessman, a late convert to philanthropy, has trumped them all with his $21 billion foundation which will provide vaccines for the Third World and education for its children. In real terms this is almost four times the total donation made by the hitherto greatest philanthropist, John D. Rockefeller, who started giving away his money when he was a clerk in Cleveland and by the end of his life had handed over $550 million, around $6 billion in today's terms, to various causes.

There are obvious parallels between nineteenth-century American robber barons like Rockefeller and Andrew Mellon, and the twenty-first-century philanthropists: a desire to gild their reputations, to influence the future of their country and, as Andrew Carnegie put it, to provide 'ladders within reach upon which the aspiring can rise'. But they differ in other respects. Their predecessors donated locally, today's philanthropists aim to make an impact all over the world. The robber barons had to be careful of their standing with government, their modern counterparts need to pay far less attention. Once, if powerful men overstepped the mark, governments eventually stepped in to curb their power; but today, apart from the recent Microsoft ruling, we see little evidence of that. The earlier entrepreneurs were rich, but today's are richer, owing partly to the significant rise in the real GNP of developed countries. Which makes the issue of what the super-rich are to do with their money only more acute. Harvard Business School now offers a workshop in strategic philanthropy to address this very problem, and the most successful high-tech companies have full time philanthropic counsellors to advise stock-rich employees.

Unelected statesmen

Philanthropic funding is not only going the way of the arts and culture, museums and galleries or charitable institutions. Today's philanthropists are much more political than their predecessors. With personal fortunes rivalling those of states, and a global presence that mocks states' limited reach, they are bypassing mainstream electoral politics to achieve political ends. Rather than seek election to office, many of them clearly believe that they can achieve much more as business people than as politicians,[2] using the leverage of their business empires to gain access to world leaders and using that access to further their own diverse aspirations.

As Ted Turner has said,

I would only run for president if it was the only way I could get this country to turn around . . . I'm a deeper thinker. I've travelled all over. I have more access to information than anyone on the planet. When you realise your family, your friends, your society and your planet is in a dire state of emergency, that has to change anyone with a responsible world outlook. I've thought about being president from time to time, and people have asked me about it from time to time, but I like my present job a lot more. I said back in the early 1980s that I want to be Jiminy Cricket for America. You know, the country's conscience.[3]

These real-life Citizen Kanes are effectively becoming a class of unelected politicians, ambassadors and advocates, raising popular support, acting in defiance of government policy, donating money to supranational organisations, playing the role of unofficial diplomats, and using their power, wealth and influence to effect political and social change to an unprecedented degree. Having made hundreds of millions or even billions of dollars in the corporate world, they now want to leave their mark in the public sphere. Peter Lampl has often said when questioned about his motivation, 'What do you think I should do with my money, buy myself a plane?'

These new stars on the global stage, 'chiefs' of 'pan-global fiefdoms', are deferred to more than most world political leaders. Bill Gates had two summit meetings with President Jiang Zemin of China in eighteen months; Bill Clinton, by contrast, had only one.

Thanks to their wealth, acumen and access, these businessmen are able to promote their beliefs and further their values. Beyond lobbying for changes that will directly benefit their business holdings, increasingly a significant number of leading business people are lobbying for changes that will, in their opinion, better the world.

Take the case of the ice cream maker Ben Cohen, co-founder of the Ben & Jerry's chain, who launched a grassroots campaign to derail plans for Hungary, Poland and the Czech Republic to join NATO. He heads a business group, Business Leaders for Sensible Priorities; other members include Ted Turner, Paul Newman and Alan Hassenfeld, chairman and CEO of Hasbro. The group broadcast a 30-second commercial on several US network talk shows in 1997, warning that NATO expansion would alienate Russia and rekindle cold war tensions. Cohen voiced concern about antagonising Russia and the costs of NATO expansion. 'Why would the US expand a cold-war alliance against a democratic Russia that wants to be part of western Europe when those resources could be used at home and abroad so much more productively?' he asked. 'It's crazy.'[4,5]

In January 1999 Business Leaders for Sensible Priorities began an advertising campaign opposing President Clinton's proposed $112 billion increase in defence spending. The US, Cohen argued, is already spending over three times as much on defence as Russia, China, and 'rogue' states such as Iraq, Iran and North Korea combined. 'Far and away, we already have the strongest military in the world. That's just not where we need to put our limited resources.' He continued, 'The real concerns we have as people are education and health care,' and promised a 'long-term campaign' to block the increase sought by Clinton.[6] While the American government was as usual lining up with the business interests of the arms manufacturers, a group of extremely powerful businessmen were declaring that this was not the best use of the state's resources.

Paul Fireman, Robert Haas and Bruce Klatsky, CEOs of Reebok, Levis and Philips Van Heusen respectively, are also men with a mission. Recognising that it is no longer enough for them to create 'islands of sanity' – production facilities that uphold human rights – in countries where human rights abuses are the norm, the trio have crossed a line that both most of their fellow CEOs and governments have until now been unwilling to cross. 'I don't believe business should stand up and lecture governments on human rights,' said Peter Sutherland, former Director General of the WTO and now Chairman of Goldman Sachs and Co-Chairman of BP. Nor, as we have seen, do governments seem to see this as their responsibility in any effective or forceful way. But these three corporate activists are taking a stronger line.

In April 1999 they wrote to President Jiang Zemin, their goal being to persuade him to broaden union rights for the estimated four million workers who toil in China's 44,000 garment factories for as little as 13 cents a day – at present only one powerless union is allowed. Levis even hired a former US Assistant Secretary of State for Human Rights, Gare Smith, as their point man. Over the next thirteen months they sent numerous letters and called several unconventional meetings with Chinese diplomats. At the time of writing, however, the meeting with Jiang has yet to take place. 'We got the big brush-off,' said one executive, summarising a letter of 10 March 2000 from Beijing's ambassador in Washington. 'He said, Jiang is busy for the rest of his life. Mind your own business.'[7]

Their efforts give the lie to the claim – which, as we saw earlier, is used by many businessmen and politicians to justify continuing co-operation with repressive regimes – that the greater the access to foreign investment and influence the Chinese have, the more speedily their position on human rights will be reformed.

These CEOs are as yet unwilling to threaten pulling out of China, and the $500 million in annual exports and tens of thousands of jobs that they generate do not seem to carry sufficient weight with the Chinese regime. But at least they are nevertheless trying to use their insider status to good effect in raising with the Chinese government issues that politicians, afraid of jeopardising trade interests, have in effect given up on years ago. A spokesman for the group said, 'When you're doing international diplomacy on human rights with a country that hasn't respected them in a thousand years, just raising the issues must be viewed as a success.'

But many of these unelected and self-appointed 'politicians' are not just attempting to reshape the world, they are actually succeeding. The same traits that have enabled them to succeed in business – aggressiveness, self-confidence, acumen – coupled with their individual wealth, make them well suited to pivotal roles in the political arena.

Ted Turner, for example, is not only an environmental crusader and social reformer who actively campaigns for cleaner transportation, wilderness conservation and greener business; who over the past few years has given millions of dollars to environmental groups and has set up the Turner Endangered Species Fund to promote the conservation of US species such as desert bighorn sheep, Mexican wolves, Californian condors, and black-tailed prairie dogs. He is also overtly political.

On 18 September 1997 he pledged to donate $1 billion to the United Nations, an amount roughly equivalent to the UN's annual budget and well over half the amount the US government was in arrears at the time. Rather than donating money to a party in order to help his business interests, Turner has earmarked funds for his favoured causes: the environment, children, population control and women's projects. 'My main concern is to be a benefit to the world . . . to control population, to stop the arms race, to preserve the environment,' he said. 'It's a billion-dollar day at the United Nations,' announced a spokesman for UN Secretary General Kofi Annan, adding, 'The moral boost it gives to the organisation exceeds the financial value of Ted Turner's gift'.

Businessmen's involvement can be even more direct. Tiny Rowland, the buccaneering entrepreneur who once owned major mining interests in Africa as well as for a brief time the *Observer* newspaper, developed a plan with Scottish lawyers in 1997, which he subsequently helped to sell to Libyan leader Colonel Gadaffi, whereby Gadaffi would hand over the two men suspected of involvement in the bombing of the PanAm jet over Lockerbie in Scotland for trial in Holland under Scottish law.[8] Rowland clearly enjoyed outsmarting the British Foreign Office, but his involvement also consolidated his relationship with Gadaffi, an investment for the time when sanctions against Libya are lifted, as they undoubtedly will be.[9]

Boris Berezovsky, the Russian media mogul, has been involved in facilitating over fifty hostage releases in Chechnya, including the release in September 1998 of British aid workers Camilla Carr and Jon James after fourteen months in captivity. He has consistently denied paying cash for the hostages whose freedom he has secured, but allegedly pays instead with the latest computer equipment. It is rumoured that, thanks to Berezovsky, the residence of the Chechnyan rebel commander Salman Raduyev is now better equipped than some Russian special service units.

These and other business leaders share a desire to use their money and influence for political ends. They seem impatient with the speed of government action, and have little compunction about bypassing traditional political channels; they dismiss the notion of state sovereignty and aim to override elected officials at will. Business people are even involving themselves in peacemaking, a domain previously exclusively handled by diplomats and foreign ministers.

Monopoly diplomacy

In 1993, Omar Salah, a 25-year-old English-educated Jordanian, was driving down a Californian freeway when he heard the news that the Oslo Accord between Palestine and Israel representastives had been signed. Struck by inspiration, as he describes it, he flew to Israel, to scout out potential business partners, where he met Dov Lautman, head of Delta Gallil, Israel's biggest textile company and the largest producer of private label underwear in the world, who was himself looking at the possibility of manufacturing in Jordan. There was instant chemistry. While the Jordanian–Israeli peace process took years to negotiate and sign, Salah and Lautman's joint venture Century Wear was in business eight months after the two men first met. Today it employs 2,200 people and is the largest private sector employer in Jordan, using Egyptian cotton, spun in Turkey, knitted and cut in Israel and sewn in Jordan to make Calvin Klein underwear, Gap T-shirts, and Giorgio Armani boxer shorts that are sold in Europe and the USA.

Century Wear is only one of over forty alliances between Israeli and Jordanian businesses that have been set up over the past few years; over 50 per cent of Jordan's leading businessmen are now involved in such ventures. Co-operation with Israel is essential to Jordan's business community, providing it with opportunities to acquire expertise, leapfrog technologically, access otherwise elusive investment funds, penetrate global markets, enhance productivity, and provide employment.

The interlocking relationships created by these joint ventures are proving remarkably resilient. The business alliances have lasted, despite the antagonisms inherent in the whole Middle East peace process. Assassination and terrorism have been rife. Hundreds have been killed on both sides, a fact particularly poignant for Jordan, 70 per cent of whose population is Palestinian. Yet not only have the alliances persisted, they are also beginning to influence the political relationships between the two countries. For now that they are Jordan's biggest private sector employers (with the joint ventures typically paying employees between 30 and 40 per cent above local industry norm), no Jordanian premier can afford to jeopardise their future. Furthermore, powerful businessmen, with a vested interest in political stability, increasingly lobby for greater co-operation between the two countries and their governments. At the Sharm el-Sheikh summit in October 2000, King Abdullah's response to the Palestinian uprising earlier in the year was surprisingly muted and he did not call for sanctions, evidence that these business relationships are beginning to cement the peace in ways that politics could never achieve. After hundreds of years at war, it is business people, rather than politicians, who are most likely to cement peace between Jordan and Israel irreversible.[10]

It is not just in the Middle East that we can see the role that business can play in peacemaking. The 'Group of Seven', consisting of Northern Ireland's most significant trade and business organisations, created a second diplomatic track to the peace process when they held six meetings between October 1996 and the summer of 1998 in which they brought together representatives of all the political parties involved in the official peace talks and helped to mediate between the various factions. Shortly after the signing of the Good Friday Agreement, Sir George Quigley, chairman of Ulster Bank, one of Northern Ireland's largest financial institutions, and chair of the Group of Seven, claimed that its efforts had 'made it less easy for the parties to simply walk away.'[11] When asked why the CBI (the Confederation of British Industry) had decided to join the Group, Nigel Smyth, director of the CBI in Northern Ireland, claimed that economic self-interest was the prime motivator, and emphasised the opportunities for economic growth that the CBI felt peace would bring.

The sons of the most powerful men in China and Taiwan – Jiang Zemin, the Chinese President, and Y.C. Wang, Taiwan's biggest tycoon – have become joint venture business partners in a £4 billion project to build China's biggest computer chip plant. Indications are that this top-level alliance will have a significant influence on the resolution of the long dispute between Taiwan and China over the Taiwan Strait. One China watcher has commented, 'If the sons can work things out, then maybe so can the fathers. At the very least, the sons can pass top-level messages back and forth should China and Taiwan start a new dialogue.'[12]

But of course business people are not always driven by a desire to make peace. Civil wars in Angola and Sierra Leone have been fought on the back of diamond and oil interests for years. Black marketeers played a significant role in maintaining the Yugoslavian conflict. And Chase Manhattan's Emerging Markets Group's infamous memo on the need to 'eliminate' the Zapatista rebels in Mexico was posted on the official Zapatista website. As easily as corporations and business people can act as ambassadors of peace, they can also fuel conflict.

What is clear, however, is that when business people see it as in their commercial interest to do so, they are able to build islands of co-operation amid seas of conflict, creating links based on shared economic interests that seem to be proving remarkably durable, while politicians' efforts at peacemaking seem increasingly ineffective. In fact, business is changing the political dynamic. The evangelical entrepreneurs are not simply enacting states' foreign policy; they are determining and enacting foreign policy themselves by their own actions.

This development is a fundamental characteristic of this latest phase of the Silent Takeover. As we have seen, governments are foundering and state revenues are increasingly constrained, while the rich are getting richer. And when they do, the egoistic thrust of capitalism seems in a number of cases to be overtaken by an altruistic force. For personal reasons, often independent of their business goals, some evangelical entrepreneurs are using their wealth, as George Soros has, as a platform from which they aim to change the world – distributing welfare, championing the environment, backing economic reforms, assuming a moral stance. Are these business people an unrepresentative minority, the contemporary equivalents of nineteenth-century enlightened industrialists such as Joseph Rowntree, Robert Owen or the Cadbury brothers? Or is the seeming broadening of motivations more fundamental? While the business of government seems more than ever to be business, is the business of business by contrast increasingly becoming that of government?

MOTHER BUSINESS

Corporate carers

The AngloGold goldmine, Vaal River, South Africa, 4.30 a.m. The lifts that drop a mile below the earth's surface are packed with migrant workers who have come here from all over the country in search of work. Dark, hot and dangerous with no way out when things go wrong. Rock falls and explosions are commonplace. Yet the risks of working below ground are arguably no worse than those above. Of the 50,000 workers in this mine, 40 per cent are HIV positive. And this is not unusual. Current estimates are that half of South Africa's miners are similarly infected.[1,2]

With many of the miners hundreds or thousands of miles away from home, housed in single-sex dormitories seventy to a room, the mines represent the honeypot towards which flock South Africa's second-class citizens: women. With their earning opportunities extremely limited, many with children to feed, prostitution in the shanty towns that encircle the mines is endemic. Ten rand with a condom, 20 rand without, the illusory closeness of 'flesh on flesh' snatched in the toilets of the Saturday night mines bar, is seen by many as worth the risk.

TB is also spreading, among miners whose immune systems have been destroyed by the HIV virus. In the mine hospital four men die as a result of AIDS-related opportunistic infections every week, and this figure omits those who have been sent back home first. The reaction of the South African government has been, to say the least, inadequate, despite the fact that mining for gold, coal, diamonds and platinum remains the backbone of the South African economy. As Alan Whitehead, Director of Health Economics and HIV/AIDS research at the University of Natal in Durban, puts it, 'Our next lost generation will be children orphaned by AIDS, but what is the government doing? Nothing. They are not even thinking about it'. The annual cost per person of AZT, currently the leading anti-AIDS medication, is $1,200; South Africa spends less than $400 per person on total annual health care provision[3] – partly because after assiduously following neo-liberal economic prescriptions the state is virtually bankrupt. Meanwhile, President Mbeki has, until very recently, denied that AIDS is caused by a virus, adopting the views of US biochemist Peter Duesberg, who is widely viewed by AIDS experts as at best misguided, at worst as a heretic.

While the South African government is largely failing to provide basic health education and care, Anglo Gold, Gold Fields, Iscor, and other privately held corporations are taking on these roles themselves. Companies, rather than the state, have set up clinics to tend to the dying; companies, rather than the state, are producing poster campaigns to explain the dangers of unsafe sex, and are financing free-condom dispensing machines, and sponsoring and running AIDS education classes for junior managers, encouraging them to pass on the information to their workers.

The companies' health activities are clearly not only motivated by a sense of moral purpose but, more centrally perhaps, by pragmatic business considerations. Each employee infected by HIV costs a mining company approximately £10,000 a year once AIDS develops.[4] Workers with AIDS are less productive, often absent from work, present a greater health care burden, and result in a higher turnover of personnel. Experienced specialist labour is not easy to replace. Morale is eroded among the survivors.

Unless a cure is found, which currently seems unlikely, 40 per cent of Gold Fields mining company's 50,000 miners will be dead within the next ten years; it is easier for the South African government in effect to ignore the problem than it is for the mining companies, for which the cost of inactivity is likely to prove prohibitively high.

Denationalising compassion

There are an increasing number of examples of corporations assuming responsibility on a much wider basis in this latest phase of the Silent Takeover. Many of the roles that governments are increasingly unable to play effectively, many of the responsibilities they are less and less able to meet, are now beginning to be met not only by individual businesspeople but by companies themselves. An increasing number of corporations – the same ones that lobby for favours, that irresistibly pressurise governments, that can in effect refuse to pay increased taxes and angle for subsidies and privileges, even, in some cases, that in the past have shown little regard for the communities in which they operate – are nowadays showing signs of a caring face; and not simply as a reaction to consumer and shareholder pressure or government legislation.

This is not simply a matter of contracting out government services to the private sector – the collection of garbage, the provision of school meals, the delivery of welfare, even the running of prisons. In these cases government remains the client. It sets the terms of performance, determines the agenda, can replace the service provider if it fails to meet given criteria, and still, at least in theory, remains ultimately in control.

Rather, there is emerging a new dimension to corporate activity, one that puts corporations in the role of welfare providers and social engineers, environmentalists and mediators, in which corporations assume the traditional functions of the nation state. Business takes over the role of government.

Poor communities – bad business

In parts of the Third World, in countries in which the state is so moribund that it cannot deliver even the most fundamental of public goods such as education, basic health, roads and infrastructure, corporations are deciding to meet the shortfall themselves.

In Nigeria, for example, Shell spent $52 million in 1999[5] on a social investment programme, building schools, hospitals, roads and bridges, supplying electricity and water to areas that the government effectively abandoned in the early 1980s. In fact, the company now employs more development specialists than the government. 'Things are back to front here,' said Brian Anderson, who ran Shell's operations there in the mid-1990s. 'The government's in the oil business and we are in local government.'

Shell has learnt, from experience, that it is not ultimately to its advantage to perpetuate the corrupt systems that have characterised Nigeria for most of the past thirty years. In the past, 70 per cent or more of upstream revenues from its oil projects typically went in taxes and royalties to the government, and it has been claimed that Shell alone was responsible for three quarters of the Nigerian government's revenues and about a third of the country's GNP. Much of this money went into offshore bank accounts. Virtually nothing was put into building Nigeria for Nigerians. Corruption was virtually universal. After Ken Saro-Wiwa's execution in 1995, protests increased, not least against the major multinationals, especially Shell in particular, which had been working with the corrupt regime.

The damage to its image in the First World has not been the only cost to the corporation. Resentment, civil unrest and instability in Nigeria have also proved costly. Pipelines have been blown up, oil installations have been invaded, work equipment seized, and rigs blockaded.[6] In the autumn of 1998, the unrest cut Nigeria's daily oil production by a third.[7] In June 1999, fifty young Nigerian men invaded a Shell station and closed it for five days, costing the company $2.4 million. During 1999 alone, Shell faced forty-five separate incidents of hostage taking, involving over 200 staff.

By not facilitating trickle-down in the past, by being perceived as not building infra-structure, tackling inequalities of wealth or respecting the needs of the communities in which it operates, Shell has paid a price. The company has slowly come to realise that it does not serve its own interests if it is seen as ignoring the way the proceeds of ventures remain undisbursed to citizens of the Third World countries in which it operates. Instead, it is beginning to ensure that benefits actually reach the communities in which it operates, and to meet at least some of the local basic needs. Where people cannot turn to their governments for support, Shell is showing itself prepared to set up in dialogue directly with the local people. Where the state is corroded or in collapse, men whose trade is oil exploration and drilling are now needing to act as diplomats, politicians and mediators.

Unrest, instability, and poverty are not conducive to doing effective long-term business anywhere in the world. Jaime Augusto Zobel de Ayala II, President of the Ayala Corporation, one of the Philippines' largest conglomerates, said in a speech to Asian business people in 1995:

We all pay for poverty and unemployment and illiteracy. If a large percentage of society falls into a disadvantaged class, investors will find it hard to source skilled and alert workers; manufacturers will have a limited market for their products; criminality will scare away foreign investments, and internal migrants to limited areas of opportunities will strain basic service and lead to urban blight. Under these conditions, no country can move forward economically and sustain development . . . It therefore makes business sense for corporations to complement the efforts of government in contributing to social development.

In the West too, the environment in which business operates does matter, and companies are beginning to recognise that poor communities make poor business. Yet Conservatives and

New Labour, Republicans and New Democrats alike have made it clear that they are either not prepared or are unable to tackle the negative consequences of the system they continue to champion. 'The state cannot solve all our economic and social problems. Nor should it try,' said John Reid, Labour's Scottish Secretary in May 2000.

Given that the current consensus, from both right and left, is that the answer to poverty is not welfare payments and government handouts – for governments are not prepared to fund social programmes by running up deficits – many corporations are increasingly seeing it as good business practice to take on the role of societal custodian themselves. Sir John Browne, Chairman of BP, said, 'The simple fact is that business needs sustainable societies in order to protect its own sustainability.'[8]

Companies are beginning to realise that social and environmental issues cannot just be tacked on to their overall strategy as insignificant addenda; they bear directly on company performance. In the short term, corporate interests can ignore the wider interests of society, but if society breaks down altogether, corporations also have to bear the cost. Jack Welch, Chairman and CEO of General Electric, remarks:

I've always believed that the greatest contribution a business could make to society was its own success, which is a fountainhead of jobs, taxes and spending in the community. I still believe that – but I don't think that is enough anymore. And I don't believe that even generous financial philanthropy on top of that prosperity is enough . . . These times . . . will not allow companies to remain aloof and prosperous while the surrounding communities decline and decay.

In an attempt to address the issues of urban decay alluded to by Jack Welch, the founders of Ben & Jerry's, Ben Cohen and Jerry Greenfield, made it a condition of the sale of their ice cream business to Unilever in April 2000 that Unilever create a $5 million fund to help minority-owned businesses and others in poor neighbourhoods. Rite Aid, the American drug store chain, has committed 580 of its 4,000 stores across America to inner city areas that are in need of revitalisation, contracting with local developers, hiring local employees, and creating knock-on effects in the local economy. There is no reason to imagine it is doing this only for compassionate reasons, however; it makes good business sense too. CEO Martin Grass acknowledges that inner city involvement can be attractive to the company because the disposable income of such areas has been undervalued in the past. There are 7.7 million households in depressed inner city areas of the USA, spending more than $85 billion per year on retail items, even though many are without access to local quality goods and services;[9] inner city areas thus present a huge and unexploited commerical opportunity.[10] And also a huge unexploited political opportunity for politicians, for this same market also consists of areas with the greatest latent and untapped voting power.[11]

The corporate nation

Government's retreat has presented business with an opportunity. As politics becomes an ever more fuzzily branded product, corporations can both take the moral high ground and gain real business advantage by assuming social and environmental responsibilities.

Schools have become a prominent battleground for corporate marketers who want to maximise the potential value of social contributions. While governments, in today's environment of low taxes and redirected priorities, are ever more pressed to find sufficient resources for education, companies are seizing on new business opportunities. Go into any classroom now, and the quantity of products 'donated' by corporations is startling. In countless British classrooms, the Tesco computer stands next to one bought with vouchers from packets of Golden Wonder crisps.[12] United Biscuits has distributed to 800 British playgroups and primary schools a kit that urges children to get to grips with reading and arithmetic by discussing 'their favourite Penguin biscuit' and copying the 'P-p-pick up a Penguin' slogan. In the US McDonald's has supported literacy programmes by attaching booklets with tips for reading aloud to 13 million Happy Meal bags. Nike is among the biggest contributors to parks, recreation facilities and other youth-related projects. 'Give me a child before the age of seven . . .' said the Jesuit priest; companies are taking this maxim literally, some by producing 'grab bags' of branded items for nursery school age children.

Proctor & Gamble, Toyota, and Marks & Spencer are just a few of the many companies that are providing advice, funding and managerial support to help children to develop basic skills and education. Levis runs schemes aimed at young truants, seeking to provide them with routes back into the school system. Accountancy firm KPMG runs a head teacher mentoring system in the UK and South Africa. BP's 'Science Across the World' initiative operates in thirty-seven countries on six continents, reaching 65,000 students. Bill Gates has announced his intention to put a computer on every British child's desk. And in 1993 Honda spent $17 million to set up a remarkable school in Colorado for students whom the public school system is failing, providing residential care for 80 high school seniors from all over the USA in a 640-acre setting on the eastern slopes of the Rocky Mountains.

Here wayward kids, children who have skirted the mainstream of society, persistent truants, many with problems with drink or drug, teens with nose-rings, mohawk hairs dos, and platform shoes, benefit from Honda management's mandate to make a social impact in ways that will not be perceived as too self serving, in ways 'that go beyond what one would expect of a corporation.'[13] The school is a resort-like campus that not only has six housing units but also a full-length soccer field, three classroom buildings, a gym complete with weight room, basketball court, swimming pool and climbing wall; and an all-purpose lodge where pupils watch TV, eat, and attend daily morning gatherings at which they confess their misdemeanors, hug and make clear when things are outside of their 'comfort zones'. The school doctrine is 'tough love', and students soon develop a firm sense of right and wrong. Over half of the school's graduates have gone on to college. All but a few of the rest are either working or in the military.

Honda contrives to support the school to the tune of $3.5 million a year which guarantees free year-round tuition for the students. This works out at roughly $25,000 per student each year, a figure several times the average in US public schools. The children are provided with all their essential needs from books to gym clothes as well as some non-essentials such as long-distance phone time. And the school has become a model for other alternative schools elsewhere. Each year as many teachers as 2,000 teachers, principals and scholars pass through the campus, sitting in on classes and meeting with students, staying in a bunkhouse specially built to accommodate them.[14]

Other corporations are working to foster other social needs. By investing in such non-business related areas, by addressing the downsides of capitalism and globalisation, companies aim to distinguish themselves as caring about more than simply making another sale. By investing in the community, they can improve their images, lower employee turnover and increase their chances of getting the people's 'vote'.

Entrepreneur Anita Roddick's entire business is focused on the virtues of ethical behaviour and social engagement. Her Body Shop brand has become synonymous with social activism, support for human rights and the protection of the environment and animals, all through selling toiletries and cosmetics.

BT, the telecommunications company, published a paper in 1998 entitled *Changing Values*. The values referred to were not shareholder value, or the value of the brand, but those concerning world poverty and the widening gap between rich and poor.[15]

Proctor & Gamble tackles education, crime prevention and economic regeneration, and is using its skills in marketing, communication, project management and staff mentoring to contribute to the communities in which it operates. In parts of Newcastle, for example, in which three quarters of the children live in households with no earned income, P&G has developed a mentoring and business skills programme for local schools and used its marketing expertise in efforts to combat drug abuse in the area.

Avon, the American beauty products company, has tackled health issues and launched the Breast Cancer Awareness Crusade, which raises money for breast cancer programmes through sales of Avon 'pink ribbon' products and lobbies for more government funded research.

British Gas targeted the needs of the elderly when in 1999 it announced a partnership with the charity Help the Aged to reduce the number of older people in the UK who die each winter of hypothermia through lack of fuel. At the same time as a Labour government was being criticised by pensioners for inadequately addressing their needs, one in three single pensioners were spending 10 per cent of their weekly pension trying to keep warm – and 44,000 elderly people were dying of cold-related illnesses each year 'faced with the dilemma of whether to heat their homes or eat a meal over winter'. Such deaths are entirely preventable, and once again business was taking the initiative.[16]

What motivates these companies? Why is Honda, a Japanese car corporation, funding a school in Colorado? Proctor & Gamble tackling drug abuse in Newcastle? British Gas championing the elderly poor?

In part because employees and managers do not leave their values as individuals at home when they arrive at work. Now that belief in the integrity of political parties is at an all-time low, employers can foster staff loyalty by espousing employees' values. And those employees who are in demand, the skilled, those with highly-developed and specialist skills, are becoming increasingly selective about who they choose to work for. While the choice of political parties is in effect highly restricted, this elite can choose to join organisations whose values they find sympathetic.

Several multinational oil company managers are finding that during job interviews many of the most promising university graduate engineers are now asking about policy on the environment and human rights, questions which were rarely raised in the past. Numerous studies conducted in recent years[17] have shown that 'employees prefer to work for a company that has a good reputation as a corporate citizen', and that allegations of corporate irresponsibility have a serious effect on morale.[18] Directors of both BP and Shell, for example, report being overwhelmed by the large number of concerned e-mails they received from staff following adverse TV and press coverage[19] of their operations in Colombia and Nigeria. As *Fortune* magazine has noted, the single most reliable predictor of overall excellence in a company is its ability to attract and retain talented employees. In this new era of knowledge-based business, when human capital is the dominant factor of production, it is essential that companies be able to recruit and retain talented staff, few of whom wish to work for corporations derided as pariahs.

Companies have also realised that by playing a greater role in the welfare of the communities in which they are active, they can improve the bottom line: 86 per cent of British consumers say they have a more positive image of a company if they see it is 'doing something to make the world a better place'.[20] A third of American consumers said that the primary goal of business should be building a better society[21] – and are willing to support those that do, seizing the chance to make a positive contribution through their purchasing decisions. Coca-Cola calculated that in 1997 it experienced a 490 per cent increase in sales of its products at 450 Wal-Mart stores during a six-week campaign allied with Mothers Against Drunk Driving, to whom the company donated a proportion of its sales. Diageo plc, the food and drinks company whose brands include Johnnie Walker and Smirnoff, reported that between 1994 and 1998 twenty-two cause-related marketing projects helped it raise $600,000 for causes while increasing the sales of tracked brands by 37 per cent. Wendy's International in Denver increased sales of jumbo fries by more than a third in 1998 when it contributed a percentage of each purchase to the city's Mercy Medical Centre. Unlike the payment of taxes, whereby people have little sense of where their money is being spent, cause-related purchases enable them to earmark where their spending is going. Consumers will change brands, switch retailers, be more accepting of price rises and have a better perception of a company when businesses or brands are linked to a good cause. Cause-related marketing enhances corporate image, builds brands, generates PR and increases sales. No wonder the linking of sales to good causes has increased threefold over the past decade, and over 85 per cent of American corporations now use cause marketing.[22]

Sheep in wolves' clothing

In the world of the Silent Takeover corporations are beginning to realise that customers will reward them, not only for not doing ill, but also for being seen to do good. Consumers and workers 'no longer buy the product, they buy the entire company ethos. What companies do, make or sell is inseparable from what they are.' Corporations are discovering that by taking on some of the costs that governments have relinquished, they can improve their standing in society and consequently their profits. Does this represent a win-win solution?

It is precisely with regard to those issues that the state finds hardest to regulate, issues that transcend international borders and that could be addressed by politicians only through hard-to-enforce international protocols and international agreements, that we see the inherent advantage that corporations have in tackling world issues. Operating globally, companies can assume responsibilities, make decisions, and stimulate concern in ways that governments find extremely hard to attain, and at a speed that government bureaucracies are unable to equal. Companies can even take the initiative. As it says on the BP website, 'It is not enough . . . to rely on the leadership of politicians. Business needs to play a responsible, active role and to show leadership in finding solutions and putting them into practice.'

So while the US government has still not ratified the Kyoto Protocol on climate change which was agreed on in principle back in 1997, a number of oil and chemical companies are already putting its aims into practice. Sir John Browne, CEO of BP and the first oilman to declare that global warming may be a real issue, has led the way with his pledge that BP will decrease emissions of the greenhouse gas carbon dioxide by 10 per cent from 1990 levels by 2010, which is significantly more than both the US's promise of 7 per cent and even the EU's more aggressive 8 per cent; and also with his implementation of an internal emissions trading system whereby BP divisions can trade pollution credits with each other, a system discussed at Kyoto, but still not implemented at any national level. Other companies, fearful of being singled out as environmentally unsound, are following suit – with Shell, Dupont, Alcan and Pechiney and others agreeing to match BP's targets, and either also trading pollution permits between their subsidiaries or developing trading systems themselves. As Browne has said, 'A lot of companies work in partnership . . . which means that the influence of thinking, technology and approach begins to spread.'[23]

Who is taking over who?

While politicians shirk their social and environmental responsibilities, pleading the pressures or limitations of globalisation and economic interests, corporations are, as we have seen, increasingly taking over this mandate in directly tackling the world's global issues. For the opportunities of the global market have come at a price. The greater a corporation's reach, the more visible it is, and the greater the benefits of being seen to contribute to the remedying of the world's ills.

Many of our leading companies now realise that responsible behaviour and social engagement are increasingly less of an option, and more a necessity, if a company means to safeguard its commercial interests. Big business has begun to move beyond seeing social responsibility as an effective PR tool; corporations are now being held hostage by their own marketing strategies. Not least, in the need to compete with each other, the causes they champion must be ever worthier, ever more substantial and ever more original. The innovative campaigns of the Body Shop during the 1980s have become the humdrum promotions of today's high street banks. Not only do products have to be seen to be whiter than white; company ethics, ideologies and initiatives have to be so too.

So we see the spring shoots of the latest phase of the Silent Takeover: corporations taking stands against incumbent governments, actively pushing forward political agendas, substituting for the policy failures of politicians. Corporations are beginning to right social ills and dispense justice in places where the state does not, to tackle issues of environmental degradation while governments seem paralysed, to champion human rights in those parts of the world that no politician seems prepared to speak out for. Having bankrolled a system that creates losers as well as winners, corporations rather than governments increasingly seem to be the only institutions that are attempting to address the imbalance with any effect.

Politicians are actively supporting this unexpected development. In February 2000 Bill Clinton, then president of the richest and most powerful nation, addressed a group of the world's most influential business leaders in Davos in Switzerland. 'My most important wish,' he told them 'is that the global business community could adopt a shared vision for the next ten to twenty years about what you want the world to look like, and then go about trying to create it . . . collectively you can change the world.'

The truth of the matter is that business people are often able to do more than governments can. They are not tied up with bureaucracy; they can bypass protocol, make decisions single-handedly, and have a direct impact. They are able to transcend national boundaries and to ignore the strictures of supranational organisations. They often have access where foreign ministries and diplomats cannot reach. While the British government was powerless when the human rights activist James Mawdsley was jailed in Burma for seventeen years for distributing leaflets criticising the country's military junta, it was Premier Oil, the British oil company vilified for its support of the Burmese regime, that was instrumental in securing his release. As Charles Jameson, its chief executive said, 'We are in a unique position . . . We are the only British organisation which has access at all levels.'[24]

It is in fact a double switch: politics has entered commerce, consumerism has entered politics. Politicians, by not providing the same levels of service in hospitals and schools, the same quick response to our concerns, and the same willingness to tackle the downside of the laissez-faire system as do P&G, BP and Honda, are forfeiting our custom. Corporations, realising how easily transferable our 'vote' is, are becoming more responsible and responsive in fear of our possible 'defection'. We don't have to wait four or five years for an election after all to change our product choice.

But who, in this latest phase of the takeover, is taking over whom? Politicians are spending some of their time acting like salesmen, and corporations some of their time acting like politicians. Consumers are voting with their pockets while the electorate is increasingly staying away from the polling station. Governments are emulating business and business is emulating government. The state is giving up many of its responsibilities, and corporations are beginning to take them over in its place.

Since the eighteenth century western societies have regarded politics as essential to the progressive enactment and widening of reforms. Today we are seeing that other institutions are able to take on some of these roles. As our expectations of politicians are declining, our expectations of corporations are becoming both greater and broader.

Does this mean that the companies that succeed in the twenty-first century will be those that decide that the business of business cannot solely be business? Is it just possible that corporations, whom we are used to expecting to disregard human interests in their pursuit of profit, are in fact turning out to be our reliable allies? Are their attempts to right injustice constructive? Are their remedies more effective than those of government? Is their willingness to effect our will greater than that of our elected representatives?

Can this fusion of consumer politics and corporate power provide satisfactory solutions to the problems created and encouraged by an untrammelled capitalism, or even be a satisfactory replacement for traditional politics? Or is it a chimera? And if it is a monster, will it devour us?

WHO WILL GUARD THE GUARDS?

Soylent Green

It is 2022, the earth's face has changed. The greenhouse effect has raised average temperatures significantly. In most cities, the polluted smoggy air is virtually unbreathable. New York has become an overcrowded hellhole, and now has 40 million to feed.

The rich are richer and the poor poorer than ever – sleeping wherever there's room, and fighting each other for scraps of food. For the poor, most of life's simplest pleasures are a thing of the past. The rich live in separate luxury apartments in gated communities and have access to such luxuries as paper and pencils, bars of soap, and running water. The only time people see blue skies and green forests is on video at the government-run euthanasia centres during their last twenty minutes of life.

Natural foods, fruit, vegetables and meat are almost extinct. Strawberries cost $150 a jar. The only food to which the starving masses have access is that manufactured by the Soylent

Corporation, a powerful food-processing company – concentrated nutritional wafers that come in red, yellow, or the more nutritious green produced, according to the TV commercials, 'from the finest undersea growth'. But even this is in such short supply that when it is distributed riot police need to be available to try to limit the resulting violence.

In the classic 1973 sci-fi movie, Charlton Heston plays Police Detective Thorn, a man who has known nothing but this dystopian world of overpopulation and global warming, and whose mission is to investigate the murder of an official from the Soylent Corporation. But in the course of his investigation, he discovers a much bigger crime. The executive, it is revealed, was killed because he knew something terrible: the secret ingredient of Soylent Green. For in order to meet the demand for their product, the powers that be have secretly taken to making these wafers not out of the soybeans and plankton as advertised but out of the many newly dead.

'You've got to warn everyone and tell them!' says Thorn in the final speech of the film. 'Soylent Green is made of people! You've got to tell them! Soylent Green is people!'

As the year 2022 approaches, these are essentially the issues we face. Is the world we are heading towards, this emerging world of 'evangelical entrepreneurs', 'corporate carers' and 'campaigning corporations', a world in which corporations really will safeguard the public interest? Or are we are heading towards the apocalyptic world of *Soylent Green*? A world in which the corporate interests – literally or metaphorically – feed off our carcasses? Will the corporate takeover ultimately be for good or ill?

Corporate aid

In the Third World, in places where the state has collapsed or is greatly weakened, the corporate contribution to welfare – its assumption of quasi-state roles, its ability to ensure that rights are upheld in places where the political will to do so does not prevail, its ability to mediate between warring factions – can provide a lifeline to people abandoned by their own governments.

Is it ideal that corporations, rather than host governments, perform this role? No, of course not. Corporations, and their managements, are unelected. These functions are alien to their core business – managers of multinationals operating in the Third World are often overwhelmed by the social problems they encounter, and understandably find it difficult to know which causes to prioritise. They have no expertise in distributing aid, and limited experience in the provision of state functions, even though they are often working closely with NGOs and grassroots organisations, and hiring knowledgeable people. Their contributions can be squandered. IBM provided a number of computers to South Africa schools, but these schools were highly prone to theft. In schools, computers are only useful if they are accompanied by appropriate teachers, not of course provided by IBM. So the impact of the contribution was minimal, a significant number of children did not become computer literate, and money spent on welfare was, as is often also the case in the public sphere, completely wasted.

There is a real risk that as and when corporations move on (we have seen how easily modern companies can change the location of their activities) so too will their obligations to local communities. There is a real danger that their presence, their taking on of these traditional governmental roles, will create a disincentive for governments to develop appropriate institutions themselves; and that if and when they pull out, there will be nothing at all to replace them, and no recourse to be had. There is a real danger that corporations could use this dependence to exact a stream of IOUs and quid pro quos, to demand ever more favourable terms and concessions from host governments. There is a real danger that such 'socially responsible' policies could be a form of 'greenwashing' – where, hiding behind a superficially responsible screen, corporations can abuse their considerable power and inflict damage on the society or the environment in which they operate.

All these concerns are valid, and should not be dismissed. The history of multinationals overseas has often been shameful: more often rapacious than peace-seeking or just; characteristically silent when faced with regimes that violate civil and political rights. However, the amount of money Western governments are willing to provide for overseas aid does not begin to address the needs of developing countries, and many recipient governments seem unwilling to put their people's needs first either by distributing the gains of trade among them or by enforcing regulation. In many places, where multinational corporations operate, the state lacks legitimacy and is undemocratic. We cannot afford to dismiss the fact that business is now in many ways better placed than any other institution to act as the primary agent of justice in much of the developing world.[1]

In the West also, it is again business that is increasingly appearing (and with governmental encouragement being put forward) as a potential if unlikely saviour for at least some of those whom untrammelled capitalism has failed. These developments are in their early stages. But as governments operating in global markets find it increasingly hard to raise the finances to fund social welfare programmes at appropriate levels, particularly in the context of changing populations, and the inevitable downturn in the business cycle causes the government surpluses of today to turn to deficits, we will in all likelihood see more welfare functions being provided by companies, both as standalone for-profit business ventures and as add-on features to existing product ranges.

In some respects, this is an attractive development. For not only has the private sector delivery of public services often proved superior to public provision but, given the interminable bureaucracy inseparable from traditional politics, government's loss of its monopoly on politics is probably ultimately to our advantage, should these developments be managed correctly.

Who will guard the guards?

But that is the crux – 'managed correctly'. For the more we come to depend upon corporations in areas crucial to our basic welfare, the more critical it is that if things go wrong, they can be held accountable. But if corporations take over the role of governments, 'who', as Juvenal first said in AD 100, 'will guard the guards themselves'? How will we ensure that Soylent Green is not made of people? We have already seen how governments' ability to check corporate power is under threat from supranational organisations such as the WTO. Will governments be able to be effective regulators if they become ever more dependent on corporations to deliver welfare solutions? Will companies not be able to use positive activities in one context to protect themselves from being held accountable for the harm they may be doing elsewhere?

In the Hungarian town of Pecs, where it has a large cigarette factory, British American Tobacco (BAT) has sponsored a medical clinic, a hostel for the homeless (now named BAT House), and a theatre (the BAT Theatre). While restrictions not only on cigarette advertising but also on commercial sponsorship by tobacco companies seem likely (remember Hungary's desire to join the EU), in a country in which the state is unable to provide adequate welfare provisions, a tobacco company can market its brands not only by associating with good causes, but can also use this to shape their political relationships. BAT company executives now sit on several local government committees and, as Pecs Mayor Lazlo Toller has said, are invited to all 'high-level meetings.'[2]

Ted Turner's donation to the UN, noted in Chapter 8, raises similar concerns. For although his intentions are undoubtedly philanthropic, his donation sets a dangerous precedent. With US payments to the UN in arrears of $1.6 billion, could the UN be forced to turn to wealthy businesspeople or corporations to fund itself, becoming 'a club for wealthy individuals[?] . . . scary, given that not every wealthy donor's agenda may be as benign as Turner's.'[3]

This concern was first raised in 1958 when the UK floated a proposal – immediately quashed – to allow the UN to raise money from philanthropic businesses. 'With money inherently comes ties,' explains the historian Rachel Thourt of the United Nations Research Group. 'The smaller nations asked a good question: if the UN takes money from oil companies year after year, it will grow dependent on it. Even if Standard Oil says there are no conditions, won't we have some desire to keep them happy? Then won't it be harder to sort out things in the Middle East?'[4]

As we have seen in previous chapters, the market cannot be counted upon to ensure that corporations will always act in our best interest, so we must be able to continue to count on government's ability to play the role of regulator of last resort. Regulation with teeth is clearly often needed to counter monopoly power, safeguard the rights of individuals, and protect the community from the abuse of corporate power more generally. But if government and business become 'partners', who will be there to adjudicate if things go wrong? In the early twentieth century the American government passed strong and effective anti-trust laws to protect the interests of society when business got too big and powerful. The growing dependency of government on business, and the blurring of boundaries between the public and private sector, compel us to ask who will step in now.

This latest phase of the takeover raises other questions. For example, do we want unelected businessmen and corporations stamping their opinions and views indelibly on our own lives, however seemingly benign their intent? Do we want to risk our world becoming one in which we have to depend on corporate charity?[5]

Politicians talk of 'market-based solutions', 'private delivery of public goods', and 'corporate citizenry', as if these were the answers to the failings of laissez-faire capitalism. But it was the American government, not business, that picked up the pieces after the crash and depression of the 1920s; and government money, not corporations', that rebuilt European economies after the war and created welfare states.[6] Corporations may be able to play some role in alleviating poverty and tackling conflict and inequity, but social investment and social justice will never become their core activity. Their contribution to society's overall needs will always remain at the margins, and their contribution to welfare will never be comprehensive.

Unlike politicians, who are charged with looking after their citizens' interests, business people and businesses have no such mandate. Even where wealthy individuals have other motives, those of companies will always be predominantly commercial rather than moral, and so will be subject to market vagaries. For it is, of course, those social concerns deemed most appealing to their customers that will be embraced by corporations in the West. It is charity predicated not on need but on market appeal. And in a world where welfare and social justice are increasingly left to the market, minority interests or unattractive causes may well suffer. The sick, the homeless, those of us with limited purchasing power potential, or a lack of customer appeal, those with little voice, risk being excluded even more than now.

Despite the inefficiencies of public service provision, despite the fact that many goods and services are better delivered by the private sector, when public services are taken over by the private sector profit becomes their *raison d'être*. If the government does not manage these private providers of our needs stringently, and admit that not all public goods should be for sale, tragedies like the millions of uninsured infirm of America, and the Paddington and Hatfield rail crashes in the UK which occurred as a direct result of the way in which British Rail was privatised, could become more commonplace. As Railtrack's chief executive Gerald Corbett admitted after the Hatfield disaster, 'The railway was ripped apart at privatisation. The structure that was put in place was designed, if we're honest, to maximise the proceeds to the Treasury. It was not a structure designed to optimise safety, optimise investment or cope with the huge increase in the number of passengers.' Whatever the arguments in favour of turning over social responsibility to the private sector, the parallels with the privatisation of public services provide significant cause for concern.

When the party's over

Moreover, corporations have been able to build a business case for social responsibility during a period of unprecedented economic boom. Their customers, most of whom are reaping the rewards of economic good times, have proved to be – and to be able to afford to be – socially minded. They have rewarded companies for taking on welfare roles, and in some cases have even shown that they are willing to pay more to have companies dispense global justice.[7] But will customers' priorities change in an economic downturn, and as a result corporations' priorities too? Will the business case for social responsibility be sustainable during the inevitable downturn when it comes? When cost cutting becomes essential for corporate survival, when the emphasis on price will again be paramount?

Until recently in Japan, trading groups, *keiratsu,* once provided extensive social security systems for communities. It used to be the norm that companies would spend up to 70 per cent on top of actual wages to ensure the provision of welfare systems – 'corporate communities', they used to be called. And many of the welfare functions normally associated with the state – housing, job creation, local economic development, education – were provided by corporations. But in the wake of the Asian financial crisis and faced with the demands of ever more competitive global markets, Japanese companies have been unable to continue these practices. The lifetime employment system that effectively provided social security for the nation has disappeared, and with it the security of countless families. The head of Toshiba says that they are no longer 'a charity', corporations have been selling off their company dormitories, bonuses have been reduced. Entire communities are suffering in the Nissan Towns, the Mitsubishi Villages, and Toyota Cities which have depended on the social network and security provided by the *keiratsu* system for nearly fifty years, as plants close down and firms withdraw support from the community. School vouchers, health care, and many other provisions are being reduced or withdrawn entirely. 'The suicide rate in Japan was up one third in 1999 over 1997, a testament to the social strain.'[8]

The Japanese example provides a warning to those of us who have looked to the corporate takeover of welfare as a possible solution to the social problems created by laissez-faire capitalism. For if this move towards greater responsibility and care that we are beginning to see in the West is predicated solely upon the continuing strength of the global economy, upon the fact that philanthropic acts are essentially tax write-offs against balance sheets firmly in the black, it is surely liable to be reversed when times once again become difficult. When in 1999 Nestlé withdrew from sponsoring London's Notting Hill carnival at the last minute, claiming that its new cold coffee drink which was to have featured prominently was not yet in the shops, what hope is there that in a downturn commitments will be upheld?[9] Unless the impact on their reputation of withdrawing from social commitments is deemed more costly than that of maintaining such commitments, companies will simply not be able to justify staying involved to their shareholders. The corporate provision of welfare risks dependence on the continued generation of profits.

And the future?

Despite the fact that major companies will increasingly do their business in the context of potentially critical public opinion, there remains great uncertainty about the future. What happens at the point where ethical business considerations and profit-making diverge sharply? If companies decline to pay the increased costs of social responsibility, preferring to relocate or withdraw their investment, it is not clear that either politicians, pressure groups or individual consumers wield sufficient power on their own to prevent them.

Is there a price that will be exacted for acts of corporate benevolence? Today Microsoft puts computers in our schools; will it tomorrow determine what our children learn? [10] When Mike Cameron, a 19-year-old student, turned up at Greenbriar High School in Evans, Georgia, on an official 'Coke Day' wearing a T-shirt with a Pepsi logo, he was suspended by the school authorities. 'I know it sounds bad,' said school principal Gloria Hamilton. 'It really would have been acceptable . . . if it had just been in-house, but we had the regional president here and people flew in from Atlanta to do us the honour of being resource speakers, and Coca-Cola does so many positive things for our school like helping organisation and sports. These students knew we had guests.'[11]

Tesco's Computers for Schools campaign, sponsored by 7-Up, Tango and Pepsi, may get computers into schools, but it also increases children's exposure to sugary drinks that can damage their teeth. Vending machines are generating thousands of pounds per year for some secondary schools, income that is crucial given problems of inadequate funding and lack of resources. 'It's hard for head teachers to resist,' says Joe Harvey, director of Health Education Trust, a charity dedicated to food policy development in schools. 'You suddenly think, "Great, now I can afford the part-time classroom assistant that I need for the special needs department".'[12] Yet only one in ten products targeted at children was found by the Food Commission to be healthy.[13]

The US Channel 1 network is by now notorious for having provided 12,000 American schools with money and supplies in exchange for being able to broadcast commercials into classrooms.[14] In Germany a number of schools have responded to declining government funding by turning to corporate sponsorship, with Coca-Cola, L'Oreal and Columbia Tristar only three of a number of companies now allowed to put up posters in German schools. And above Brooklyn Bridge floats a painting of a Snapple bottle, created by a non-profit arts group, and sponsored by – you guessed it – Snapple. But do we want to live in a world in which commercialism takes advantage of shortages in funding and rides off the back of children's learning? A world in which this could be the first step towards greater business influence on education? A world in which children from low-income neighbourhoods paint murals that glorify brands.

Gerald Levin, CEO of AOL-Time Warner, claimed at the time of the recent announcement of the companies' planned merger that 'This is not just about big business. This is not just about money . . . This is about making a better world for people.'[15] Yet how can the AOL merger possibly advance the good of the world? The reality remains that the business community will never place good customer service, ethical trading and social investment above moneymaking whenever the two come into conflict. Both the political choices and all the other actions of businesses will be made in the primary interests of the shareholder value and profit projections, not justice, equity or morality.[16] In fact, given the current state of the law as regards duties to shareholders, Anglo or American businesses have to do so. In the USA investors can sue a firm if they believe that it is not making best use of their money by putting it into social causes. When Kodak gave $25 million to a black civil rights organisation in Rochester, New York, it was threatened with a shareholder suit and had to withdraw its donation. Corporations can only do good if they can show that they can make more money by doing so.

So the oil companies jumped on to the environmental bandwagon, not for any ethical reasons – although the principals involved may also have believed that this was the right thing to do – but for clear commercial gain. BP viewed climate change as a 'source of business risk', and felt that by changing company policy it would gain a distinctive 'competitive advantage' and win favour with customers, regulators and legislators, and thus bring about future business benefits.[17] Diamond cartel De Beers would have been unlikely to have instructed its suppliers to stop purchasing 'blood diamonds' from Sierra Leone as it proposed in July 2000 if the UN Security Council had not banned trading in such gems until a certification process could be set up, or if it had not feared a consumer boycott of diamonds similar to that which destroyed the fur industry in the 1970s and 1980s.

For this is not about ethics, this is about business. Sometimes both sets of considerations will coincide, but clearly not always. Corporations are not society's custodians, they are commercial entities that act in the pursuit of profit. They are morally ambivalent: Siemens, Knorr, Deutsche Bank, AEG, BMW, Volkswagen and Daimler-Benz have all been cited by the Holocaust Education Trust as exploiters of slave labour from the Nazi concentration camps. Governments on the other hand are supposed to be social institutions, within which responsiveness to citizens is, or at least should be, central. Downgrading the role of the state in favour of corporate activism threatens to make societal improvements irreversibly dependent on the creation of profit. Standing back while corporations take over, without being willing to set terms of engagement or retain the upper hand, leaves governments increasingly in danger of losing the support of the people still further. Remaining mute in the face of the Silent Takeover risks leaving us ultimately without either recourse or representation.

RECLAIM THE STATE

The rise of protest

As we have seen, while the power and independence of governments withers and corporations take over, a new political movement is beginning to emerge. Rooted in protest, its advocates are not bounded by national geography, a shared culture or history, and its members comprise a veritable ragtag of by now millions of NGOs, grassroots movements, campaigning corporations, and individuals. Their concerns, while disparate, share a common assumption: that somehow the people's interests have been taken over by other interests viewed as more fundamental than their own – that the public interest has lost out to a corporate one.

These protesters are not the brown-rice-and-sandal brigade of the 1960s and 1970s: they include housewives, schoolteachers, students, business people, suburbanites and city folk, blue- and white-collar workers alike. Although their goals may be divergent and may even at times be at odds with each other, they share a scepticism about the promises and assurances given by those in authority and – thanks to the neo-liberal orthodoxy which has taught them that the state cannot solve their problems – considerable uncertainty about the role of government.

The apparent inability or unwillingness of our elected representatives to defend our interests against those of business has created a cycle of cynicism. People do not look to government to solve their problems, and politicians therefore have little to lose if they focus their attention on business rather than on voters. Low voter turnout, falling levels of trust and increasingly visible corruption have contributed to a widespread feeling that politics simply does not matter. It is almost as though both sides of the electoral equation have given up on democracy, through a suspicion that elections don't really change anything substantial. In a world where governments are proving less effectual than corporations, trust in representative government is at an all-time low. Traditional deference to politicians, along with many other experts, has evaporated, leaving a citizenry that increasingly demands an effective and decisive say in important issues, a say that seems ill-served by the electoral ballot box.[1]

These protesters believe that taking the chance that what is good for business is good for us and our communities is just too high a risk, hazarding the food we eat, the environment, and the democratic process. While some may welcome the recent attempts of various corporations to address some of the failings of the system and contribute to the social sphere, they tend to see these attempts as window-dressing or corporate PR, and remain sceptical about companies' motives. At the same time they reject representative government as an ineffective, co-opted and flawed mechanism for dealing with the failings of the market or representing their interests on the global stage, and reject the politics of today as the 'politics of Narcissus', concerned only with presentation and 'spin'. They choose to voice their concerns on the street, on the Internet, and in the shopping malls, because they feel that these are the only places that they can be heard. They will not trust either government or business except in terms of responsiveness and results.

The Pulitzer Prize winning author Thomas Friedman's 'McArches World',[2] in which countries with McDonald's in them do not go to war, is being replaced by a McConflict world, in which José Bové, the French farmer who destroyed a McDonalds construction site, has become a folk hero, while wrecked McDonald's shop fronts have become a symbol of the discord within. International order provided courtesy of multinational corporations may have been purchased at the price of domestic anarchy.

But it is not just brands that the protesters attack; governments and international organisations are targeted with equal venom. There was the forcing through of a pact on global climate at the Earth Summit in Rio de Janeiro in 1992, where NGOs 'set the original goal of negotiating an agreement to control greenhouse gases long before governments were ready to do so, proposed most of its structure and content, and lobbied and mobilized public pressure to force through a pact that virtually no one else thought possible when the talks began.'[3] And the collapse of the Multilateral Agreement on Investment (MAI), thanks to the efforts of the numerous consumer groups and environmentalists who feared the draft treaty to harmonise rules on foreign investment, would have disabled national governments' ability to protect their own citizens in the face of corporate demands. Then there was the balaclava-wearing, pipe-smoking sub-commander Marcos, who in 1994 waged cyber war against the pro-NAFTA 'Structural Adjustment Policies' of Mexico's Partido Revolucionario Institucional (PRI) government; and the pink fairies of Seattle and then Prague, who brought the IMF and WTO meetings to a standstill by dancing in drag. Jubilee 2000, the British campaigning organisation, successfully pushed for a dramatic reduction in the debts of the poorest countries; and the presidential building in Quito, Ecuador was taken over in protest in January 2000 against President Jamil Mahaud's austerity programmes. A culture of protest is emerging that threatens to overturn the status quo.

Through demonstrations, publicity campaigns and direct action schemes, the protest movement attempts to raise the costs to businesses and governments of continuing with whatever practices protesters consider damaging, and to shape the terms on which the new elites can operate. As journalists, academics, activists and ordinary citizens speak out against the omnipotence of big business and the unreliability of government, nowadays protesters log on rather than turn on and protest rather than drop out.

What makes this movement particularly remarkable is the breadth of its appeal, and the extent to which it has managed to coalesce divergent interests. Traditional and non-traditional groups have worked together in unprecedented ways to achieve solutions rather than, as in the past, seeing each other as a part of the problem. The BSE scandal in Britain, for example, was significant in the extent to which it gave former enemies a common cause:

> Civic association – the classic expression of civil society – and uncivil politics – the presumed expression of anomic democracy – joined hands against government untrustworthiness. Farmers and producers, environmentalists and consumer groups, opposition politicians and newspapers mixed conventional forms of participation with social activism in response to untrustworthy government.[4]

The debate over genetically modified foods elicited a similar response, except that agrochemical corporations joined politicians as the focus for protesters. In Britain, guerrilla gardeners – environmental activists whose tactics included night attacks on GM crops – found themselves sharing a platform with the Women's Institute, a traditional bastion of British conservatism, in condemning GM foods.

At the World Trade Organization talks in Seattle in November 1999, a similar range of divergent interests gathered outside the convention hall to express their concerns over international free trade. Trade unionists, environmentalists and anarchist groups differed in their goals but shared a common hostility to the way that global markets were being sliced up and controlled by the most powerful governments and corporations. The image of these erstwhile enemies holding hands symbolises the extent to which civil society is now speaking with a common voice, and how protest is becoming institutionalised as an acceptable form of expression.

The movement has no fixed membership, so it can mobilise support around shared concerns, national or global, as and where appropriate. This lack of permanent mass membership and of a physical base does not weaken it, rather it makes the movement more flexible and able to tackle diverse issues, many of which may cross national boundaries. Its power is widely distributed: 'One does not need an army, control over governmental bureaucracies, massive wealth or even large numbers of activists to be effective.'[5] In the age of the Internet mass action can be orchestrated with unprecedented ease. 'Sharing information and building links is easier and cheaper than ever before.' We saw the pressure corporations are now under from e-boycotts. Similarly 'A draft of the MAI text, posted on the Internet . . . allowed hundreds of hostile watchdog groups to mobilise against it. [And] the Seattle trade summit was disrupted by dozens of websites which alerted everyone (except, it seems, the Seattle police), to the protests that were planned.'[6]

As the power and credibility of politicians wanes and the power of corporations and international organisations grows, the protest movement is gaining momentum. A hundred NGOs turned up at the WTO Ministerial Meeting in 1996; three years later, in Seattle, there were over a thousand.[7] Over 100,000 Bolivians took to the streets in February 2000 in protest against their government's decision to privatise the national water supply. The Washington World Bank/IMF protests of April 2000 saw over 10,000 demonstrators. At the end of June 40,000 people gathered in France outside the court at which José Bové was being tried. In July a consumer boycott by thousands of Japanese housewives brought down Sogo, the Osaka retailer that had come to epitomise business–government cronyism and corruption in Japan.[8]

These are early days, but if people continue to feel alienated from traditional politics and distrustful of the politicians' agendas, if they continue to feel abandoned by the state, and increasingly of the opinion that politics has been co-opted by business, if people continue to feel that the only real power is in the hands of unelected institutions – huge corporations and unaccountable supranational structures – the voice of protest will only grow louder and we will continue to see a shift from the politics of acceptance towards that of dissent. In the nineteenth century workers, and in the early twentieth century women, protested to get the vote; today protest centres on the assumption that their votes have become insignificant.

Protest as the catalyst for change

As we have seen, in today's world economics has become the new politics, and the pursuit of economic goals now outweighs political and social concerns. Governments pursue market share rather than territorial gain, and politicians depend on big business to fund their campaigns and provide the jobs they need to win elections, threatening what impartiality they once had. At the same time people have become increasingly distanced from politicians, and politicians have shown themselves equally out of touch with their electorates. Even James Wolfensohn, head of the World Bank, now concedes that 'globalisation is not working at the level of the people',[9] and it is clear that wealth is not trickling down as has been predicted. Meanwhile, the IMF's 2,700 employees dictate economic terms to 1.46 billion people, and corporations are now openly in the business of politics. The democratic deficit is fast becoming a democratic chasm, and protest is emerging as the only way for other voices to be heard.

The protest movement gives a voice to people who have been denied the right to elect their governments, as well as to people who no longer feel that their representatives are acting on their behalf. It empowers people who otherwise would have no recourse, in particular the young, the group throughout the world's democracies least likely to express themselves through the traditional ballot box. By rejecting traditional notions of representative democracy it makes democracy more direct, and puts it in people's own hands. By questioning, criticising and publicising, it 'can change the terms of disclosure, and the balance of different components in the international constellation of discourses.'[10]

The movement's success has given participants a sense of empowerment, and demonstrated that there are alternatives to the frustration and alienation that many experience. They have proven that the *demos* has a clear role to play in this commerce-centred world, in applying pressure to society's decision makers, in making democracy more robust, if more uncertain.

In a world in which ideology competes with ice cream and the policies of the dominant parties are almost indistinguishable, so that there is no apparent gain from changing the government, protest places on the agenda policies that the dominant parties would not otherwise offer the electorate. In a post-cold war era in which the US has become the only 'imperial power', we see a rise in popular dissent, because people see no alternative but to take issues into their own hands.

Of course, such protest does not provide a long-term solution to the Silent Takeover. Its limitations mirror those of consumer activism – unsurprisingly so, given their shared genesis in the discontent of the early 1990s, and their similar methods of expressing discontent. The commonality of interests often centres on a shared general disillusionment, rather than specific concerns or proffered solutions. In some cases protesters are motivated by a sense of common good; but in others they are concerned only with safeguarding their own interests, or those of a limited group – the 'raise less corn and more hell' variety of protest, like the British fuel protests of autumn 2000. As we have seen, pressure groups need to play to the media, which encourages polarised posturing, the demonisation of 'enemies', the oversimplification of issues and the choosing of fashionable rather than difficult causes to champion. Issues such as soil erosion, nitrate leaching, forest biodiversity in Africa, hardly ever get a look in. And the need for media attention can inspire violence; as one of London's May Day protesters put it, 'There has to be trouble, otherwise the papers won't report it, we won't get our concerns on the front page.'

Various pressure groups that play a large role in civil society have taken up the mantle of people's champion, yet they lack any sort of democratic mandate, are often narrowly focused on the priorities of their members, or of their leadership, and work to impose their values irrespective of those of others. Some aim to speak for the poor and the marginalised, but not all. Because they concentrate on single issues, they feel no need to concern themselves with the concerns of others, as would occur in a genuine democracy. Sometimes the coalitions of interests are global in their concern, but often they have highly nationalistic undertones. And sometimes the wishes of the *demos* can be downright nasty, like the British hysteria about paedophiles, largely stirred up by a corporation, News International, through the pages of its *News of the World* newspaper and resulting in such fiascos as that of the Bristol paediatrician who had to go into hiding because the mob couldn't tell the difference.

Protest is far removed from any familiar notion of participatory democracy. For those who are not prepared to stand in the clouds of tear gas outside another intergovernmental conference, or to live in tunnels beneath proposed road development sites, the scope for involvement is limited. We can post off a cheque once a year to Greenpeace – or, like the majority, sit back and watch the dramas unfolding on our television screens, unsure whether we really identify with or support the tactics of the protesters. Can these masked masqueraders really be representing majority views?

Protest acts as a countervailing force to the Silent Takeover, yet because it is not fully inclusive it shares the illegitimacy of its opponent. The institutionalisation of protest risks leaving us with a political system where those with the most intensely held opinions, those who shout the loudest or are the best organised, are the people to whom politicians and CEOs respond. Anti-abortion campaigners in the United States and defenders of foxhunting in the UK have distributed pre-printed postcards to group members for them to sign and send to local representatives. E-mail allows pressure groups to mobilise thousands of members instantaneously, who can shoot off standard forms of protest to express concern about a single issue. The silent majority risks becoming disempowered by the vocal minority. Corporations risk being tried by kangaroo courts, while politics risks being permanently assigned to an arena in which the battle for political sway is fought on the one hand by corporations and on the other by pressure groups, with ordinary people's interests lost in the struggle.

But despite the limitations of protest, despite its failure to balance effective means with democratic ends, despite the fact that it can never by itself be a long-term solution, the question remains as to whether, as its powers increases, it will be able to act as a catalyst for reform. Can protest change politics in the same way as it is beginning to change the corporate agenda? Can protest pressurise governments into once again putting the people's interests first? Can it force politicians to return to true democracy and provide the stimulus for them to come up with genuine inter-party debate and politics that will mobilise voters? Can protest act to re-establish government as a democratic forum within which different social needs are weighed, and all is not reducible to either the corporation or the individual? Can protest serve to reinvent the state?

Power to the people

History suggests that it can. Democratic governments and large corporations alike need mass support to survive, and this gives an enormous power to the people to impose their own terms of co-operation.

At the beginning of the last century, the USA was enjoying a period of relative prosperity not dissimilar to our own: over the previous thirty years agricultural production had more than doubled; the production of coal had gone up five times; and that of crude petroleum had increased twelve times.[11] But farmers were facing increasingly low returns despite increases in output, industrial production was rapidly becoming concentrated in the hands of a few large corporations, and powerful political bosses at city, state and national level were giving favours to big business to win financial support for their machines. 'High tariffs, business monopolies, inequitable taxation and civic graft'[12] ate into people's incomes.

News magazines revealed cases of serious and widespread collusion and corruption involving business and politics.[13] Articles exposed the threat to public safety from contaminated food, and the extortion practised by the railroads. Newspapers overflowed with editorials deriding John D. Rockefeller, Andrew Carnegie, Jay Gould and other 'robber barons'.

An increasing proportion of the American people began to feel vulnerable, uneasy and angry.[14] There was a grassroots awakening, as the realisation that corruption, monopoly franchises and discriminatory pricing were adversely affecting the public interest spread.[15,16] Urban and rural interests combined in a rare alliance, and a public mood emerged 'generally sympathetic to calls for reform'.[17]

There was an increase in political activism, but outside traditional political channels.

Prior to 1900, it was rare for people to turn away from their political parties and find methods other than the vote for influencing government. Beginning in the early twentieth century this older structure of political participation gave way to new patterns. Voter turnout fell, ticket-splitting rose, and relatively few voters could be counted on to support the regular party candidates year after year. In the same period, a great variety of interest groups successfully pioneered new ways of influencing the government and its agencies.[18]

Citizens' organisations were formed to improve urban conditions, tackle the squalid living conditions of the poor, and address abuses of political and corporate power.[19] Groups were formed to demand rights for women or for workers, and consumers increasingly refused to buy products made by child labour. Voters demanded new powers, and popular pressure led to the introduction of various legislative reforms: the Corrupt Practices Act, which addressed the illicit relation between money and politics; the direct primary, which put the choice of political candidates in the hands of voters rather than those of the party machines; the initiative, which allowed citizens' organisations to propose legislation; the referendum, allowing citizens a vote on crucial state laws; and the recall, which allowed the removal of corrupt or incompetent officials before the end of their term of office.

Politicians realised that they could no longer depend on people to vote unthinkingly along traditional party lines, and had little choice but to respond. A third party entered the 1912 electoral race: the Progressive Party, with Theodore Roosevelt as its candidate. Its success – polling 25 per cent of the vote in a system which remains notoriously unwelcoming to third parties – led all parties to rally against the corporate domination of politics. Business was systematically regulated for the first time, and new forms of political participation emerged that downgraded party bosses and gave more powers to ordinary voters.[20]

This combination of protest with voter and consumer pressure, and the skilful use of the media, gave an irresistible momentum to the progressives' cause. Progressivism became 'the first (perhaps the only) reform movement to be experienced by the whole American nation. Wars and depressions had previously engaged the whole nation's attention, but never reform.'[21]

Fifty years later, in Europe a similar process was being played out, a process that translated broad societal disaffection into swift and effective action outside traditional political channels, focused this time not on social and political issues, but on the environment.

In the 1960s, declining levels of economic growth in combination with the new environmental problems that were facing advanced industrial democracies – nuclear power, resource shortages, toxic waste, acid rain – led to a growing sense of public concern about the environment. Scientific evidence of these concerns became available for the first time, making grimly clear the environmental and health consequences of industrial development. Front-page headlines catalogued disasters: oil spills that damaged aquatic life and the coastlines of California and Cornwall; and toxic waste that spilled into the Rhine, killing fish and poisoning drinking water. Rachel Carson's *Silent Spring*[22] galvanised popular support with a bleak depiction of a miasmatic world in which, thanks to the overuse of insecticides and pesticides, birds no longer sing.

An environmental movement emerged to fight against what was seen as corporate and political negligence. Like the progressive movement before it, it eschewed conventional, hierarchical organisation by party or interest group, and rejected traditional forms of participation and the idea that the vote alone was an adequate form of political expression. Again like the American progressives, it built its success on successfully harnessing latent public anxieties and mobilising the broad coalition of interests that gathered together under the environmental banner. In their shared goal of protecting the planet, mainstream conservationists of the 'save the whale' type united with radical groups who opposed industrialisation and preached apocalyptic messages about global destruction. Disasters such as the Chernobyl nuclear explosion in 1986 and the discovery of the link between skin cancer and the hole in the ozone layer were used to maximum effect.

Consumers stopped buying products containing CFCs and boycotted products tested on animals. Citizens' groups were formed to address local environmental problems. People joined organisations such as Greenpeace to protest about nuclear testing, ozone depletion and global warming. Membership of ecology groups in Britain rose by the mid-1980s to half a million members, and groups in both West Germany and The Netherlands had membership levels of around a quarter of a million.[23] Direct action and protest were seen as the only ways to promote the environmental cause.

And the strategy worked. Despite the success of New Right governments that came into power in much of the developed world in the early 1980s, for whom the environment was not a natural cause to champion, the environmentalists doggedly managed not only to keep the issues before the public but also, in a relatively short time, succeeded in transforming the political landscape. Soon the groundswell support for environmental issues led existing political parties to compete in demonstrating their 'green' credentials, and European leaders of both left and right – Mitterrand, Kohl, Thatcher – began to claim to be environmentalists.

New political parties were established which explicitly advocated a green agenda. 'By the beginning of the 1990s, green parties or their New Left supporters had won seats in the national Parliament or EC Parliament for most nations in Western Europe.'[24] These parties showed a remarkable ability to break the left–right mould of the established party systems and, as in the case of the American progressives, appealed to voters who had previously followed a strict partisan line. They still remain significant players in continental European politics. Green parties are currently members of governing coalitions in Germany, France, Belgium, Italy and Finland. In Britain, they maintain a strong presence in local government.[25] The Greens are the fourth largest coalition in the European Parliament. Green issues are now firmly established on the political agenda.

Whither the Takeover?

The combination of consumer activism and political protest can clearly be extremely effective. And the parallels between the eras of the American progressive movement, the European environmental movement and today are striking: a comparable disillusionment with government and a rejection of mainstream politics, a suspicion of big business, a willingness to take to the streets and protest, the use of consumer pressure as a political and economic weapon, a broad coalition of interests; avoidance of traditional economic debates in favour of debates over quality of life issues, the ability to combine idealism with self-interest, and a non-partisan and non-class based orientation.

But while the successes of the progressives and the environmentalists teach us that governments *can* respond, the question of whether they *will* respond to protest against the Silent Takeover remains unanswered. The Internet has revolutionised the speed at which businesses respond to activism – an internal memo to senior executives of a large multinational in April 2000 pointed out that 'Riots in Seattle, Washington DC and London on May Day are all evidence of rising tensions which we ignore at our peril' – yet national institutions lag behind, slowed down by traditional structures that can seem ill suited to the new millennium.

Will this groundswell, these acts of vigilantism and anger, kick-start a reform of the twenty-first century's political agenda in the same way that these earlier movements did?

To a limited extent they already are. As the rhetoric of business has changed, so has political discourse. Across party lines, if clearly in differing degrees, all political parties have begun to make use of a new jargon. Talk of the 'third way' and 'compassionate conservatism', the hijacking of the language of the left by the right, Clinton's sympathetic comments regarding the Seattle protesters,[26] the Labour government's 'Rip-Off Britain' campaign, the attempts in the recent US election by Gore to woo the Green vote, all suggest a fear of rising popular dissent and a growing acceptance by politicians that the pendulum of global capitalism may have swung too far, that the rising tide never did manage to lift all the boats, that corporations may be too powerful, that it is time to lay the 'capitalismo selvagem' (savage capitalism) of Thatcher and Reagan to rest. Social justice may be coming back into political fashion.

Yet it remains questionable whether politicians are capable of translating this new rhetoric into a sustainable reality. The 'free lunch' school of politics, in which politicians continue to make inflated claims and generate inflated expectations without admitting that trade-offs will undoubtedly need be made, has become the norm. Rather than taming increasingly vast corporations, governments turn a blind eye to billion-dollar mergers. In the USA, the Security and Exchange Commission (SEC) and the Justice Department's anti-trust division, the two institutions that have some regulatory ability to watch over global companies, have had their budgets slashed and are likely to have even less funds at their disposal under the new Bush administration. In the UK the Blair government's refusal to introduce an effective Freedom of Information Act, despite pledges made while in opposition, has been a blow not only for consumer empowerment but also for citizens, who remain unable to effectively police politicians, since they lack information that in other democratic states is in the public domain. Attempts to set national policies within supranational programmes, and moves towards more international governance – essential if national governments are to have any hope of restraining global corporations – are evolving only very slowly, and largely seem more aspirational than realisable. The US never ratified the Kyoto Protocol on climate change, thanks to the UK's veto, the EU did not ratify its social chapter, which aims to develop common policies on, amongst other things, living and working conditions and underprivileged groups, and demands for a global financial architecture in the wake of the Asian financial crisis produced no results. We are far from having a World Environmental Organisation or a World Ethics Organisation to counter the WTO.

Politicians have a vested interest in maintaining the status quo, and are unlikely to volunteer to initiate changes that threaten the interests that helped them be elected. The financial dependence of political parties and candidates on big business has been discussed in earlier chapters. The cost of elections in many democracies can no longer be met by the state or from party membership revenues, requiring politicians to seek alternative backing in the private sector. Governments rely on business to address the problems that they do not want to or cannot take on, and thus become ever more dependent. Considering, too, the ability of multinational corporations to threaten to withdraw their capital from a state if governmental decisions are unfavourable or if tax rates are too high, and the market's predilection for punishing those governments it deems fiscally irresponsible, it seems almost impossible that individual states will alter the balance of power in a way that disadvantages business.

This is the short-term perspective on change. But if governments are not farsighted enough to confront the Silent Takeover; if they are not prepared to learn from the lessons of the progressive and environmental eras, to search for solutions, to resist pressure from big business when the market mechanism fails or when the pursuit of corporate profit is against the public interest, and use their coercive powers to demand compliance from corporations; if they remain out of touch with the public and do not work to give people a greater say in the system, using new technologies to consult voters and allow increased levels of participation; if they forget that people will no longer support a world which is exclusively about growth rates and private capital flows; if they fail in all this they will sign their own death warrant, and the world we live in will be one in which corporations rule, markets are above the law, and voting becomes a thing of the past. The final stage of the Takeover is the end of politics itself – the takeover of politics by protest.

Given the short-term factors sustaining the status quo, there is no guarantee that states will respond to these longer-term dangers. Radical policies are not the currency of mainstream politics, and politicians are predisposed to preserve the system that produced them. This is something that we must view with real concern. Once, it took the Wall Street crash, the Great Depression, the rise of fascism and World War II to make us reconsider how we managed our global affairs. If we are to avoid permanent marginalisation in the key decisions that shape our lives, now is the time for decisive action.

Since neither business nor politics can survive without popular support, we are in a powerful position if we unite and press for change. As consumers we must be both vigilant and active; as protesters we must force our politicians to realise the dangers of inaction and respond appropriately. And as citizens we must make it clear to government that unless politics focuses on people as well as business, unless government's love affair with big corporations ends, unless politicians offer us a product worth buying, we will continue to scorn representative democracy, and will choose to shop and protest rather than vote. Until the state reclaims us, we will not reclaim the state.

NOTES

Chapter 1

1. Of particular note is the fact that the World Bank's World Development Report 2000 acknowledged that inequality was bad for growth, economic growth does not automatically reduce poverty, and that poverty is not simply an economic problem but also a political one.

2. Interestingly, the Death Row campaign badly misfired. After victims' rights groups picketed a Texas Sears store in February 2000, Sears, the second largest retailer in the US, dropped its contract with Benetton for a private label line. The line had been expected to generate some $100 million in sales in its first year. Olivero Toscani, Benetton's longtime creative director, was another casualty of the campaign. A joint statement with Benetton owner Luciano Benetton implied he left to 'take on new projects'.

3. According to the World Bank's 1999 *World Development Indicators,* there were 654 television sets per 1000 people in highly developed countries. In the USA this is as high as 847 per 1000.

4. Ben Bagdikian, *The Media Monopoly,* 4th edn (Boston, 1992) p. 157; 'Buy-nothings discover a cure for affluenza', *The New York Times, 29* November, 1997.

5. E. Herman and R. McChesney, *The Global Media: The New Visionaries of Corporate*

Capitalism (London, 1997)

6. www.adbusters.org; see also: www.oneworld.org/ni/issue278/jamming.html
7. 'Shoppers are pigs', *Wall Street Journal,* 19 November 1997. See also: 'Consumer republic', *Adweek,* 22 November 1999.
8. Anderson and Cavanagh, 'Top 200: The rise of global corporate power', Institute for Policy Studies (Washington, 1999)
9. Compiled from country and company data from *Economist* and *Fortune 500* lists, 2000.
10. 'Business: Rupert laid bare', *The Economist,* 20 March 1999.
11. Stephen Byers speech transcript, Mansion House, 2 February 1999. http://www.dti.gov.uk/ministers/archived/byers02021999.html
12. *Pulling Apart: A State-by-State Analysis of Income Trends,* Center on Budget and Policy Priorities and the Economic Policy Institute (2000).
13. Federal Election Commission Data, 18 December 2000.
14. Robert D. Putnam, Susan J. Pharr, and Russell J. Dalton, 'Introduction: What's Troubling the Trilateral Democracies', in Putnam and Pharr (eds.), *Disaffected Democracies,* (Princeton, 2000), p. 14.
15. 'Too much corporate power', *Business Week,* 11 September 2000.
16. Remarks by Eric Hobsbawm in 'Roundtable: The Global Order in the 21st Century', *Prospect,* Issue 44, August/September 1999.
17. J. Stiglitz, 'The economic consequences of income inequality', Federal Reserve Bank of Kansas City (1999).

Chapter 2

1. William Greider, *One World, Ready or Not,* (1997), p. 362.
2. Chris Pierson, 'Social Policy', in David Marquand and Anthony Seldon, *The Ideas that Shaped Post-War Britain,* (1996), p. 151.

3. Desmond S. King, *The New Right: Politics, Markets and Citizenship*, (1987), p. 58.

4. Nigel Lawson, 'The Frontiers of Privatisation', speech to Adam Smith Institute conference on privatisation (1988), quoted in Peter Riddell, *The Thatcher Era and its Legacy*, (1991), p. 6.

5. Desmond S. King, *The New Right: Politics, Markets and Citizenship*, p. 68.

6. David Marquand, 'Moralists and Hedonists', in Marquand and Seldon, *The Ideas that Shaped Post-War Britain*, p. 14.

7. Ibid., p. 15.

8. 'The Thatcher Record', *The Economist*, 24 November 1990; Economic Report of the President, January 1993, Table 13-59, p. 462; 'The trouble with theories: Assessing Reaganomics', *The Economist*, 21 January 1989.

9. John Gray, *Beyond the New Right*, (1993), p. vii.

10. John Moore, Social Services Secretary, speech in London, 26 September 1987, quoted in Peter Riddell, *The Thatcher Era and its Legacy*, p. 127.

11. Peter Riddell, *The Thatcher Era and Its Legacy*, p. 150.

12. Ibid, p. 151.

13. Quoted in Peter Jenkins, *Mrs Thatcher's Revolution*, (1987), p. 326.

14. Ibid.

15. Chris Pierson, 'Social Policy', in Marquand and Seldon, *The Ideas that Shaped Post-War Britain*, p. 140.

16. Desmond S. King, *The New Right: Politics, Markets and Citizenship*, p. 139.

17. It was former prime minister Harold Macmillan who described it as a sell-off of the family silver: 'First of all the Georgian silver goes, and then all the nice furniture that used to be in the salon. Then the Canalettos go.' Harold Macmillan, first Earl of Stockton, speech to the Tory Reform Group, 8 November 1985, quoted in Peter Riddell, *The Thatcher Era and its Legacy*, pp. 27–9.

18. I am using £67 billion to refer to £67,104 million.

19. David Butler and Gareth Butler, *Twentieth Century British Political Facts*, (2000), pp. 430–33.

20. John Gray, *False Dawn: The Delusions of Global Capitalism*, (New York, 1998), pp. 27–8.

21. Peter Riddell, *The Thatcher Era and its Legacy*, p. 92.

22. Madsen Pirie, 'Reasons for privatization', in Philip Morgan (ed.), *Privatization and the Welfare State*, (1995), p. 26.

23. Peter Riddell, *The Thatcher Era and its Legacy*, pp. 27–9.

24. Richard P. Nathan, 'The Reagan Presidency in Domestic Affairs', in *The Reagan Presidency: An Early Assessment*, Fred. I. Greenstein (ed.), (1983), p. 49.

25. Philip Morgan, 'The privatization of the welfare state: A case of back to the future?', in Phillip Morgan (ed.), *Privatization and the Welfare State*, p. 12.

26. Ibid., p. 152.

27. See for example Peter Huber, 'Technology: the great deregulator', *Forbes*, vol. 15, no. 6, (1995).

28. Desmond S. King, *The New Right: Politics, Markets and Citizenship*, p. 155.

29. Ibid., p. 139.

30. John Burton, 'Taxation Policy and the New Right', in Grant Jordan and Nigel Ashford (eds.), *Public Policy and the Impact of the New Right*, (1993), p. 103.

31. Riddell, Peter, *The Thatcher Era and its Legacy*, pp. 112–3.

32. Friedrich Hayek, *Law, Legislation and Liberty*, (1979), p. 139.

33. David A. Stockman, *The Triumph of Politics,* (London, 1986), p. 6.

34. Michael Moran and Tony Prosser, 'Introduction: Politics, Privatization and Constitutions', in Michael Moran and Tony Prosser (eds.), *Privatization and Regulatory Change in Europe*, (1994), p. 1.

35. John Gray, *False Dawn: The Delusions of Global Capitalism*, p. 39.

36. Francis Fukuyama, *The End of History and the Last Man*, (1992), p. 42.

37. See for example J. Toye, *Dilemmas of development: Reflections on the counter-revolution in development theory and policy*, (Oxford, 1987).

38. Vincent Wright, 'Industrial Privatization in Western Europe: Pressures, Problems and Paradoxes', in Vincent Wright (ed.), *Privatization in Western Europe*, (1994), p. 3.

39. 'Twilight of a god', *The Economist,* 17 September 1994.

40. Edward Carr, 'Survey of Business in Europe: What the ministry managed', *The Economist,* 23 November 1996.

41. 'The Future Surveyed: The future of capitalism', *The Economist,* 11 September 1993.

42. 'The Post-Soviet world: The resumption of history', *The Economist,* 26 December 1992.

43 Francis Fukuyama, *The End of History and the Last Man*, p. 41.

44. For a comprehensive review of dependency theory literature, see Robert A. Packenham, *The Dependency Movement: Scholarship and politics in development studies,* (Cambridge MA, 1992).

45. Robert Skidelsky, 'Bring back Keynes', *Prospect,* May 1997, p. 30.

46. Tony Blair, leader of the opposition, speech to the News Corporation Leadership Conference, Hayman Island, Australia, 17 July 1995.

47. Martin Walker, 'No argument', *Prospect,* March 2000, p. 35.

48. John Gray, *False Dawn: The Delusions of Global Capitalism.*

49. Martin Rhodes, 'The Welfare State', in Martin Rhodes, Paul Heyward and Vincent Wright (eds.), *Developments in West European Politics*, (London 1997).

50. 'Europe's New Left: Free to bloom', *New Economist,* 12 February 2000.

51. Ibid.

52. Ibid.

53. John Gray, *False Dawn: The Delusions of Global Capitalism*, p. 29.

54. 'Europe wheels to the right', *The Economist,* 10 May 1997.

55. John Gray, *False Dawn: The Delusions of Global Capitalism*, p. 87.

56. 'The left's new start: a future for socialism', *The Economist,* 11 June 1994.

57. 'Displaced, defeated and not sure what to do next: The plight of Europe's right', *The Economist,* 23 January 1999.

58. Robert Taylor, 'The social democrats come roaring back', *New Statesman,* 20 December 1999, p. 26.

59. 'Europe's new left: Free to bloom', *The Economist,* 12 February 2000.

60. Madsen Pirie, 'Reasons for privatization', in Philip Morgan (ed.), *Privatization and the Welfare State*, p. 26.

61. Michael Maclay, 'A mission for Britain', *Prospect,* March 2000, p. 24.

62. Margaret Thatcher, chief opposition spokesman on power, Conservative Political Centre address, Blackpool, 10 October 1968, quoted in Peter Riddell, *The Thatcher Era and its Legacy*, (1991), p. 1.

63. Kenichi Ohmae, *The Borderless World: Power and strategy in the global marketplace*, (London, 1990).

64. 'One world?: The growing integration of national economies', *The Economist,* 18 October 1997.

65. Astonishingly, more than 50 per cent of Britain's net investment went abroad in 1885–94 (Kevin O'Rourke and Jeffrey Williamson).

66. This is redolent of the Barings crisis of 1890 when the merchant bank had to be rescued by the Bank of England after dabbling in South American securities. The same Barings, that is, that went under in 1995 after their Singapore-based trader Nick Leeson bet the wrong way on Japanese equity futures.

67. Globalisation theorists like R. Barnet and J. Cavanaugh, *Global Dreams: Imperial Corporations and the New World Order* (New York, 1995), and Raymond Vernon,

Sovereignty at Bay: The Multinational Spread of U.S. Enterprises (1971), see the current pattern of MNC expansion to be qualitatively new, whereas globalisation sceptics like Hirst and Thompson, *Globalisation in Question: The International Economy and the Possibilities of Governance* (Cambridge, UK, 1996) take a contrary view and claim that an internationalised economy is not unprecedented, that multinationals are not new and that markets are not necessarily more open or more expansive than they have been through history.

68. World Trade Organisation, 'Trade and Foreign Direct Investment', 1996, http://www.wto.org/english/news_e/pres96_e/pr057_e.htm

69. All figures from the World Bank's World Development Indicators 1999.

70. Francis Fukuyama, *The End of History and the Last Man*, p. xiii.

71. Peter Riddell, *The Thatcher Era and its Legacy*, p. 234.

72. Charlie Leadbeater, 'Thatcherism and progress', in Stuart Hall and Martin Jacques (eds.), *New Times: The Changing Face of Politics in the 1990s*, (1989), p. 396.

73. Office of National Statistics, *Social Trends*, (London, 1999).

74. 'Kiwis turn sour', *The Economist,* 19 October 1996.

75. 'Latin America and the Market: The free society on trial', *The Economist,* 21 November 1998.

76. Bill Clinton, 'The Year 2000 State of the Union: The economy, education and healthcare', address by Bill Clinton, President of the United States, delivered to Congress and the nation, Washington DC, 27 January 2000.

77. Focus on the Corporation, 'Michael Eisner vs. Vietnamese Laborers', 24 March 1998; www.essential.org/monitor.focus/focus.9812.html

78. Paul Krugman, 'Some Don't Want to Be Saved From Globalization', *International Herald Tribune,* 17 February 2000.

79. Francis Fukuyama, *The End of History and the Last Man*, p. 41.

80. Debora Spar, 'Foreign investment and human rights', *Challenge,* January/February 1999. See also Debora Spar, 'China(B): Polaroid of Shanghai Ltd.', Harvard Business School Case Study no. 794-089.

Chapter 3

1.   See Giovanni Andrea Cornia, 'Inequality and poverty trends in the era of liberalization and globalization' (United Nations University publication, 1999).
2.   Lamia Kamal-Chaoui, 'Halving Poverty', OECD Observer Paris, April 2000; also see UN Human Development Report 2000.
3.   For details of South Africa transition, see W. Munro, V. Padayachee, F. Lund and I. Valodia, 'The state in a changing world: plus ça change?', *Journal of International Development,* vol. 11, (1999).
4.   Lamia Kamal-Chaoui, ibid.
5.   Peter Nolan, *China and the global business revolution* and *China and the global economy* (2001).
6.   See the UN Human Development Programme's 1999 and 2000 Human Development Reports.
7.   K. Newland, 'Workers of the world, now what? On the disappearance of organized labor', *Foreign Policy,* Spring 1999.
8.   For a review of this literature, see Arik Levinson, 'Environmental Regulations and Manufacturers' Location Choices: Evidence from the Census of Manufacturers,' *Journal of Public Economics,* 62, (1996), pp. 5–29.
9.   Support for the 'race to the bottom' hypothesis can be found in: T. & F. Collingsworth, William Goold and Pharis F. Harvey, 'Time for a Global New Deal' *Foreign Affairs*, January/February 1994; J. G. Ruggie (1995), 'At Home Abroad, Abroad at Home: International Liberalisation and Domestic Stability in the New World

Economy', *Millennum*, vol. 24, no. 3, pp. 507–527; Susan Strange, *The Retreat of the State: The Diffusion of Power in the World Economy* (Cambridge, 1996); P. Cerny, 'Globalization and the changing logic of collective action', International Organization, vol. 49, (1995), pp. 595–625. However, there is also a body of literature which contradicts this view and even points to the fact that some firms choose to locate in areas of high unionisation: J. Friedman, D. Gerlowski and J. Silberman, 'What Attracts Foreign Multinational Corporations? Evidence from Branch Plant Location in the United States', *Journal of Regional Science*, vol. 32, (1992), p. 4; C. Coughlin, J. V. Terza and V. Arromdee, 'State Characteristics and the location of foreign direct investment within the United States', *Review of Economics and Statistics*, vol. 73, (1991), pp. 675–683; Timothy J. Bartik, 'Business Location Decisions in the United States: Estimation of the Effects of Unionization, Taxes, and Other Characteristics of States', *Journal of Business and Economic Statistics*, vol. 3, no. 1, pp. 14–22. Others suggest that regulatory differences in free trade regimes such as the NAFTA countries only have a minimal impact on firm investment decisions: Gene M. Grossman, and Alan B. Krueger, 'Environmental Impacts of a North American Free Trade Agreement', unpublished manuscript prepared for the Conference on the US–Mexico Free Trade Agreement, 1991. Some also have found no correlation between the intensity of environmental regulation, for example, and the investment decisions of firms; see G. Knogden, 'Environment and Industrial Siting', *Zeitschrift fur Umweltpolitik*. But as Spar and Yoffie point out (D. L. Spar and D. B. Yoffe, 'A Race to the Bottom or Governance from the Top?', in Aseem Prakash and Jeffrey A. Hart (eds.), *Coping with Globalization*, (London, 2000), pp. 31–51) it is diffcult to disaggregate the data and establish causal links and patterns of decision-making, therefore it is unclear whether or not corporate movements were or were not spurred by differentials in environmental regulation or wage rates. As they point out, 'even if the empirical evidence is somewhat dismissive . . . theoretically they are also quite plausible. Firms undeniably seek to increase profits and create competitive advantage and if moving to less expensive or less onerous locations would serve these aims, it is only logical to expect them to do so.'

10. 'Human Rights Alert', *Business Ethics,* May/June 1999.

11. See Sen's works on development and welfare economics, including *Poverty and Famines* (1984), and *Development as Freedom* (2000).

12. Centre on Budget and Policy Initiatives and the Economic Policy Institute (2000) in G. Koretz, 'Not Enough is Trickling Down', *Business Week,* 31 January 2000. Within-state income inequality continued to grow in most states in the 1990s despite economic growth and tight labour markets. See also United for a Fair Economy and Institute for Policy Studies report, 'A decade of executive excess: the 1990s: Sixth annual executive compensation survey'.

13. 'Pay: Winners and losers', *The Economist,* 8 May 1999.

14. 'Divines opine', *The Economist,* 12 April 1997.

15. P. Barclay (chair), *Income and Wealth, Volume 1: Report of the Inquiry Group* (1995), Joseph Rowntree Foundation report in C. Pantazis and D. Gordon, *Tackling inequalities: Where are we now and what can be done?* (Bristol, 2000).

16. United Nations Human Development Report (1999), p. 37; http://www.undp.org/hdro/Chapter1.pdf.

17. Complementary massages and free snacks are just some of the perks now on offer at internet companies.

18. See for example, 'Benefits dwindle for the unskilled along with wages', *The New York Times,* 14 June 1998.

19. The 1999 Human Development Report, UN Development Programme.

20. W. Greider, *One World, Ready or Not: The Manic Logic of Global Capitalism* (New York, 1997).

21. Quoted in H. Martin and H. Schumann, *Global Trap: Globalization and the assault on democracy and prosperity* (London, 1996); from the *Financial Times*, 14 May 1996.

22. Conversations with Hepatitis C sufferers.

23. IMS Health Report, 'Pharmacast and beyond: a study of the G7 anti-depressant market' (1998).

24. Robert Whymant, *The Times*, 27 February 1998 (Tokyo).

25. R. G. Wilkinson, 'Unhealthy Societies: The Afflictions of Inequality' (London, 1996).

26. R. G. Wilkinson, 'Income, inequality and social cohesion', *American Journal of Public Health*, September 1997; and McDonough et al, 'Income dynamics and adult mortality in the United States 1972 through 1989', *American Journal of Public Health,* September 1997.

27. Richard Freeman, 'Solving the new inequality', *Boston Review*, December/January 1996/97.

28. Avery F. Gordon, 'Globalism and the prison industrial complex: an interview with Angela Davis', *Race and Class: the threat of globalism,* October 1998 – March 1999.

29. Quoted in Greider, ibid.

30. Rt Hon. Stephen Byers' Mansion House speech.

31. Quoted in Alain Lipietz, *La société en sablier,* (Paris, 1996), p. 313.

32. Ulrich Beck, 'Beyond the Nation State', *New Statesman,* 6 December 1999, p. 25.

33. Freeman, ibid.

34. See 'The Economist survey: Globalization and Tax: The Vanishing taxpayer', *The Economist*, 29 January 2000.

35. Quoted in Ulrich Beck, 'Beyond the Nation State'.

36. Quoted in Robert Boyes, 'Bonn warned of cash flight by industry', *The Times,* 2 March 1999.

37. Quoted in the *Guardian,* 'Left is where the heart is, warns Lafontaine', 15 March 1999.

38. 'Schröder to review tax', *Independent,* 4 March 1999.

39. *The Economist,* 5 August 2000.

40. *The Times,* 12 May 1999.

41. Ibid.

42. 'The tap runs dry: Disappearing taxes', *The Economist,* 31 May 1997.

43. 'Rupert laid bare', *The Economist,* 20 March 1999.

44. See 'Cradle to grave: what should become of the welfare state?', *The Economist,* 21 September 1996; and 'The tap runs dry: disappearing taxes', *The Economist,* 31 May 1997.

45. Philip Gould, *The Unfinished Revolution* (1998), pp. 283–4.

46. Moore and Stansel, *How Corporate Welfare Won: Clinton and Congress Retreat from Cutting Business Subsidies,* CATO Institute Report, 1996.

47. Donald L. Bartlett and James B. Steele, 'Paying a price for polluters', *Time Magazine,* 23 November 1998.

48. Donald L. Bartlett and James B. Steele, 'States at War', *Time Magazine,* 9 November 1998, vol. 152.

49. 'A User's Guide: Investment Agencies', *Corporate Location,* November/December 1996.

50. J. Lloyd-Smith, 'Dobson poised to approve use of Relenza in limited cases', *Independent,* 7 October 1999. Note that although the drug wasn't approved, Glaxo did not pull out.

51. 'The equality trap', *Financial Times,* 19 April 1999.

Chapter 4

1. 'European Union Report on the NSA', *Daily Telegraph,* 16 December 1997.

2. Adam Smith, *The Wealth of Nations,* (1776).

3. See for example, S. Huntingdon, 'The Erosion of National Interests', *Foreign Affairs,*

September/October 1997 and Jeffrey Garten, 'Business and foreign policy', *Foreign Affairs*, vol. 76, no. 3.

4. Susan Strange, *The Retreat of the State: The Diffusion of Power in the World Economy* (Cambridge, 1996).

5. William Greider, *One World, Ready or Not* (1997), p. 24.

6. Madeline Albright, 'First-class diplomacy', statement at confirmation hearing before the Senate Foreign Relations Committee, 8 January 1998.

7. See S. Dryden, *Trade Warriors: USTR and the American Crusade for Free Trade* (1994).

8. Edward Luttwak, *Turbo-Capitalism: Winners and Losers in the Global Economy* (1999).

9. *Financial Times,* 7 April 1999. With regard to the beef and bananas disputes, at the time it was argued that 'beef will make bananas look like peanuts' – see *Financial Times,* 17 May 1999.

10. *Financial Times,* 17 May 1997.

11. *Financial Times,* 4 March 1999.

12. *Financial Times,* 7 April 1999.

13. Analysed in the following pages.

14. The Russian argument was that the Caspian is a closed water system with a fragile ecological balance and all decisions concerning its economic exploitation have to be taken jointly by all states that participate in the Caspian littoral. Russia has demonstrated a 'proprietary attitude' towards the Caspian oil deposits and towards energy ventures in the Commonwealth. See 'Moscow pressures neighbours to share oil, gas revenues', *Washington Post,* 18 March 1994, p. A24. We should also note that shortly after the dissolution of the USSR, a first inter-republican agreement on distribution of Caspian resources took place with Azeri, Kazakh, Turkmen and Russian officials at the Ministry of Fuel and Energy in Moscow. See also Angela Spatharou, 'Geopolitics of Caspian Oil: The Role of the Integration of the Caspian Region into World Economy in

Maintaining Stability in the Caucasus', in B. Gokay (ed.), *The Politics of Caspian Oil* (Basingstoke, 2001).

15. *Interfax*, 16 and 20 September 1994. (Source: *Russian Press Digest* database search).

16. Baku, Azerbaijan Radio, news conference by H. Aliev, 20 September 1994. (Source: *Russian Press Digest* database search).

17. *Interfax,* 20 September 1994. (Source: *Russian Press Digest* database database search).

18. Series of articles in the *Financial Times;* see 18 July 1997, 29 July, 30 August, and 4 October when the contracts were actually approved.

19. *Financial Times,* 30 August 1997.

20. *Financial Times,* 18 July 1997.

21. 'Britain: addicted to the arms trade', *The Economist,* 18 September 1999.

22. *Financial Times,* 30 August 1997.

23. The USA is the world's biggest arms exporter, accounting for nearly 50 per cent of the $53.4bn (£37bn) annual market in 1999. (Richard Norton-Taylor, 'US sells half the world's arms exports', *Guardian,* 20 October 2000).

24. Cited in 'Cook's aide accuses DTI over Indonesian arms', *Independent,* 17 September 1999. See also 'Cook bans arms for Indonesia', *The Times,* 26 September 1997 and 'Britain still selling Indonesia arms', *Independent,* 15 May 1998.

25. http://www.gn.apc.org/tapol/home.htm

26. Michael Ignatieff, 'Human rights: The midlife crisis', *The New York Review,* 20 May 1999.

27. Ahmed Rashid, *The Taliban, Islam, Oil, and the New Great Game in Central Asia* (2000). Also see *The Economist,* 16 December 1995; 2 December 1995.

28. http://www.amnesty.org.uk/action/camp/saudi/repression.shtml

29. *The Economist,* 3 April 1999.

30. *The Economist,* 3 April 1999; *Financial Times,* 8 April 1999.

31. W. Meyer, 'Human Rights and MNCs: theory vs. quantitative analysis', *Human Rights*

Quarterly, vol. 18, no. 2. (1996); Han Park, 'Correlates of human rights: Global tendencies', *Human Rights Quarterly*, vol. 9 (1987).

32. Debora Spar, 'The Spotlight and the Bottom Line', *Foreign Affairs*, March/April 1998.

33. OECD, *Trade, Employment, and Labour standards* (1996), www.oecd.org

34. I take the position that there are certain universal human rights that ought to be defended at all costs and that in the defence of them the principle of state sovereignty can and should be overridden.

35. Quoted in Christopher Avery, *Business and Human Rights in a Time of Change* (London, 2000).

36. Ibid.

37. Derek Brown, 'Iraq sanctions', *Guardian*, 1 August 2000.

38. 'China's snake charmer – Zhu returns to China', *The Economist*, 24 April 1999.

39. See for instance *The Times*, 21 October 1999; *Daily Telegraph*, 25 October 1999. Also Gill Bates, 'Limited engagement', *Foreign Affairs*, July/August 1999, vol. 78, no.4, pp. 65–76.

40. James Baker, 'Personal View', *Financial Times*, 7 April 1999.

41. David Acheson, 'Personal View', *Financial Times*, 30 June 1999.

42. Philip Cerny, 'Globalising the political and politicising the global', *New Political Economy*, March 1999.

43. MORI polls Archive, Human Rights, www.mori.com/polls/1998/una.htm

44. Eurobarometer, Report No. 51, July 1999; http://europa.eu.int/comm/dg10/epo/eb/eb51

45. Allan Hogarth, Amnesty International UK Info office.

46. Gallup poll, 3 June 1999: 'Americans' unfavourable attitude towards China unchanged ten years after Tienanmen', www.gallup.com/polls/releases/pr990603.asp

47. This observation is based upon the time I spent working in Russia in 1991–3 for the

International Finance Corporation and CS First Boston.

48. W. LaFeber, 'The tension between democracy and capitalism during the American century', *Diplomatic History*, vol. 23, no. 2 (Malden, MA, 1999)

49. LaFeber, ibid.

50. T. E. Vadney, *The World Since 1945* (1992).

51. LaFeber, ibid.

52. LaFeber, ibid.

53. LaFeber, ibid.

54. LaFeber, ibid.

55. Straight to Knox, 12 February 1911, Willard Straight Papers, Cornell University, Ithaca, New York.

56. R. Mokhiber and R. Weissman, 'Sanctioning Burma, Sanctioning the United States', Focus on the Corporation, 23 December 1997; http://www.essential.org/monitor/focusfocus.9707.html

57. 'Feeding Mammon – World Trade Organisation: Special Report', *Guardian,* 30 November 1999.

58. Mark Lynas, *The World Trade Organisation and GMOs,* Consumer Policy Review, London, November/December 1999.

59. 'Feeding Mammon – World Trade Organisation: Special Report', *Guardian,* 30 November 1999.

60. 'Media Advisory: Initial Reports from Seattle gloss over WTO issues', *Fairness and Accuracy in Reporting (FAIR)*, 1 December 1999.

61. See Carol Miller and Jennifer L. Croston, 'WTO Scrutiny v. Environmental Objectives: Assessment of the International Dolphin Conservation Program Act', *American Business Law Journal*, vol. 37 (1999). See also 'Focus: Trade Wars, the hidden tentacles of the world's most secret body', *Independent on Sunday*, 11 July 1999. See also

Mark Lynas, 'The World Trade Organisation and GMOS', *Consumer Policy Review*, November/December 1999.

62. David Korten, *When Corporations Rule the World* (1995).

63. Carol J. Miller and Jennifer L. Croston, 'WTO Scrutiny v. Environmental Objectives: Assessment of the International Dolphin Conservation Program Act', *American Business Law Journal*.

64. Hilary Clarke, 'The Superpower elite that sidelines the poorest nations', *Independent on Sunday*, 18 July 1999.

65. 'Focus: Trade wars, The hidden tentacles of the world's most secret body', *Independent on Sunday*; Clarke, 'The Superpower elite that sidelines the poorest nations', *Independent on Sunday*, ibid.

66. John Madeley, 'There's a food fight in Seattle', *New Statesman*, 22 November 1999. It was finally resolved, however, that Supachia would share the post with Michael Moore. Supachia was in line to take over from Moore in 2002 for a further three years.

67. Mark Lynas, ibid. And see also George Monbiot, 'Britain and America have given big business an inhuman bonus', *Guardian*, 28 October 1999.

68. Mark D. Fefer, 'Not-so-free Trade', *Seattle Weekly*, 22–28 April 1998. Note that the organisation that solicited large contributions from the private sector for preparations for the Seattle WTO round, the Seattle Host Organisation, was co-chaired by Bill Gates and Boeing CEO Phil Condit.

69. Mark Lynas, ibid.

70. See also Marceau Gabriell and Peter N. Pederson, 'Is the WTO open and transparent?', *Journal of World Trade*, February 1999.

71. Mark Milner and Stephen Bates, 'Trade rules flouted in banana dispute', *Guardian*, 11 March 1999.

72. Donald E. Barlett and James B. Steele, 'How the Little Guy Gets Crunched', *Time*

Magazine, 7 February 2000.

73. Ibid.

74. Ibid.

75. www.corporatewatch.org. Corporate Watch is a corporation-monitoring organization.

76. World Development Movement 'DBCP Legal Action Report', August 1997.

77. Samuel Huntingdon, 'The Erosion of American National Interests', *Foreign Affairs,* September/October 1997.

Chapter 5

1. Michael Ellison and Martin Kettle, 'Back-door donations shatter all spending records', *Guardian,* 7 November 2000.

2. 'Money and politics: Politicians for rent', *The Economist,* 8 February 1997.

3. Ibid.

4. Margaret Scammell, 'Political Marketing: Lessons for Political Science', *Political Studies,* XLVII, p. 720.

5. Martin Harrop, 'Political Marketing' in *Parliamentary Affairs,* vol. 43, no. 3. Quoted in Margaret Scammell, *Designer Politics: How Elections are Won* (1995), p. 3.

6. Margaret Scammell, *Designer Politics,* p. 4.

7. Charles Lewis, 'Keeping Government Accountable', Centre for Public Integrity, speech to the Institute of Security Studies, 12 April 1999.

8. Julian Borger, 'For sale: the race for the White House', *Guardian,* 7 January 2000.

9. Ibid.

10. 'Fuelling the political machine', *The Economist,* 15 November 1997.

11. Paul Heywood, 'Political Corruption: Problems and Perspectives', *Political Studies,* vol. 45, no. 3 (1997), pp. 430–31.

12. Charles Lewis, 'Capital Gains on Capitol Hill', Centre for Public Integrity (2000);

http://www.publicintegrity.org/PressRoom_Fatcat.html

13. See 'Are Corporations/Business people abusing the power they wield in Politics?', *Forbes,* 8 February 1999; 'Do Corporate PAC's restrict competition?', *Business and Society Journal,* Chicago, June 1998.

14. Donald E. Barlett and James B. Steel, 'How the Little Guy Gets Crunched', *Time Magazine,* 7 February 2000.

15. A report from the US General Accounting Office in 1996 put the cost to the taxpayer at $126.4 billion for resolution costs and $285.2 billion for interest expenses, a total of $411.6 billion.

16. 'You pays your money', *The Economist,* 31 July 1999.

17. Centre for Public Integrity, 'The Buying of the President' (2000); http://www.publicintegrity.org/buying_questions.html. See also John Bores, 'Money Business and the State: Material interests, Fortune 500 Corporations and the size of the Political Action Committee', *American Sociological Review,* Vol. 154, pp. 821–33.

18. Ibid.

19. Ibid.

20. Lars-Erik Nelson, 'Democracy for Sale', *New York Review of Books,* 3 December 1998.

21. Julian Borger, 'For sale: the race for the White House', *Guardian,* 7 January 2000.

22. Ibid.

23. Lars-Erik Nelson, 'Democracy for Sale', *New York Review of Books,* 3 December 1998.

24. Jeffrey Birnbaum, 'Microsoft's capital offence', *Fortune,* 2 February 1998.

25. 'US and Canada Satellite companies accused of inadequate safeguards', *Financial Times,* 26 May 1993, p.3. See also 'Unlovey-dovey: China's blocked satellite deal' *The Economist,* 27 February 1999. Paul Mann, 'High tech dispute dogs US/Sino summit', *Aviation Week Space Technology,* 11 May 1998.

26. Lars-Erik Nelson, 'Democracy for Sale', *New York Review of Books,* 3 December 1998.

27. Andrew Jack, 'Struggle to get pact banning bribery', *Financial Times,* 21 November 1997.
28. *Guardian,* 4 December 1999.
29. *The Economist,* 10 April 1999.
30. Hans-Dieter Klingemann, 'Mapping Political Support in the 1990s: A Global Analysis', in Pippa Norris (ed.), *Critical Citizens* (1999), p. 50.
31. 'Money and politics: Politicians for rent', *The Economist,* 8 February 1997.
32. Ibid.
33. John Curtice and Roger Jowell, 'The Sceptical Electorate', *British Social Attitudes, the 12th Report,* Social and Community Planning Research (1995), p. 141.
34. Transcript from the case of Mostyn Neil Hamilton v. Mohamed Al Fayed, 19 November 1999.
35. Lars-Erik Nelson, 'Democracy for Sale', *New York Review of Books,* 3 December 1998.
36. 'The globalisation of communications', *The Economist,* 29 November 1997.
37. Nicholas Watt, 'Soccer decision leaves Murdoch's backing for New Labour in doubt', *Guardian,* 10 April 1999.
38. *Sun,* 18 March 1997.
39. 'The Sun also sets', *The Economist,* 22 March 1997.
40. Quoted in Richard Belfield, Christopher Hird and Sharon Kelly, *Murdoch: the Decline of the Empire* (London, 1991).
41. Ibid.
42. Quoted in David Korten, *When Corporations Rule the World* (1995).
43. Matthew Josephson, *The Robber Barons: The Great American Capitalists, 1861–1901* (1934).
44. Russell, J. Dalton, 'Political Support in Advanced Industrial Democracies', in Pippa Norris (ed.) *Critical Citizens,* p. 74.

45. See Gallup *Political and Economic Index,* 1991–9.

46. In the 1998-9 Gallup surveys health, unemployment, and education scored consistently high as the most urgent problems facing Britain. In a survey of bills debated in the House of Commons in the 1998–9 session, only 22 out of a total of 144 (15 per cent) related to these issues.

47. Henley Centre, *Planning for Social Change, 1996–97* (1996), quoted in Mark Leonard, *Britain*™ (1997), p. 28.

48. The Gallup Organization – Poll Releases, 3 January 1997; www.gallup.com/poll/releases/pr970103.asp

49. World Values Surveys, quoted in Pippa Norris, 'Institutions and Political Support', in Pippa Norris (ed.), *Critical Citizens,* (1999), p. 229.

50. Robert Putnam, Susan Pharr and Russell Dalton, *What is Troubling the Trilateral Democracies?,* (2000).

51. *Voter Turnout from 1945 to 1997: A Global Report on Political Participation,* pp. 81 and 94.

52. Charles Lewis, 'Keeping Government Accountable', Centre for Public Integrity, speech to the Institute of Security Studies, 12 April 1999.

53. *Financial Times,* 15 June 1999.

54. Susan E. Scarrow, *Parties and their Members,* (1996), p. 57.

55. *L'Etat de la France 1993/94,* (Paris, 1993), quoted in Jeremy Richardson, 'The Market for Political Activism: Interest Groups as a Challenge to Political Parties', *West European Politics,* vol. 18, no. 1, p.121.

56. Susan E. Scarrow, Centre for German and European Studies Working Paper 2, 59, University of California, Berkeley (1996).

Chapter 6

1. 'Protests against "corporate evil" take root across small town America', *Financial Times*, 8 August 2000.
2. Peter Melchett, *New Statesman*, 10 January 2000, p. xiii.
3. Tony Jackson, 'The Global Company: Facing up to a challenging opposition', *Financial Times*, 31 October 1997, p. 16.
4. Christopher Avery, *Business and Human Rights in a Time of Change* (London, 2000).
5. *New Start Worship*, New Start 2000.
6. www.thehungersite.com
7. Neil Buckley, 'Rise of the ethical consumer', *Financial Times*, 27 April 1995.
8. Nancy Dunne and Stella Burch, 'Clinton moves on sweatshops', *Financial Times*, 5 August 1996, p. 3.
9. Roger Cowe, 'Caring attitudes out of fashion', *Guardian*, 12 March 1999.
10. Co-op America, Harwood Group.
11. Tony Jackson, 'The Global Company: Facing up to a challenging opposition,' *Financial Times*, 31 October 1997, p. 16.
12. 'The Enron Corporation: Corporate Complicity in Human Rights Violations', Human Rights Watch January 1999. Although this was not the first time that Human Rights Watch had condemned the role of corporations, the Enron report was distinct in that the corporation was the focus of the report and named in its title.
13. Peter Melchett, *New Statesman*, 10 January 2000.
14. John Vidal, 'Consumer power ready to take on corporations', *Guardian*, 27 November 1999; 'Germany: Market for Green/Ethical Investment Products Booms', Handelsblatt.
15. Thomas Bauer, 'New market report: Green's shares and funds – a growth area', *Öko-Zentrum NRW*, 23 January 1999.
16. Richard Johnson and Daniel Greening, 'The effects of corporate governance and

institutional ownership types on corporate social performance', *Academy of Management Journal,* October 1999.

17. 'Pru to put investments through ethical screening', *The Times,* 24 November 1999.
18. Conversations with CEOs, 2000–2001.
19. Debora Spar, 'Foreign Investment and the Pursuit of Human Rights', *Challenge,* January/February 1999.
20. Conversations with the author.
21. Debora Spa, 'The spotlight and the Bottom Line', *Foreign Affairs,* March/April 1998.
22. A. Maitland, 'The Value of Virtue in a Transparent World', *Financial Times,* 5 August 1999.
23. Joanna Bale and Valerie Elliott, 'Byers calls on consumers to use their power', *The Times,* 23 July 1999. See also White Paper, 'Modern Markets: Confident Consumers', Stephen Byers, July 1999.
24. Bale and Elliott, ibid.

Chapter 7

1. Quoted in DFID, *Viewing the World,* July 2000.
2. Robin Anderson, *Consumer Culture and TV Programming* (1995).
3. 'News going nowhere', *Observer,* 20 August 2000.
4. Robin Anderson, *Consumer Culture and TV Programming* (1995).
5. 'Turning off the presses', *The Economist,* 11 October 1997.
6. Anderson, ibid.
7. Reuters, 'Journalists' federation warns on AOL-Time merger', 11 January 2000.
8. Lynda Morris, *The Ethical Consumer: A New Force in the Food Sector,* Leatherhead Food Research Association, executive summary (1996).
9. 'Sainsbury's in bid to develop new GM foods', *Sunday Times,* 4, June 2000.

10. A. Maitland, 'The Value of Virtue in a Transparent World', *Financial Times,* 5 August 1999.

11. Institute of Business Ethics, Company Use of Codes of Business Conduct, (1998).

12. Sustain-Ability, *The Oil Sector Report: A review of environmental disclosure* (1999).

13. KPMG, *International Survey of Environmental Reporting 1999.*

14. B. Dennis, C. Neck and M. Goldsby, 'The Body Shop International: An Exploration of Corporate Social Responsibility', *Management Decision,* vol. 36, no. 10 (1998).

15. 'Science for sale', *Forbes*, Network 17 May 1999.

16. Z. Monkheiber, 'Science for Sale', *Forbes*, 163 (10), pp. 136–144.

17. See for example 'Think Tanks sell firms EU access', *Sunday Times*, 2 April 2000.

18. K. Maguire, 'University takes tobacco "blood money"' *Guardian*, 7 December 2000.

19. 'Focus on the Corporation', 2 April 1998; www.essential.org/monitor/focus

20. Ron Nixon, 'The corporate assault on the Food and Drug Administration', *International Journal of Health Services,* vol. 26, no. 3, (1996), pp. 561–8.

21. Conversation with CEO.

22. The Boycott Board and Microsoft Boycott Campaign; www.boycott.2street.com;www.vcnet.com

23. www.corpwatch.org, www.igc.org and www.mcspotlight.org

24. Although Judge Thomas Penfold Jackson's ruling of June 2000 in the Microsoft anti-trust trial means that Microsoft should no longer be able to direct customers to its own websites, products and services whenever they go online for help, given that the ruling is to be appealed, all has been frozen until the appeal is heard.

25. 220 on Alta Vista.

26. *Guardian*, 27 August 1998.

27. Diane Summers, 'Charities accused of exaggerating advert claims', *Financial Times*, 4 October 1995, p. 11.

28. Michael Shaw Bond, 'The Backlash Against NGOs', *Prospect*, April 2000.

29. Frank Furedi, 'It's just a failure of nerve', *New Statesman*, 10 January 2000, p. xxviii.

30. Wyn Grant, *Pressure Groups, Politics and Democracy in Britian*, 2nd edn, (London, 1995).

31. Lynda Morris, *The Ethical Consumer: A New Force in the Food Sector*, Leatherhead Food Research Association, executive summary (1996).

32. National Consumer Council, Annual Review 1999; www.ncc.org/underst.htm

33. Neil Buckley and Peter Marsh, 'Tesco bows to plastic pressure', 25 April 1995, p. 12.

34. *A Sporting Chance; Tackling child labour in India's sports goods industry*, Christian Aid Report, 1997.

35. *The Apparel Industry and Codes of Conduct: A Solution to the International Child Labour Problem?*, Bureau of International Labor Affairs, US Department of Labor, 1996.

36. *Child Labour: The Way Business Can Help Children*, Anti-Slavery International, 1996.

37. Committee of Inquiry, *A New Vision for Business* (1999), p.54; www.business-impact.org.

38. Frank Furedi, 'It's just a failure of nerve', *New Statesman,* 10 January 2000, p. xxviii.

39. Robert Shrimsley, 'Customer power will help tackle "rip-off" Britain', *Daily Telegraph*, 23 July 1999.

Chapter 8

1. 'Top of the form', *Sunday Times*, 23 May 1999. See for example 'United States – Gates the Good', *The Economist*, December 1999; 'Gates' fortune to combat Aids', *Sunday Times*, August 1999.

2. There are, of course, exceptions, such as Steve Rubin and Silvio Berlusconi.

3. Bibb Porter, *Ted Turner's Amazing Story; It ain't*, (1994), p. 415.

4. 'Ben & Jerry & Nato', *New York Times*, 28 April 1998,

5. 'Military excess from the Executive office', 13 June 1999. 'NATO expansion foes rally

for Senate votes – Debate in Eastern European countries', *Washington Post*, 27 April 1998. 'Large scoops of social values', *Financial Times*, 9 Feb 1998.

6.   'Clinton's defense budget hike targeted – Many consider his spending priorities out of place', *San Francisco Examiner*, 30 January 1999,

7.   T. Emerson, 'A Letter to Jian Zemin', *Newsweek International*, 29 May 2000.

8.   Conversation with Paul Spicer, former Deputy Chairman, Lonrho.

9.   The UK suspended its sanctions against Libya in July 1999 when the Lockerbie suspects were extradited to stand trial. A decision to permanently suspend the sanctions will not be taken until after the verdict.

10. See Noreena Hertz and Michael Porter, 'The Bottom Up Solution', *Financial Times*, 16 September 1997.

11. Conor O'Clery, *Greening of the White House*, (Dublin 1996).

Chapter 9

1.   'Australian Business Intelligence: HIV sweeps through the mining industry', *Sydney Morning Herald*, 26 November 1999.

2.   Schuettler, AIDS threatens to bury SA mining industry, 28 July 1999; http://www.wozainternet.co.za

3.   World Health Organisation's World Health Report 2000.

4.   Bekker, Jacoline, 'The Weave of Business and Government' (1998), Judge Institute of Management Studies, unpublished dissertation.

5.   The Shell Petroleum Development Company of Nigeria Limited, '1999: People and the Environment Annual Report'.

6.   'Nigerian tribes cut oil lines', *The Times*, 22 February 1999,

7.   *New York Times,* July 1999.

8. John Brown, Reith Lecture, *The Times*, 29 April 2000.

9. J. Bennet, 'Franchises for Inner City: Economic Development Tool', *Planning*, November 1998.

10. M. Hickins, 'Rite Aid in the City', *Management Review*, March 1999.

11. At the last local British elections in 1999, the Benwell ward of Newcastle, one of the UK's most deprived inner city areas, an area where three-quarters of children live in households with no earned income, saw a turnout of only 19.4 per cent.

12. More than 98 per cent of British schools participate in Tesco's Computers for Schools and Walkers' Free Books scheme.

13. Eagle Rock brochure – American Honda Education Corporation.

14. 'The High School at the end of the Road', *New York Times Magazine*, 5 July 1998.

15. 'Analysis: Corporate responsibility: The cannibals adopt cutlery', *Guardian,* 18 March 1999; and BT, 'Changing Values', http://www.bt.com/world/sus.dev/; 1998.

16. www.helptheaged.org.uk

17. See for example Walker Information and Council of Foundations. 'Measuring the Business Value of Corporate Philanthropy', http://www.walkerinfo.com' or *Crossborder Monitor*, 'The corporate citizen: Adoptin a socially responsible image', 28 September 1994.

18. Chris Marsdenand Jörg Andriof, 'Towards an understanding of corporate citizenship and how to influence it', *Journal of Citizenship Studies*, July 1998.

19. Chris Marsden and Jörg Andriof, ibid.

20. 1997 Access Omnibus Survey by Business and the Community.

21. 'Millennium Poll on Corporate Society Responsibility', Environics, 1999.

22. '85 per cent of corporations use cause marketing tactics', *Direct Marketing*, September 2000.

23. Brown, Reith Lecture, ibid.

24. 'Oil firm's secret deal to free Burma prisoner', *The Times*, 7 December 2000.

Chapter 10

1.   Premier Oil, for example, is playing the role of partner and conduit to NGOs in Burma such as Amnesty International and Save the Children, who otherwise could not legally function in the country.
2.   'Where there's smoke', *Guardian*, 18 September 2000.
3.   Stephen Glass, 'Gift of the Magnate', New *Republic,* 26 January 1998.
4.   Ibid.
5.   For a good summary of the general problems of depending on philathropy, 'A major transfer of government responsibility to voluntary organisations. Proceed with caution,' *Public Administration Review*, Washington, May/June 1996.
6.   Charles Leadbeater and Geoff Mulgan, 'Lean democracy and the leadership vacuum', *Lean Democracy,* (1994), p. 14.
7.   I am referring here to the willingness to pay $1 more on a $20 item of clothing for one not made with sweatshop labour.
8.   I. Fuyuno, 'A silent epidemic', *Far Eastern Economic Review,* Hong Kong, 28 September 2000, vol. 163, no. 39, pp 78–80.
9.   Virgin Atlantic Airways, which had just started flights to the Caribbean, stepped in.
10. Already started: the computers come with the MS Encarta Encyclopaedia and other MS education software.
11. Naomi Klein, *No Logo: Taking Aim at the Brand Bullies* (2000).
12. A few countries recognise the potential conflicts, and regulate marketing to children so as to disallow such practices. Denmark prohibits any kind of commercially sponsored material or activity in schools. In Belgium companies can produce materials, but schools are prohibited from using them. Most countries leave industry to regulate itself.

13. Naomi Klein, *No Logo: Taking Aim at the Brand Bullies*.

14. Ibid.

15. 'AOL, *Time*, cite social goals', Yahoo! headlines, 11 January 2000; http:\\uk.news.yahoo.com/000111/22/dayw.html

16. In the United States companies face a significant liability if their shareholders believe that they are not making the best use of their investment by putting it towards social causes, and investors can sue for damages.

17. BP Harvard Business School Case Study: F. Reinhardt, *Global Climate Change and BP Amoco*, (Cambridge MA, 2000).

Chapter 11

1. John S. Dryzek, 'Transnational democracy', *Journal of Political Philosophy,* vol. 7, no. 1 (1999), p. 38.

2. Thomas Friedman, *The Lexus and the Olive Tree* (1999): Thomas Friedman puts forth 'The Golden Arches Theory of Conflict Prevention' which states that 'no two countries that both had McDonald's had fought a war against each other since each got its McDonald's.'

3. Jessica Matthews, *Foreign Affairs*.

4. Sydney Tarrow, Sidney 'Mad cows and social activists', in Susan J. Pharr and Robert D. Putnam (eds.), *Disaffected Democracies,* (2000), p. 286.

5. John S. Dryzek, 'Transnational democracy', *Journal of Political Philosophy,* vol. 7, no. 1 (1999), pp. 45–6.

6. 'The Non Government Order', *The Economist*, 9 December 1999.

7. For an illuminating description of the Seattle protest see Jeffrey St. Clair, 'Seattle Diary: It's a Gas, Gas, Gas', *New Left Review,* no. 238, November/December 1999.

8. 'Housewives' Revolt Rocks Japan', *The Times*, 22 July 2000.

9.   W. Hutton and A. Giddens (eds.), *On the Edge: Living with Global Capitalism* (London, 2000).

10. John S. Dryzet, 'Transitional Democracy', Journal of Political Philosophy, vol. 7, no. 1, (1999) pp. 45–6.

11. Richard Hofstadter (ed.), *The Progressive Movement 1900–1915*, (1963), p. 2, and J. A. Thompson, *Progressivism,* British Association for American Studies (1979), p. 7.

12. Ibid., p. 349.

13. Ibid., p. 349.

14. Richard L. McCormick, *The Party Period and Public Policy*, (1986), pp. 326–7.

15. Ibid., p. 377.

16. Richard McCormick, *The Party Period and Public Policy,* p. 327.

17. J. A. Thompson, *Progressivism*, p. 37.

18. Richard McCormick, *The Party Period and Public Policy*, p. 274.

19. Ibid., p. 283.

20. Ibid., p. 276.

21. Ibid., p. 272.

22. Rachel Carson, *Silent Spring*, (Boston 1962).

23. Russell Dalton, *The Green Rainbow,* (1994), p. 90.

24. Ibid.

25. 'Greens grow up', *The Economist,* 7 August 1999.

26. 'I am very sympathetic with a lot of the causes being raised by all the people that are there demonstrating.' Bill Clinton, 1 December 1999. Quoted in *The Times,* 2 December 1999.